CAMBR...
AND OTHER ...

CAMBRIDGE
AND OTHER MEMORIES
1920 - 1953

By

Basil Willey

1968

CHATTO & WINDUS

LONDON

Published by
Chatto & Windus Ltd
40 William IV Street
London W.C.2

*

Clarke, Irwin & Co. Ltd
Toronto

Printed in Great Britain
by William Lewis (Printers) Ltd, Cardiff

Contents

Cambridge and other Memories

Preface

In my previous book, *Spots of Time*, which was a retrospect of the early years of my life (1897-1920), I said that I might some day continue the story onwards through the middle and later years. The present volume contains my attempt to do this.

Before I began I knew that the second book, if ever written, would be quite different from the first, and much more difficult to write. I already knew, in theory and from the experience of other autobiographers, what hazards and pitfalls await the author who tries to re-create his own adult life. In writing of childhood and early youth one can almost regard oneself as another person, of whom one can speak objectively and for whom one is not responsible. Any account of adult life, on the other hand, must needs lack this sort of detachment. And there are other difficulties, which, although foreseen, only reveal themselves fully when the writing has actually begun. There is, for example, the problem of avoiding all reference to living persons which might give pain or annoyance. There is the difficulty of writing about controversial matters without falling into the tone and style of a public report, a leading article, a letter to *The Times* or a speech at a committee meeting. Above all there is the problem of giving unity to the multitudinousness of middle life — of making the narrative an imaginative whole and not a mere series of separate essays. The auroral gleams, the sparkle and the dew-drops, which lent enchantment to memories of childhood and youth, have now given place to 'the light of common day'.

This book is not intended to be a contribution to any of the debates or issues mentioned in it, though I sometimes have to take sides and say what I think about them. My chief hope of keeping the story imaginatively alive as well as factually true lies in this: that all the while I shall be trying to convey the *feel* of events and ideas rather than to formulate them intellectually or to affirm convictions.

My life, uneventful as it may have been, and to others unimportant, has at least been of importance to myself; it has seemed full of meanings, hints and intimations which I must try to capture, if I can, before they slip from my grasp. Do what I may, however, this book is bound to be an *Excursion* rather than a *Prelude*.

When I retired (1964) from the King Edward VII Professorship of English Literature at Cambridge on reaching the statutory age of 67, my chief feeling was one of unspeakable relief. It is this feeling that is uppermost in the ensuing chapter, in which I give a rapid survey of the Cambridge English School, of its history and of my association with it. The Chapter was written immediately after my liberation, and formed the text of the Ballard Mathews Lectures (1964) at the University College of North Wales, Bangor. To the authorities of that College, and above all to the Principal, Dr. Charles Evans, I am indebted, both for the incentive given me by their invitation, and now for their permission to publish the lectures in the present book.

Let me not be misunderstood when I speak of 'relief' and 'liberation'. I was immensely pleased and proud, as well as astonished, when I was appointed by the Crown to succeed Sir Arthur Quiller-Couch in 1946. My life as Professor was on the whole happy, serene and comparatively free from the entanglements, administrative and other, which afflict most Professors in other places and in some other subjects. I enjoyed the friendship, confidence and loyal support of many of my colleagues. For all this I am humbly grateful and should hate my former colleagues and ex-pupils to think otherwise. No: but the point is that I had for some time been in what I increasingly felt to be a false position. I represented the 'Q' tradition, genteel and amateurish, in a Faculty (and a world) which was becoming more and more specialised, doctrinaire and sectarian. My own interests, too, as a 'history-of-ideas' man and a 'moralist', led me to read things not read by my colleagues, and to neglect things which they regarded as of first importance. Gradually I came to feel that I did not belong to the world of professional 'Eng. Lit.' at all; I was like Teufelsdröckh – a 'Professor of Things in General', and out of sympathy with a great deal of modern literature, criticism and scholarship. Moreover, although the Professor of English is not 'Head of a Department' in Cambridge, and is therefore not responsible for policy, he is yet ex officio a member of the Faculty Board. Thus for nearly twenty years, although I lacked talent for administration, and was always dazed and distracted by contending arguments and voices, I had to attend the ever-lengthening Board Meetings, and listen to endless discussions, recapitulated over the years, of such matters as Tripos reform, and more recently, of the vast and complex reports on University and College administrative and educational re-organisation which have come up for analysis and comment. I am not denying the interest and importance of these matters, and I am second to none in my admiration for those who, for no reward and with small thanks, have given so much of their time and thought to them. It was simply that I considered myself a very poor hand at academic statesmanship, and felt embarrassed by my inability to give the sort of lead which, as Professor, I might be expected to give. Fortunately for the world, there are many who have a gift for these things, who enjoy discussion, and who even look forward to every meeting as to another of their 'finest hours'. For my own part, I can participate fruitfully in – and even, if necessary, lead – a discussion with one or two non-contentious friends. But at a full Board Meeting I always felt like an operator in a telephone exchange, with all the bells ringing at once, and unable to find any of the plugs. I am sure that many others besides me have felt this sort of distraction, and I salute them for their patience, public-spirit and clear-headedness in acquiring, as I seemed unable or un-willing to do, the art of manipulating the plugs. Considering my short-comings as a committee-man, I often marvel at the number of Chair-manships of various kinds, inside and outside the University, that have fallen to my lot over the years. However, I think I have almost pre-ferred, as a lesser evil, the Chair to any other place at a meeting; there one was forced to be alert and (ostensibly) efficient; and, what matter-ed most, one could control the tempo of the discussions.

With all these and other reasons for desiring retirement, imagine how touched and surprised I was when in June 1964, a few months before the date, a group of my colleagues (many of them ex-pupils) presented me with the *Festschrift* called *The English Mind*. The Cam-bridge University Press had produced for me an exquisitely-bound copy, which was handed to me at a delightful *vin d'honner* held – with what appropriateness readers of *Spots of Time* will know – in the Wordsworth Room at St. John's College.

I am grateful to Dr. Charles S. Duthie (Principal of New College, University of London) and the other Trustees of the Drew Foundation for allowing me to reproduce, as the last chapter of this book, my Drew Lecture called 'Thoughts of a Layman about Immortality', (given in October, 1967).

Chapter One

Cambridge English, 1919-64

I came up to Peterhouse, Cambridge, on demobilisation in January, 1919, when the University, after having been at a very low ebb for four years — indeed almost non-existent except for youths under military age, Asiatics, and the physically unfit ('infants, Indians and invalids') — was suddenly overwhelmed by the incoming tide of returned warriors, and freshmen straight from school. After reading History Part II, I switched over to English in 1920. That sounds very simple and natural, but in fact it was a big and decisive transition. I wonder how many people realise that the first English Tripos examination was held as recently as 1919? The Cambridge Chair of Greek was founded in 1540; that of English in 1910 (by Sir Harold Harmsworth, afterwards Lord Rothermere). Arthur Verrall was the first holder of the King Edward VII Chair; and he, during the whole of his brief tenure and 'Q' during the first four years of his long reign, had no autonomous English School to preside over; English was merely one section of Medieval and Modern Languages. Neither the Chair nor the Tripos was started without vigorous opposition from the academic Old Guard. When Harmsworth's offer was first received, Dr. M'Taggart said 'it seemed to him that a Professorship of such a subject would not only be useless but positively harmful to the University'. Another don, Dr. J. Mayo, said he was afraid 'that this Professorship . . . would be simply a Professorship of English Literature dating from the beginning of the latter half of the nineteenth century, and the effect of that would be that it would be a Professorship of English fiction, and that of a light and comic character. For that reason, he thought that the Professorship was a Professorship unworthy of the University'. Similarly, when the Report proposing an independent English Tripos was being discussed (Spring of 1917), Dr. Mayo quoted Plato: 'I do not teach Hellenic to the Hellenes: the fact that they are born Hellenes precludes the necessity for Hellenising them; they are Hellenes all their lives'. In the same way, thought Dr. Mayo, 'an Englishman was English all his life and did not need to be taught English'.

But, during 1916 and 1917, in wartime Cambridge, while the few remaining dons were being jeered at by occupying armies, talks were going on in a quiet backwater (Chadwick's garden in Gresham Road) which were big with future promise. The participants were H.M. Chadwick, who had succeeded Skeat in 1912 as Professor of Anglo-Saxon; H.F. Stewart of the Special Board for Mediaeval and Modern Languages, and Sir Arthur Quiller-Couch who had succeeded Verrall the same year as King Edward VII Professor of English Literature. It was to the foresight and insight of these men, chiefly – and perhaps above all to the statesmanship and doggedness of Chadwick – that the Cambridge English School and Tripos owed its independent existence. They knew that, directly the war was over, there would be a deluge which would sweep away many landmarks. A hungry generation of young men and not so young, disillusioned, scarred and seared in mind and body, quick to detect humbug yet still eager for culture, would rush in and tread down many traditional sanctities. They would stand no nonsense; they would be impatient of the pedantries and the textual minutiae of classical scholarship; they would insist on something more modern and actual; they might even think that English Literature, after having had time to produce Shakespeare, Donne, Milton, Pope, Johnson, Wordsworth and a few others, might now have come of age, and be ready to mediate some of the values hitherto only attainable through Greek or Latin.

It may seem odd to present-day eyes that this *praeparatio evangelica* (or should we say *anglistica?)* should have been so largely the work of Chadwick the Anglo-Saxon scholar and Stewart the parson and French scholar. Well! they happened to be men of vision and courage – it took plenty of both in those days to sling a pebble at the Goliath of academic authority – but one may add that each had his own good private reasons too. To Stewart the Modern Linguist, saintly as he was, and graced with the countenance of a seraph, English may well have seemed the cuckoo's egg in the linguistic nest. It was safer to have it out in time. And, what was more important for Cambridge English, Chadwick held the view – highly unusual if not unique in a man of his type of interests and learning, in which he was pre-eminent – that Anglo-Saxon was important as a branch of Archaeology and Anthropology rather than as the foundation of English Literature, and could be more fruitfully studied in connexion with the history of early cultures – Norse, Celtic etc. – than as a preliminary to the understanding of modern English literature, a literature which had drawn so much of its sap from Greece, Rome, Italy, Spain and France rather than from Beowulf. He believed in his own subject, and thought that it could only survive in independence of Eng. Lit.; tied to the latter, it would be like a dinghy towed in the wake of a great galleon. So he, too, had his own good reasons. And his view, of course, chimed in wonderfully with those of 'Q', who knew no Anglo-Saxon, hated pedantry and the Germanic type of scholarship which had produced the Anglo-Saxon cult, and was anxious above all to liberate English studies from the clutches of philology. Left to himself, 'Q' might have been no more than the persuasive and graceful public apologist for English that in fact he actually was. It needed the toughness of Chadwick, and the sanctified worldliness of Stewart, to push the thing through the University machine. But it was the fortunate conjunction of these three bright, particular stars which produced the English Tripos we have known: the first English honours examination in any English University, I believe, in which students and lovers of our literature could pursue their chosen subject without having to endure the alien yoke of Teutonic Philology. Anglo-Saxon studies were never excluded, but they were optional from the start. Optional, that is, in what was at first called Section A of the Tripos, the literary-critical Section; the man who proposed to take his degree in English and no other subject had to take Section B, which included Anglo-Saxon and Old Norse. A great many, of whom I was one, took Section A after having taken a part of another Tripos, such as History, Modern Languages or Classics. It has never been possible in Cambridge to graduate in English without qualifying also (in Part II which superseded Section B) in some other language, which might be Anglo-Saxon but was more often French or Italian or Mediaeval Latin.

To switch over from History to English, as I did, was academically rash in 1920. The new subject was very much a Cinderella, and the elder sisters thought very meanly of her. Many, indeed most, of the Colleges had no Fellow and no entrance scholarships in English, and discouraged their undergraduates from taking it. My own College sighed, shook its head, and sent me for advice to A.J. Wyatt, who had hitherto supervised in English for almost the whole University. Wyatt was an exact scholar of the old philological school; he had helped William Morris with the Kelmscott translation of *Beowulf*, and he was bitterly opposed to the new literary and critical approach. Accordingly, at the interview, he prophesied disaster for the new Tripos, and unemployment for me or anyone else deluded enough to take it. I came away deeply dejected, and what or who put it into my head to go and see Chadwick I cannot now remember. But go I did, and Chadwick, in his asthmatic whisper and Yorkshire accent, and with much blinking of the eyelids, uttered the memorable words "Eh, er, ye see – you ought to go to Tillyard!" I went, and from that moment I never looked back. Tillyard accepted me (as he was accepting many others from all Colleges at that time), and quickly inspired me with his own confidence and zeal. Those supervisions of his, for two or three of us at a time, are unforgettable. We felt ourselves to be a happy band of pioneers, united by a common faith, despised perhaps by the older academics, but sure of triumph in a glorious future. This was the spirit that prevailed in most parts of the English School in those early years, when it was flooded with returned soldiers, many of them nearly as old as their supervisors, and most of them swift to distinguish the genuine from the counterfeit, fruitful study from sterile pedantry. We felt that we were in at the start of an important new movement in University history, and nobody radiated this feeling more abundantly than Tillyard. From the start his method was to direct our attention to particular texts and passages, to make us taste their diverse qualities, comparing and distinguishing. In our essays we were to avoid mere gossip, metaphorical vapourings and woolly mysticism. Tillyard seemed to us immensely wise and well read; I can see now, of course, that he was improvising valiantly, and was often hard-pressed to keep up with the supervisions.

2

But though Tillyard may have been the soundest and sanest of the early Fathers, there were others more glamorous — and none more so than the legendary 'Q' himself. It may, I suppose, be hard for the present generation to understand, and impossible to feel, the influence he then exerted. Who reads him now? His books, many of them, are hard to come by in the bookshops. About fifteen years after his death, Herbert Butterfield and I set "Arthur Quiller-Couch" as the subject for a University Prize Essay, and I found that the candidates were inclined to treat him with kindly disdain. The old man was a period piece — though one had to admit that he had done quite a useful job of work when one considered the suffocating atmosphere of sentimentality, gentility, prudery and patriotism in which he lived, moved and had his being. But in those early days he was a spell-binder, who by sheer force of style and prestige brought *réclame* and faith to the new School. Always impeccably clad for every occasion — for lectures, in full morning dress, for the tow-path, the C.U. Gig Club, or the Midsummer Fair, in a loud check-suit, brown bowler rakishly tilted, a tie of carefully chosen hue, and brown leather gaiters — he nothing common did or mean, and even the routine of Board Meetings was enlivened by his presence.

None of this sprang from mere affectation: it was, like his prose style, the outward and visible sign of an inward and spiritual grace. It proceeded from a fastidious sense of what was decorous, of what, in all the uses and occasions of life, was most proper to be said and done. 'Q' was a perfectionist in the Art of Living, as well as in the Arts of Reading and Writing. His lectures were social and ceremonial functions, like royal visits, and attracted crowds such as Cambridge had never before known. They were of rare occurrence, never delivered more than once, and carefully composed for publication. Entering the packed lecture-room, he would step carefully through the recumbent forms on the floor, ascend to the rostrum, glance up at the serried ranks on benches, window-sills and ledges, spread out his manuscript with a hand that trembled a little at first, and begin — always with the word

"Gentlemen", although his audience was often predominantly, and during the war years almost exclusively, feminine. 'Q' was no anti-feminist, but the University was still technically a male institution, and he was appointed to lecture before the University; decorum therefore demanded that he should address himself formally to its members only.

In substance the lectures were sometimes a little light-weight, though ballasted and enriched with the allusions, classical and modern, that came so abundantly from his copious reading and spiced with the wit, epigrams and *bon mots* that delighted his hearers and kept them triumphantly immune from the normal lassitudes of the lecture-room. In style, too, they were mannered, self-conscious and olympian, though never pompous. But the spirit of them was incomparable. Life, for 'Q', was a thing to be enjoyed; an exploit to be achieved with chivalry, resolution and gaiety, a glorious opportunity for adventure and fun. And literature was a function of life, a finer distillation of its essence. You were to savour it, relish it, consorting with masterpieces, catching from them something of the nobility which made their writers immortal, and something of the articulateness and stylishness which had made their speech memorable. In English literature, which 'Q' loved and idolised, there were infinite riches to be found — "My God, what treasures!" he would exclaim — and English, as an academic discipline, could therefore do everything, and more than everything, which Classics were supposed to have done in the past. It could turn out men and women who were sane, wise, balanced, free from specialisms and all kinds of lopsidedness, sensitive to beauty and trained to discriminate between the good and the shoddy both in literature and in living. A touching but unrealistic faith, you say? Ought I to have introduced undertones of irony into my summary, as I expect most of my younger readers would have done? I have not done so, because I wanted to convey the quality of the faith, the conviction, with which Cambridge English, thanks largely to 'Q''s evangelical zeal, began its pilgrimage. 'Q' was a Christian humanist, and even the 1914 war, in which he lost his only son, had not shattered his faith in God and his love of man, his love of his country, or his belief that the study of English Literature was conducive in the highest degree to the good life.

'Q' is best remembered by the world at large as a novelist, as the compiler of the *Oxford Book of English Verse,* as an exponent and teacher of what is called 'Style', and as a crusader against Jargon and journalese. I have already mentioned his distaste for dry-as-dust scholarship, and for every form of study which drained away the life-blood of literature. No one hated all pedantic preoccupation with trends, tendencies, forces, influences and movements more than he did; just as no one more vigorously defended honest, racy English against the cloudy obfuscations of officialese. ' "Tendencies" did not write *The Canter-*

bury Tales; Chaucer wrote them'. "Naturalism" did not write *Tintern Abbey;* a man called William Wordsworth wrote it.' In the days of 'Q's' greatest influence and popularity, that is, the decade following the first great war, all things Teutonic were at a discount, and 'Q' was able to score points off philology, off all accumulations of mere *facts about* literature, and all pseudo-philosophical classifications of literary types and epochs, by calling them 'Germanic'. 'God made man in his own image; Germans make generalisations in theirs.' But 'Q's' very sense of literature as the memorable speech of real men and women led him to see that you cannot study it in isolation from their lives and times. 'Literature cannot be divorced from life', he said; 'you cannot understand Chaucer aright, unless you have the background, unless you know the kind of men for whom Chaucer wrote, and the kind of men whom he made speak.' And so, surprisingly as it may seem, Cambridge English owes to 'Q' another of its characteristics: its emphasis, not only upon training in critical discrimination, but also upon background studies. 'Q' always insisted that the Tripos was the English Tripos, not the English Literature Tripos. It was to take due account, that is to say, of all that had gone to the building of our civilisation, especially of those master-currents of religious, philosophical and ethical thought which had controlled the lives, and so also the writing, of each historical period. From the very beginning the period-papers in the Tripos were called "Literature, Life and Thought".

But already in 1922, only five years from the birth of the Tripos, 'Q' was meditating the creation of a Part II of the Tripos which should be not philological, like the old "Section B", but theoretical and philosophical in bias. 'Q' was always anxious that the English Tripos should produce men of well-rounded culture, not merely men with one lobe of their brain over-developed. 'The man we are proud to send forth from our Schools', he said, 'will be remarkable less for something he can take out of his pocket and exhibit as knowledge, than for being something, and that something recognizable for a man of unmistakable intellectual breeding, whose trained judgment we can trust to choose the better and reject the worse.' 'What I'm groping after', he wrote to a friend in 1922, 'is a second Part of the Tripos which shall (1) mainly concern itself with English *thought,* and (2) be a stiff test of our men's capacity to *write* (which includes thinking). What we want is a Part II that will turn out men provided with some useful principles for statesmanship, the better journalism, etc., and some knowledge of what Englishmen have thought from time to time.'

'Q's' design was realised in 1928, when Part II was started. His special contribution to it was an optional paper called The English Moralists — a paper which, after more than thirty-five years, is still going strong, and being taken with apparent enthusiasm and profit, by large numbers of students. Broadly, the syllabus still follows (or did until 1964) the main lines he indicated. Beginning with the classical and Christian sources from which our civilization springs (Plato, Aristotle, the Bible) it invited attention to what was 'thought from time to time', on God, on Nature and on Human Life, by such Englishmen as Hooker, Bacon, Milton, Hobbes, the Cambridge Platonists, Locke, Shaftesbury, Hume, Burke, Wordsworth, Coleridge, Carlyle, Newman, Mill, Arnold, Ruskin and others down to the present age. I could say much more about this paper, but I am checked by the fear of seeming to cry my own wares — for this has been the main field of my own activity ever since Part II began. I will merely venture to say that I believe many students have found in it both profit and delight. It exacts a more than usually stubborn effort to think clearly — a discipline, perhaps, especially valuable for literary students who are bound, in the ordinary way, to be using subjective and shifting standards of judgment. Moreover, the study of moral ideas and their history not only helps to define the spiritual climate of each age, the climate which moulded its literature, but helps to make people more aware of those criteria by which all value, whether in literature or in life, must ultimately be judged.

When we remember these wider concerns of his, we can see that 'Q's' propaganda for 'Style' was no mere 'ninetyish' fastidiousness or affectation; it was central to his whole message. Matthew Arnold once said: 'People think I can teach them style. What stuff it all is! Have something to say, and say it as clearly as you can. That is the only secret of style.' 'Q' was of the same mind, but he developed the theme much further. Style is the index of the man, and we have seen what kind of man he wanted to produce. Style is emphatically not extraneous ornament or bogus 'fine' writing: 'Whenever you feel an impulse to perpetrate a piece of exceptionally fine writing, obey it — wholeheartedly — and delete it before sending your manuscript to the press. *Murder your darlings.*' Style is simply the outward expression of the inward man; the thing is to *be* a Christian scholar-and-gentleman, and then you will write like one. In this so-called 'century of the common man' 'Q's' doctrine may sound like snobbery, or rather class-*un*consciousness, but in reality it went deeper than this. Good style indicates and accompanies qualities which every man, however common, should be proud to possess or aspire after: honesty, clear thought, good manners, clear sightedness, imagination, the power to 'think with the heart as well as with the head'. Or, as 'Q' put it in one of his rather more rhetorical utterances: Style, like character, 'has its altar within; to that retires for counsel, from that fetches its illumination, to ray outwards'.

And this leads me, before I cease speaking of 'Q', to say a word about his campaign against Jargon. His 'Interlude on Jargon' (in *The Art of Writing*) is the best-remembered of all his Professorial pronouncements, though the memory of it has not exterminated the ogre. With the enormous new growths of bureaucracy and journalism, and with the spread of English as a world-language – with the consequent re-absorption into the mother-tongue of all kinds of corruptions and monstrosities of overseas origin – Jargon has swollen to vast proportions; and men like Sir Ifor Evans and Sir Ernest Gowers have had to re-iterate 'Q's' warnings in other terms. Jargon, which 'Q' defined as a flux or determination of words to the pen, is the language of Committees, Blue Books, Official Reports, leading articles, business letters; it is what the Americans, who use their own forms of it to excess, call 'gobbledygook'. The vice of it is that it is the exact opposite of good prose style, and thus indicates a state of mind the reverse of that which a liberal education aims to produce. 'Q's' dislike of it, therefore, was not just a fad springing from preciosity, or any affected love of undefiled English in the abstract; he hated it simply as an honest man and a writer. Jargon is bogus; it cloaks muddled or banal thought in pretentious circumlocutions; it imparts a spurious mystery and pomp to what is plain and ordinary; it is evasive and vague; it is general and abstract where it should be concrete and direct. It says 'the answer is in the negative' instead of 'No'; 'he was conveyed to his place of residence in an intoxicated condition' instead of 'he was taken home drunk'; 'prior to the implementation of the scheme' instead of 'before it was carried out'.

I think 'Q's' masterpiece in this lecture is his translation into Jargon of Hamlet's soliloquy 'To be or not to be':

'To be, or the contrary? Whether the former or the latter be preferable would seem to admit of some difference of opinion; the answer in the present case being of an affirmative or of a negative character according as to whether one elects on the one hand to mentally suffer the disfavour of fortune, albeit in an extreme degree, or on the other to boldly envisage adverse conditions in the prospect of eventually bringing them to a conclusion. The condition of sleep is similar to, if not indistinguishable from, that of death; and with the addition of finality the former might be considered identical with the latter: so that in this connexion it might be argued with regard to sleep that, could the addition be effected, a termination might be put to the endurance of a multiplicity of inconveniences, not to mention a number of downright evils incidental to our fallen humanity, and thus a consummation achieved of a most gratifying nature.'

That is Jargon: 'shuffling around in the fog and cotton-wool of abstract terms', 'beating the air because it is easier than fleshing your sword in the thing'. For 'Q', all the best of English Literature was a continual corrective and antidote against viciousness of style; and for prose, above all, the Authorized Version of the Bible: 'You have received it [the Bible] by inheritance, Gentlemen: it is yours, freely yours — to direct your words through life as well as your hearts.'

'Q' was a product of the last phase of England's greatness — the era of Kipling and Elgar and Edward VII; he was intensely and even sentimentally patriotic; unobtrusively but sincerely Christian; a passionate believer in liberal education, liberal politics, and the idea of the gentleman. All that he thought and said presupposed the unbroken continuity of the old Christian-Humanist tradition, the old class structure of society, the old sense of decorum, propriety and ceremony in human relationships as in literature. And so, with these certainties behind him, he could speak with an assurance, a security, denied to our own more sceptical, disillusioned and disordered age.

I have spoken at some length about 'Q' because I can think of no better way of conveying the ethos of those early years of Cambridge English. At that time 'Q' really was its prophet, propagandist and spokesman; he provided it with a creed, he proclaimed its saving power, and he uttered what was latent in our own minds and thoughts.

3

But there were two other men of great originality and importance teaching in the middle and later '20's and the earlier '30's, one of whom in particular, I.A. Richards, soon eclipsed 'Q' in the public eye and has probably left a deeper mark upon Cambridge English than anyone else. The other was Mansfield Forbes ('Manny'), who, as Chadwick's colleague at Clare, was his ideal co-worker in the preliminary stages of creation, supplying as he did the needful elements of air and fire. Manny was a most unusual being, hard to describe convincingly to anyone who never knew him. Someone called him the 'little wizened old boy of forty', and indeed both his face, which was wrinkled yet childlike and ingenuous, and his manner, which was at once naive and sophisticated, justified that description. He answered to Coleridge's description of the man of genius, who is able 'to carry on the feelings of childhood into the powers of manhood; to combine the child's sense of wonder and novelty with the appearances, which every day . . . had rendered familiar' [B.L. (Shawcross) Vol. 1, Ch. IV, p. 59]. Appropriately enough, he lectured on ideas of childhood and parenthood in Blake and Wordsworth, and for sheer brilliance, unexpectedness, insight and originality these lectures were unrivalled. They were also extremely funny, Forbes possessing amongst his many gifts the power of inventing whole terminologies and classifications of his own, such as "Nor-Petal" for poets like Wordsworth who think that Skiddaw pours forth streams more sweet than Castaly, and "Sou-Petal" for those like Byron or

Shelley who fly either imaginatively or actually (or both) to Italy or Greece. In more ways than one Forbes was a Coleridgean type; his lectures were a tissue of digressions; they eddied, but progressed little and had little orientation. As likely as not, half-way through a course on the Romantics he would still be talking about the early Blake. And so it is not surprising that, if ever he planned a *magnum opus*, he never achieved one; indeed, he left nothing behind him at his early death but an eccentric *History of Clare College* and an eccentrically-decorated house in Queen's Road. But none of this mattered; Manny had a truly seminal mind, an imagination from which ours caught fire, and an extraordinary sureness of taste and rightness of judgment.

Of Ivor Richards I do not propose to speak at length; he is better known by his work and influence than the others, and in any case it is not my plan to discuss or appraise the living at all fully. I was, however, one of the lucky hearers of his early lectures, those which went into the building of his book *Principles of Literary Criticism*, and I want to testify to their electrifying effect — on me and on many others, including many senior listeners. One was accustomed to finding that one's teachers were men of learning, sensibility, critical perception and perhaps noble ideals; but here was a man lecturing on literary criticism who had actually done some fundamental *thinking*! Metaphysician and psychologist, Richards had meditated deeply upon the relationships between Thoughts, Words and Things; upon the different kinds and levels of meaning; upon the different ways in which meaning can be communicated; and, most excitingly for us, upon what goes on in the mind when we read a poem. In the course of lectures in which his dry, toneless voice was amply compensated by his splendid cranium and the panoramic sweep of his intellect, he would turn continually to the blackboard and elaborate cross-sections of a reader's mind, full of springs, pulleys, and arrows indicating emotions, images and incipient impulses to act. From all this we learnt to think of a poem not merely as black marks on a page but as a state of mind in the reader, an ordering of our own impulses, corresponding (as one hoped) to that of the poet himself on the far side of the printed marks. Most significant was the realisation, springing from this, that the experience called a poem was not different *in kind* from any other experience which life might offer; thus doctrines about art-for-art's sake, and about the necessary antagonism of art and morality, were seen to be beside the point. We took over from Richards, what I suppose he had taken over partly from G.E. Moore and partly from experimental psychology, the idea that what mattered most was valuable states of mind; that a poem is to be appraised according to the value of the experience it embodies and communicates; and that 'value' itself is to be thought of in terms of the ordering and balancing of the impulses, with due subordination of the less important to the more important. We did not then pause to enquire what was the criterion of 'importance', or whether it was quantitative or qualitative; in those days this did not matter, since a fundamental scale of values could be taken for granted as shared by all. But what a revelation all this was to our generation, brought up as we had been on the gossip of a Saintsbury or the elegant posturings of an Edmund Gosse! If it does not seem a revelation now, it is because Richards's teaching has passed into circulation as part of our common heritage. How many who speak of 'stock responses', 'pseudo-statements', or 'emotive' language, know that they are using his terms? And how many remember that it was he who, in his courses and book on *Practical Criticism*, founded the modern school of 'new criticism' and the modern technique of close reading and analysis?

With all his mental and physical athleticism – for Ivor was a famous Alpinist as well as a scaler of mental mountains – he combined an extraordinary modesty and gentleness: the unassumingness, in fact, of a man who cares much more about his work than about himself. It is for these amongst other reasons that he made and makes, upon all who know him, an impression of true greatness.

4

We often hear today, from people then in or not yet in their cradles, about the levity, cynicism and desperation of the 1920's; and it is doubtless true that the 19th century – or the Victorian age – died about the year 1920 rather than in 1900. It was the 1914-18 war that killed it. And yet, for a man of my generation, how innocent, virginal and hopeful that decade now appears to the backward glance! How misleading, how distorted an impression is conveyed by that type of radio-retrospect, or highbrow potted-history, which has no eye for anything but night-clubs, avant-garde coteries, advanced art and advanced morals!

To come back to Cambridge in the early post-war years: it still seemed possible to pick up the threads where they had been dropped. The 19th century might have died overnight, but the fact was not yet generally known. The prevailing winds in the English School were still romantic, liberal, progressive; the old valuations persisted; the history of English Literature had not yet been re-written. The teaching of men like Forbes and Richards, though it was immensely stimulating and though it greatly deepened and widened our notions about the imaginative uses of language, did not of itself, or immediately, let in the rough winds of change. True, there had been subversive influences, of which we had heard. There had been, for instance, Samuel Butler who had de-bunked Victorian morality, religion, family-life, Darwin and Homer – indeed very nearly everything except money, good looks, good health,

Handel and Lamarck. But then one did not take him very seriously. There had been, of course, and there still was, Bernard Shaw, who for time out of mind had been following up Butler's attack and reinforcing it with Socialist artillery. But then he was so amusing that one didn't take him seriously either. There might be a lot in what he said, but after all Englishmen enjoy being laughed at, and Shaw *was* an Irishman. There had also been Lytton Strachey, the impact of whose *Eminent Victorians* upon some readers was certainly very strong. I remember reading it before I was out of khaki, and I relished it as I used to relish Voltaire, and for the same qualities — those of a very dry, sparkling intellectual wine. But although Strachey had turned all his Victorians into Pecksniffs he had done it in a prose not only elegant but frequently tinged with the true Victorian purple; he was, moreover, so obviously a gentleman.

But, of the major corrosives of the century, of Marx and Freud for example, hardly more than a *soupçon* had as yet trickled through into our fool's paradise. I shall never forget the amazement, the incredulity, with which I first heard from one of my own pupils (who was a Communist, or about to become one) that a poem, an image, an emotion or an ideal could be *bourgeois* — or indeed could have any connection with economics or class at all. Similarly, I remember what a joke we all thought it when Ernest Jones psycho-analysed Hamlet, and diagnosed him as a sufferer from something called an Oedipus-complex; I can hear 'Q's' snort to this day. Perhaps I was more *naif* in those days than some others — but not much, I think; my experience, I suspect, was fairly general and typical. We none of us looked instinctively, and primarily, for Freudian or sociological explanations of writers or their works; ideas, theories, and works of art, were supposed to live and move and have their being in a world of their own. They influenced each other, but it was not taken for granted that all were epiphenomena, derived from and determined by underlying psychological, historical and social forces.

The later '20's, and the pre-Hitler '30's were, I think, the golden or heroic age of Cambridge English. I say this in spite of knowing that many would reserve that title for the *Scrutiny* era, and in spite of remembering that E.M.W. Tillyard's book, *The Muse Unchained*, was severely criticised for stopping short before that era. Tillyard's judgment, I think, was at fault in one thing only: in giving that book the sub-title of "A Revolution in English Studies". This led many to expect that he meant to deal with what they regarded as the true revolutionary movement in Cambridge English: the launching of *Scrutiny* and the work of Dr. Leavis in general. But to Tillyard and the other founders and pioneers, and to many of their pupils of the earliest vintages, it seemed that the most significant thing, the genuine revolution, was the

War of Independence whereby English became an autonomous discipline, free from all alien tyrannies and ancient prejudices. It took English most of these ten years, from 1920 to 1930, to become academically respectable; at first, it was looked at askance by the traditionalists as a Cinderella subject and a 'soft option'. It is a common observation that religious and political creeds are never held with livelier conviction than when their adherents are under persecution. And so it was with Cambridge English in that decade; fighting for recognition against powerful vested interests, it believed in its own cause and presented a united front to all its critics. Later, when English had itself become an 'Establishment', the Scrutineers in their turn derived energy and solidarity from their sense of being a persecuted minority. But this meant that the original joyous unity and momentum had been lost; Cambridge English was now like Christendom after the Reformation: re-invigorated, perhaps, but rent asunder and inly racked.

But this is anticipating; and moreover, though I could say a great deal on this fascinating subject, I want as far as possible to avoid speaking about living persons. Let me instead point to some of the outside influences which, as the years went by, broke in upon the freshness of that early world and rubbed off some of its bloom. First I would mention a minor matter, a matter of organization, which yet has its meaning and its period interest. In these present times of bureaucratic regimentation, when University affairs are controlled by a vast central academic Civil Service, it is difficult to believe that all this is of rather recent growth. When I began lecturing for the English Tripos in 1923 there was no Faculty Establishment to speak of – only a Professorship and one Lectureship dating from the old regime – and the lecturing situation was a 'free-for-all'. Anybody with reasonable qualifications could offer courses; one simply had to persuade the Secretary that one's offer was respectable, and then one was put on the lecture-list. Such lecturers (of whom I was one) were not salaried teaching-officers: we simply collected our own fees by keeping a roll of names and then sending in bills to the various College Tutors at the end of each Term. This meant that popular lecturers did very well, and others not so well. All the early lectures I have mentioned were given under this system (or lack of system), and although I am not defending such extreme anarchy it produced a certain sense of excitement, and a certain freshness and flexibility, which have been lost under regular government. New courses appeared and disappeared with intriguing frequency, and people were interested to taste them. Some were naturally eccentric or worthless, but others might be by Forbes, Richards, Lucas, Downs, Tillyard, Attwater or Bennett.

How different is the picture nowadays! We now have a large staff of salaried University Lecturers and Assistant Lecturers, all most carefully and competitively hand-picked, all acknowledged experts, all bound by statute to deliver a stated minimum of lectures a year — and nobody goes to hear them! That is a vivacious statement, of course, and needs qualifying, but it contains too much truth if not the whole of it. Some lectures are well-attended sometimes: those which the current fashion fixes for the time being as 'O.K.'. Others, most others, however famous and brilliant the lecturer may be, attract only a handful. There are several possible explanations of this. One is that there are far too many lecture-courses; the undergraduates are dazed, bewildered, and give up in despair. So many luminaries crowded together create a general blur, and rob each other of brightness and particularity. Remove any one of them into the outer darkness of an Extension Course in the provinces, or even in Cambridge itself so long as it is not on the lecture-list, and its beams will radiate far and wide.

This plethora of lectures is partly due to the lack of co-ordination between College and University teaching. Lecturers are appointed by the University to do University teaching, and this has traditionally meant lecturing. Yet everybody knows that the really important thing is College supervision, and that these same lecturers, as Fellows of Colleges, will be performing their most useful function in that capacity. The individual attention given in College supervisions or tutorials has always been reckoned one of the distinctive advantages of Oxbridge education, and no doubt it has been and often still is so. In former times each College aimed at being a miniature University, providing its own teaching and lecturing in all the main subjects as well as serving its other purposes as an independent community. Today, owing to the vast increase in numbers and the proliferation of new subjects, they can no longer do this, and we have the absurd situation in which the University multiplies unwanted lectures in order (though one mustn't say so) to provide the Colleges with supervisors. Even that is not enough, and many Colleges are being forced to elect, as teaching Fellows in the big subjects, men who neither are nor have much chance of becoming University lecturers. I have tried by a rapid flash-forward to bring out by contrast the tone and quality of those earlier years which I have called golden. Over-concern — inevitable no doubt, but deplorable — with problems of organization, and apathy about lectures: these are the first to be mentioned of the clouds which have dimmed the original brightness.

I come back now to more important influences: forces affecting the spirit and ethos of Cambridge English, and of much else besides. I ought perhaps to change the metaphor, and speak not of clouds overspreading a clear sky, but of the serpent entering our Eden. It would be discourteous to call Mr. T.S. Eliot a serpent, and it must have been a very bogus sort of Eden in which he could appear in that guise. Moreover, he was only one of many intruders into pre-lapsarian Cambridge. Yet I date the beginning of the climatic change from the day when Tillyard casually observed, to me, at the end of a walk round Grantchester, that there was a new chap called T.S. Eliot for whom one should be on the look-out. It was the first time I had heard of him. What followed? It would be absurd and presumptuous to try to summarise the effects produced upon English studies by Eliot's criticism and poetry. It would also be unnecessary, for most people know all about it. Let me rather, pursuing my autobiographical line, describe how I began to notice it.

Well, I noticed it more and more in supervisions. Old and familiar intellectual clothes were being discarded, and new styles coming into fashion. Old literary luminaries were sinking below the horizon, and others rising into the sky. It was now to be down with Milton, and up with Donne. Milton, we learnt to our amazement, was a Chinese Wall blocking the onward course of English poetry; or in the other metaphor, he had applied to it surgery so drastic that it had never really recovered. Donne, on the other hand, was everything that a poet should be; he was witty, subtle, argumentative, ironical, had his intellect at the tips of his senses, could think passionately and feel intellectually, had a unified sensibility, and so forth. Or Dryden: in place of the accepted Arnoldian view of him as a brassy rhetorician, whose poetry proceeded from the wits and not from the soul, and who could never show us things in their truth and beauty, we were invited to pay him homage as a master-craftsman − the utmost that a mere poet should presume to be. Other divinities of the romantic century were ignored, or treated to passing lip-service. Shelley became a reproach and a hissing; and Arnold, though respectfully saluted, was found to be a muddled thinker after all.

Beyond and beneath all this there were corrosives at work, the acids of anti-liberalism and anti-romanticism, eating away the very foundations on which we had built. Mr. Eliot put into currency the phrase "worm-eaten with liberalism"; it was now the turn of liberalism itself to be worm-eaten. All our basic valuations, all our presuppositions about God, Nature and Man, and consequently our notions about poetry, were to be revised or even reversed. Man, we now learnt either straight from T.E. Hulme or indirectly from Hulme through Eliot, was not a well flowing with infinite and godlike potentialities (the Romantic view), but a bucket capable of holding just so much (and no more) of what was poured into him from without (the Classical view). God was transcendent and not immanent, and consequently he was not to be sought in Nature but only in a Super-Nature separated from Nature by an unbridgeable metaphysical gulf. The notion that man, and especially the child, is a heavenly visitant sent from on high to dwell awhile in a divine Universe, to commune with it and enjoy it, and return through it to God, was nonsense. And if it was nonsense, so also was much of the poetry which presupposed it (a great deal of English poetry).

And so, also, was that powerful and hitherto almost unchallenged tradition in literary criticism, which regarded poetry as in some sort a revelation of truth, the breath and finer spirit of all knowledge, the impassioned expression in the face of science, the disimprisoning of the soul of fact, the wielder of moral and natural magic, the ally or even heir-presumptive of religion. All this is the babble and froth of overweening romanticism. There is only one revelation, the Christian religion; its receptacle is the Church, and its formulation is in her dogmas. A poet is not a *vates*, a prophet or inspired hierophant or seer; he is a maker, building things with words. He must be valued, not for any supposed power of giving us glimpses into the life of things, of lightening the weight of all this unintelligible world, or of consoling or sustaining us after the loss of creeds — not for anything of this kind, but simply for his skill as a craftsman, his rhetorical expertise, his mastery in the art of making words do their various kinds of work. Hence, quite naturally and logically, T.E. Hulme disparaged the Coleridgean Imagination, which at once sees and makes the truth, keeps truth living, and sees all things as one in the life of God; and cried up the Fancy, which knows its place and doesn't pretend to do more than be clever, hard and glittering. Imagination leads off into the Romantic fogs where all clear outlines are blurred; Fancy sits preening herself contentedly in the Classical sunshine.

So that when Mr. Eliot proclaimed himself a royalist in politics, an Anglo-Catholic in religion, and a classicist in art we were not as much taken aback as we might have been by this extraordinary assertion, and as we should have been if anyone had made it during the previous half-century (or century). Mr. Eliot's position was made very clear in two of his early essays, *Macchiavelli* and *Shakespeare and the Stoicism of Seneca* (to both of which I have referred in an earlier publication). Macchiavelli, he argued, was not brutal, cynical or fiendish in his political thought; he was merely realistic. He told the truth about man, and had no illusions about human nature since the Fall. But for the past 300 years liberal-humanism and romanticism have been trying hard to obliterate this true image, and to replace it with the myth of man as naturally good. To the liberal, Macchiavelli is therefore intolerable; it is only to the orthodox believer, who accepts the Fall and Original Sin, that Macchiavelli's wisdom is revealed. Similarly with Stoicism: the Stoic, said Mr. Eliot, tried to support the strain of living the life of Reason by joining himself with the Universe — which is what Wordsworth and most of the romantics also did. But, said Mr. Eliot, a man does not join himself with the Universe if he has anything better to join; an Athenian of the best period had something better, his *polis*, and Christians have had something better, their *ecclesia*.

Why do I dwell upon all this in a retrospect of Cambridge English? It will be said that this anti-liberal drive was a mere eddy in the powerful current which was sweeping the world towards the dogmatisms, the intolerance, the tyrannies, the dictatorships and the armed conflicts of the thirties. And this is true; as the bright dawn of the '20's darkened into the '30's there was everywhere a hardening of hearts and of arteries, a commitment to party or creed, a sharpening of swords for battle. How did this show itself in the little backwater of Cambridge English?

It showed itself, I think, in the loss of the first fine careless rapture, the confident faith that in English Literature could be found the liberal and humane education *par excellence*, that by steeping oneself in its masterpieces one could gain wisdom, liberation and elevation of spirit. Parties and cliques began to show themselves in our midst. There were a few who followed Eliot into Anglo-Catholicism, and who found the Metaphysicals and Hopkins and C.S. Lewis very much to their taste. On the whole, however, it was surprising how few of Eliot's many disciples at that time (it was the time when innumerable undergraduate essay-writers tried to justify their remarks by the phrase 'as Mr. Eliot has said' — Shakespeare was a very great poet, etc.) — how few of them did follow him as far as that. They seemed to regard his religion as a mere item in his intellectual panoply; interesting and curious, perhaps, but important only in so far as it might affect (perhaps distort) his critical evaluations, or provide a framework for his own poetry. There were, on the other hand, a good many — and their numbers and influence increased steadily up to 1939 — who were either avowed Communists or who (more often) found in Marxism a new and exciting way of understanding not only the dialectic of history but also the origin and true significance of literature. It was now that 'decaying feudal order', 'control of means of production', 'rising bourgeoisie' and the rest entered the currency of literary criticism. One no longer heard phrases like *praecipitandus est liber spiritus*, or 'man's unconquerable mind; it was now the vogue to consider all literature as determined and conditioned by social and economic and psychological forces. It was as much an end-product of its own climate and soil as the vegetation. In a sense this was a reversal of 'Q's' doctrine: 'tendencies' *did* produce *The Canterbury Tales*; 'naturalism' *did* write *Tintern Abbey*, provided always, of course, that you interpreted 'tendencies' and 'naturalism' not as ideas, but in terms of historical materialism.

Lastly there were the Freudians and Jungians, who found literature useful and interesting as an explanation or illustration of other things more interesting still, namely case-histories and the collective unconscious. Why do people write at all? Probably because they are neurotic; a perfectly well-adjusted person would not need to seek this sort of compensation. So the thing to look for, the clue to any given poem, is the particular conflict — domestic, filial, sexual, social etc. etc. — which the poem was written to resolve. Or, you might be able to show that certain symbols, or patterns of symbols, were derived from archetypes buried deep in unconscious race-memory.

Apart from all these stood, in splendid isolation, the most vigorous, self-confident, self-conscious of all the sects, the Scrutineers under the leadership of F.R. Leavis. It is to their lasting credit that at a time when the centre was ceasing to hold, and people were beginning to follow strange gods, the Leavisites did keep the flag of the true faith bravely flying. It was they who went on insisting, tirelessly and in ever more strident tones, that English must be kept up; English as a discipline for mind and heart and soul; English as a co-operative enterprise, a search by a band of intelligent and sensitive people for the genuine and the authentic; English as a stronghold for minority culture in its struggle against mass civilization; English as the religion of the chosen people, the remnant, in their holy war against all Philistines — including the academic establishment, Bloomsbury, and the weekly reviews. Never for a moment straying to right or to left, never seeking refuge in religious or political dogma or in psychological explanations, they kept to the straight and narrow path, scrutinising each literary work as such and not as a product of something else, and judging it by standards which, though doubtless derived in the last analysis from religion or ethics, could yet plausibly be applied as if they were autonomous. I was often, as all non-Leavisites were, irritated by their arrogance, self-righteousness, disdainfulness and rudeness. Yet I recognised their integrity and zeal, and above all, of course, the distinguished critical perceptiveness of Leavis himself, as repeatedly shown in his subtle analyses of particular writers and passages. In those days, the days when he was still outside the Faculty and accounting himself ostracised, I always defended him against his detractors, even though sharing their exasperation at his obsessions. He always seemed to me so much more expert than most of us in a very important part of our job.

I have said that they upheld the 'true faith' against the infidels and miscreants: yes, but it was the true faith with a difference. The original faith had been Catholic; theirs was Protestant, Puritan, separatist; it even had affinities with that of the Peculiar People or the Exclusive Brethren. The original faith had been liberal, tolerant, genial; theirs was fanatical, intolerant and ascetic. This ferocity, this belligerency, was all very well — it was splendid, in fact — while they were waging war on the Gentile hordes who threatened the holy land from outside. What many of us deplored was that their fire was directed so continually against the citadel itself, against their natural allies — their colleagues and the English Faculty itself. Ah, but we, the so-called Establishment, were really traitors in league with the enemy; they themselves, the outsiders, the persecuted remnant, were the true Israel, the real Cambridge.

I had not meant to say as much as this, and perhaps I have said too much on this topic. But I could hardly give a true picture without some reference to what has, after all, figured so prominently in the history of Cambridge English during the past thirty-five years. Now that the Cambridge University Press has re-issued *Scrutiny* in bound volumes, perhaps honour is satisfied on both sides.

The very last thing I want to be or seem is egoistic, but since I have been speaking in a semi-autobiographical vein I suppose I ought to refer briefly to my own small contribution to Cambridge English. I do this reluctantly, and I do it chiefly because by means of it I can conveniently lead up to my final observations on English as an academic discipline. My route has lain, for the most part, off what most people would consider the main track. Perhaps because of my upbringing, and the special orientation it gave, I have always been a bit of a moralist — by which I mean that the art which has interested me most has been the art of living, and the good life has seemed the object best worth pursuing. Literature had this advantage over other studies, that its subject-matter happened to be life — not some sub-section or specialised department of it, but the whole of it; life as lived and reported upon by the most sensitive, intelligent, imaginative and articulate people. Literature has always seemed to me both a by-product of life and a means of life; the outcome of other people's experience, communicated to us so that we might have life and have it more abundantly. Matthew Arnold said that conduct made up three-fourths of life, but what an understatement that was! It makes up nine-tenths if not the whole of it.

So naturally I considered myself lucky to have come to English just at the close of the art-for-art's sake era, and naturally I saluted Richards as a kindred spirit when I found him bridging the imagined gulf between art and life, and showing art to *be* life, life in its most finely ordered form. Fortunately for me, also, the subject-matter of the English Tripos had been defined, not as Literature, but as Literature, Life and Thought. 'Q' had always insisted, as I said, that literature cannot be divorced from life; by this he meant that literature had been produced by flesh-and-blood human beings in the course of their lives, loves, joys and sorrows, and could best be savoured, not by pallid academics or earnest researchers, but by other human beings of like constitution, ready to accept life as an adventure and live it with gusto. I agreed with 'Q', but being a less full-blooded creature, and one more at home on the mountain-tops than in the hurly-burly of life, I turned my attention to the intellectual climates which have moulded opinion in the various centuries, and tried to see and to explain literary events and movements as the outcome of those — and not as something autonomous to be studied in isolation. It seemed to me superficial and uninteresting to say, for example, that the condition of verse in the 18th century was due to something that Milton or Dryden had done with their rhetoric, and to leave it at that. Milton and Dryden, and the 18th century, were all what they were because of certain changes in the prevailing winds of doctrine.

I started lecturing in 1923, and it was not long before I began to see in that part of the syllabus called 'Life and Thought' the sphere in which I could work most happily. But I lectured on other things too. My first course was on The Essay, and ran from Montaigne to Max Beerbohm, taking in on its way such writers as Bacon, Browne, Cowley, Addison, Lamb, Hazlitt, De Quincey, Stevenson, Chesterton, etc. I also gave a course on American writers: Emerson, Thoreau and Hawthorne — probably the first course, humble as it was, ever given on American literature in an English University. Emerson and Thoreau, in particular, had been my staple reading (believe it or not) in trenches and dug-outs during the war; in those days I had found their transcendental doctrines an admirable corrective to the mud and blood, and the brutal ethos, of army life. The same doctrines appeared pretty spectral when expounded in a lecture-room, but I owe to the Thoreau lecture one of the finest friendships of my life — with an American, now eminent in the publishing world, who attended it and liked it. In later years I lectured also on Wordsworth and Coleridge, who have always been the two great lights in my literary firmament. Indeed, a fellow-Professor who shall be nameless said to me recently: 'You do admit, don't you Basil, that all your books have really been about Wordsworth? All that stuff about Bacon and Locke, and the other later chaps, was all either leading up to him or down from him, wasn't it?'

I continued lecturing on 17th and 18th century Life and Thought until the substance of the lectures appeared in print. And then, when 'Q' introduced the English Moralists as an option in the new Part II, I devoted myself to that for the rest of my Cambridge time.

Enough, and more than enough, of these personal matters. I feel as if I had been composing a *curriculum vitae* to be used in an application for one of those posts sometimes available, *in partibus infidelium*, to Professors over the Oxbridge retiring age — which God forbid.

5

I turn with alacrity to another subject, not directly connected with Cambridge English but not without bearing upon it. For the first ten years of my teaching life, i.e. from 1923 to 1933, I was actively engaged, generally two nights a week but sometimes three, in taking

W.E.A. Tutorial Classes under the Cambridge University Extra-Mural Board. These took me to Bedford, Luton, Peterborough, Desborough, Rugby and Cambridge itself. I don't know what W.E.A. class-members are like today, or how the tremendous social, economic and educational changes of the past thirty years may have affected their approach. But in my day they were wonderful; I have never had such rewarding audiences anywhere else and certainly not inside Cambridge or any University. They were, of course, adult, mature and serious, but above all they were eager to learn, hungry and thirsty for the knowledge and wisdom that their circumstances had denied them, or allowed only sparingly. In these classes the individual who learnt most (I am sure) was myself. To speak to and hold the attention of such splendid people for two hours a week in 24-week courses, and to repeat this for three or sometimes four years, meant an effort of reading and preparation, and an expenditure of energy in expounding, such as I had never made before. There was hardly a writer or subject from classical antiquity to the present day on which I had not to be ready to say something not patently absurd or ignorant. Also, I learnt in these classes to swim without a rubber-belt – I mean, to speak extempore. I soon found that the essence of the Tutor-class relationship lay in personal friendship and mutual confidence, and reading from a prepared script would have destroyed this completely. So, with great trepidation at first, but with increasing confidence as time went on, I used to plunge in at the deep end, and found – to my astonishment and relief – that the waters bore me up. Nevertheless, I never risked this in University lecturing; the human rapport was wanting, the standards more exacting, and the need to appear omniscient more imperative.

My experience in these Classes probably confirmed me in my own original approach, for people seemed to desire just what I was readiest to give – pointers and signposts leading towards life, and life more abundant. Books and authors were valued or rejected by them, I found, in proportion to their success or failure in coming home to their business and bosoms, and serving for the uses and occasions of life. These were busy, responsible people: mothers of families, schoolteachers, tradespeople, factory hands, clerks and so on; how could I feed them on the husks of pedantry or the acorns of highbrow sophistication? What they wanted was good wholesome brown bread. They were also predominantly Christian, and especially non-comformist; and the few agnostics among them were generally, in the usual way of those times, the most serious moralists of them all. How, then, could I recommend for their approval writers who, however fine their technique, had leprous minds? How could I ask them to keep company with and share the standpoint of, fictitious characters of the kinds that both they and I would have gone a hundred miles to avoid in real life? Oh, I knew all the stock jargon and tried all the usual dodges: I talked about sincerity, awareness, first-hand experience and all the rest of it. But it did not work. They were as simple-minded as Plato, who thought that some art improved the soul and other art corrupted the soul. They were as simple-minded as Dr. Johnson, who asked what books were for if not to teach us how to live. In contact with such people one could never make the mistake, so incident to dons, of confusing means and ends, and regarding literature as an end in itself, or even as the end of life itself.

6

My concentration on background-studies, or what is sometimes called the History of Ideas, kept me immune from the academic storms that raged over various authors and reputations. But it made me, in the end, a very peculiar sort of Professor of English. After 1946 it was no longer my business to supervise undergraduates, and my lectures were mostly about writers my colleagues didn't read, and didn't regard as 'Eng. Lit.' at all. Nor did I, on my side, make it my business to keep abreast, as a real 'Eng. Lit.' Professor should, with all the latest books and articles on all the principal 'Eng. Lit.' writers – though I did in fact read a great many of these in addition to 'my own stuff'. This isolation, or even alienation, naturally grew more marked as the years went by; it was due, I think, not merely to the remoteness of my own interests but to the advent of wave after wave of younger people – both students and colleagues – whose starting-point, upbringing, standards and assumptions all differed from my own, who read different books, and who almost spoke a different language.

But I was not blind to the social, intellectual and spiritual changes going on in the '30's, '40's and '50's. For example, in the early years I had taught and emphasised the importance of ideas, especially scientific, religious, philosophical and political ideas, in forming the climates of opinion in each period. But during the later '30's, when economic and sociological types of explanation were being applied to everything, including religion and even science, and of course to the arts, it began to be questioned whether ideas as such were ever the *causes* of historical change. Were they not themselves mirages or spectra, phantoms and will o' the wisps thrown off by the earth and mud of reality; epiphenomena, translations into idealist language of the underlying economic struggle of the class war?

This worried me a bit at first, because although I didn't believe it, I didn't at once see how it could be disproved. But I was soon consoled by coming across a remark from an Encyclical by one of the Marxist Popes – Engels, I think – to the effect that ideas, once generated, could and did often affect history as if they were genuine material causes. This was good enough to be going on with. But in fact, despite

c

my lifelong interest in backgrounds and climates, I have never been a determinist; I have always considered man to be the moulder, as well as the product, of his environment.

Hitler's war never affected University life as the Kaiser's had done; the system of deferments maintained a steady continuity of teaching and study throughout, and the presence of evacuated students from London kept the numbers up. The postwar decade 1944-1954 differed greatly from the earlier one, 1920-30; there was none of the old optimism, no expectation of reviving the old world, and not much hope of producing a better one: the ghastly shadow of Hiroshima lay for years across our hearts. We had destroyed Nazism only to be left with this haunting dread.

Perhaps for these reasons amongst others the second postwar decade saw a remarkable religious revival in the University. I don't mean a revival in the old evangelistic sense, with highly-wrought emotions and conversions; I mean a serious disposition to enquire whether religion did not perhaps, after all, explain the riddle of the world better than anything else; whether its estimate of man's unregenerate nature was not the most realistic, its policy of repentance, faith and love the most promising of any. Churches and College Chapels were packed and religious study-groups showed a vitality equalling, and entirely superseding, the Marxian counterparts of the pre-war years. It was at that time that the Faculty of Divinity started its Saturday morning lectures on theological subjects, a series to which men like J.S. Whale, Professor Hodges, Professor Butterfield and Alec Vidler contributed. I also had the privilege of contributing a course, and I can at least say this, that never have I lectured to such numbers before or since; the great hall of the Examination School was full week after week for nearly all the courses in this series. The outcome of my own course was a little book called *Christianity Past and Present*, which, not being published by Chatto and Windus, never appeared in the list "By the Same Author" and was speedily forgotten. This I could not help slightly regretting, for I consider it one of the best, as well as one of the shortest, things I have ever written.

It is difficult to say how all this affected English studies. There were some attempts, rather half-hearted, to start a Christian school of literary criticism, and there was a great deal of discussion as to how, if at all, an English don who happened to be a Christian should allow his beliefs to affect his work. There were, however, so few of these that the debate died of inanition. Those who remained shy of Christianity, both teachers and taught, may have been − I think they were − impelled once again to try and make a religion out of English, complete with Spiritual Exercises (Practical Criticism), Private Devotion (poetry readings), a prophet (Leavis) and a Messiah (D.H. Lawrence).

I will conclude by indicating briefly and dogmatically what seem to me some of the hazards besetting English as an academic discipline. First, it cannot provide the balanced and well-rounded humanist education that its founders dreamed of. It does not know enough about the world in which we live, and needs supplementing with other kinds of study — linguistic, economic, historical, philosophical, scientific. Secondly, although I have called it a discipline, I now add that it does not in itself provide an adequate discipline for the intellect or for the spirit. In a sense the original objectors to an English Tripos were right, though they could not know why. For a long time it was hoped and claimed, and firmly believed by many, that in Practical Criticism we had a discipline of the whole man, mind and heart, the total sensibility, which though vaguer than those of mathematics or the sciences or linguistics was none the less exacting and bracing, and likely to produce finer human beings. But has this proved true? I think not. It leads young people to indulge in the wildest extravagances of conceit, presumption and exhibitionism in the hope of showing how clever, how perceptive, they are; or — and this is the normal, the really depressing thing — to serve up pre-fabricated and pre-digested reactions which they believe to be records of Their Master's Voice. Thirdly, scholarship has moved in upon English like an occupying army; 'Gone is the calm of her earlier shore' — the innocence, the amateurish zest, the flower-culling and garland-weaving excitement of the prime. There is now hardly an author, hardly a subject not so barricaded within double and triple walls of scholarship, variorum editions, complete letters and note-books, and all the rest of it, as to make general teaching seem imposture, and profitable learning almost impossible. Only the special-ist can feel that he is master of his subject, and thus the school which prided itself precisely on transcending specialisms has ended by re-admitting them in an extreme form. Fourthly, although vastly greater numbers now read English, why do they read it? Very few, I think, would (if they were honest) give 'Q's' sort of answer to this question. They read it, not to become finer human beings, but to get a degree with the minimum of effort and so get a job. For although it is very hard to get a First in English it is terribly easy, far too easy, to get a Third in it.

Similarly, at a higher level, what is called 'research' has become dreary and mechanical. People who embark on it do so, not because they are interested in discovering some truth, but because they are interested in getting a Ph.D., the passport to academic appointments. And as aspirants swarm in ever more thickly, the difficulty of finding any subject not already hackneyed, not futile, or not bogus, becomes desperate. I could go on much longer, but I must not. Just one further comment. 'The man we are proud to send forth . . . ' I refer to 'Q's' remark above-quoted. What sort of man do we now send forth? Often his character and mentality have already been irremediably fixed by the indiscipline, the aimlessness, the boredom and the hubris of this age; but what has University English done to correct all this? Something, let us hope and believe. But, in itself and by itself, not enough. It encourages intellectual arrogance and shallowness by its slick habit of 'placing' and 'debunking' great men. And by making young people conversant with a great variety of opinions, attitudes and beliefs, not with a view to considering their truth or their usefulness for present living, but in order to note their period characteristics and to arrange them like butterflies in a museum — by doing this, it produces in them an aggravation of the scepticism, the fecklessness and the irreverence already so prevalent in this age. It does not even give them, what it is the glory of science to give its devotees, reverence for *fact*.

There! now I have put most of my cards on the table. Make allowances for my mood if you will, but not to the extent of discounting all my points: they are, I think, worth considering, even if it is only to refute them, or to suggest how the dangers can be avoided. I would not have spent a lifetime teaching English, and some anxious recent years diagnosing its ailments, if I did not think it a magnificent study, and if I were not sure that the defects can be remedied. In saying 'Goodbye To All That' I may have seemed a bit brusque; but my final gesture is not a shrug, but an affectionate farewell kiss.

Chapter Two

1923 – 1930

I

These were years of happy domesticity and academic apprenticeship. I was married in 1923, and the first three of our family of four arrived at suitable intervals during that time. We began our married life in the small box-like villa 282 Hills Road, just near the Long Road turning. It was newly-built, and we were its first occupants. In those days we were on the very edge of the open country; there were no houses beyond the Long Road, only two or three along Queen Edith's Way, and none in the Long Road beyond what was then the level-crossing. The housing 'explosion' which by now has spread bricks and mortar the whole way from the Newmarket Road to the Gogs was still undreamed of, and the hills rose to their modest height from immemorial East Anglian cornfields. There was so little traffic along Hills Road that each September, when Mr. Gray opened the grounds of Gog Magog House for the annual Fete, we noticed the special stream of vehicles as a violation of our rural tranquillity. From our back windows we looked across poppied fields to the farmhouse, barns and ricks of Trinity Farm (now replaced by a Telephone Exchange).

We soon became extremely fond of our little house, and added to it twice in later years, to accommodate the children, rather than move to a larger one. For a long time we lived very much on the outer fringe of Cambridge, both geographically and academically. At first my only connection with the University was supervising for Peterhouse and some other Colleges, and the delivery of the above-mentioned courses of Lectures on The English Essayists and Some American Writers. These lectures, as I have explained, represented no regular University appointment; indeed, the Faculty system was not set up till several years later. I merely managed to persuade whoever was then Secretary to the Board (it was probably E.M.W. Tillyard) to put me down on the published lecture-list. I still remember my blank dismay, when, on opening the *Reporter* which was to announce my course, I found that it was not mentioned. I sat on the stairs momentarily despairing, but was immediately roused to action and renewed hope by my new ally, my newly-wedded wife. Probably nothing but good came of this mishap; the emergency-notices sent round to Tutors doubtless produced a larger audience than the routine announcement would have done.

The preparation of those lectures was a hand-to-mouth business. During the first year of their delivery, when I had nothing ready, and only my war-time and Tripos reading to draw upon, I used to write each one on Wednesday afternoons and evenings for delivery on Thursdays at 12. The sessions began after lunch and often continued far into the night; and at a later stage my wife typed them all out on the small Underwood portable which is still the only typewriter I have ever owned, and which I have never learned to use without great agony.

For the first decade after 1923, having no sort of academic security, I undertook all kinds of jobs to swell our slender income, and had no time to think of literary or scholarly ventures. I 'supervised' many hours a week, and was soon asked to examine in the Tripos. This examining, which was repeated every June for years, brought me into close and stimulating contact with some of the leading men of that time in the English School: Tillyard, Attwater, Forbes, Lucas, Richards and 'Q'; and through the examiners' meetings and the accompanying lunches I began to taste something of the flavour of College life at the senior level. But the actual reading of the scripts – small though the task can now be seen to have been compared with the monstrous proportions it has attained today – was always a penance to me. I was morbidly conscientious about justice to every candidate; prone to be easily impressed by a show of cleverness, and to see merit where little existed; and at the same time very quickly surfeited with the intake of indigestible matter, so that the daily ration of scripts could only be got through by the sternest efforts of will. What made things worse was that this agony always coincided with the annual onset of my hay-fever; thus, by the time the class-list was published I was fit for nothing except to rush away to the Lakes and there seek relief, which never failed to come – relief from both the hay-fever and the exhaustion. After the most exacting of these experiences (examining for the 'Moralists' paper in Part II, at its debut in 1929) I find the following significant entry in the very scrappy diary I then kept: 'The sheepbells on Helvellyn, heard as I lay awake the first night at Grasmere'.

It looked for a time as if my main work in life was to be 'Extra-Mural', i.e. W.E.A. Tutorial Classes. In 1924 I began a three-year class at Bedford; in 1925 one at Rugby, which overlapped the Bedford class for two years, and in 1926 one in Cambridge itself, so that by that year I had three nights a week (two-hour sessions) occupied in this way. Others followed, at Peterborough, Luton and Desborough. The Rugby class was extended to a fourth year at the request of the class. I have already spoken of the immense benefit I derived from these classes, in broadening my knowledge, giving me facility in extempore lecturing, and developing my insight into the needs and aspirations of some of the best people then in the world. To these fine people I have paid tribute above. But it was hard work keeping up with the syllabuses of three classes at once, even though they over-

lapped somewhat. And I was all the while composing new lectures for
Cambridge University, on Life, Literature and Thought in the Eighteenth Century (beginning 1927), and in the Seventeenth Century (1928).
At stated intervals there would arrive, from the Local Examinations
Syndicate, corded bales of scripts from school-children all over Britain
and the world. I have sometimes gone off to Bedford or Rugby, with
no lecture prepared except what I could concoct at desperate speed in
the train, and with several pounds avoirdupois of scripts in my suit-
case. After the two-hour class (the second hour, nominally for discussion, generally meant further draughts from my dwindling well),
and after being polite to my host and hostess (if, as often happened, I
had to stay the night away), I would retire to my bedroom and there
toil at scripts till I could no longer keep awake. The next morning —
back to Cambridge by an early train, in time to give a lecture on (say)
Bacon, or Hume, to a very different sort of audience.

Looking back on all this from a distance of forty years I must own
that I am amazed at the capacity for work that I seem in those days to
have possessed. No wonder my wife, and the young children, saw little
of me. But as long as I remained a mere free-lance at the University I
had to go on with it all. I did, indeed, hold for a short time a newly-
formed and now long obsolete post called 'Probationary Faculty
Lecturer', but this soon lapsed, and I had no permanent appointment
until 1934. Before that, however, the introduction by 'Q' of the
paper on "The English Moralists" gave me a new opportunity. Here
was something which my interests and cast of mind fitted me to
attempt. I began to lecture on the Moralists in the Lent Term of 1929,
and the measure of acceptance my lectures received gave me the feeling
that at last I was providing something that was genuinely wanted. In
view of this, and of the mounting numbers of my undergraduate
pupils at many Colleges, I ventured to discontinue the W.E.A. Classes
in 1931, although 'security' was still three years off, and lay on the
far side of my first book.

In many ways I was very sorry to give up the extra-mural work. In
those classes, I was welcome as a bringer of light; in Cambridge, my
little taper was unseen amid the glare of the greater luminaries. In the
classes, I was looked-up to, and hung-upon, as a bringer of life as well
as light — as a sort of lay-parson as well as teacher; in Cambridge, how
deplorable, how inconceivable would any such attitude have been held
to be! And rightly so, for of course in University lecturing ideas and
works of art are to be tested and pounded in the crucible, not put to
use in the process of daily living. Also, in the classes, I was treated as a
human being and a friend, whereas Cambridge seemed to consist, with
a few notable exceptions, of human icebergs. However, I could not
continue indefinitely under the strain of living in divided and dis-

tinguished worlds, and as soon as I felt pretty sure that Cambridge could do with me, I plumped for Cambridge.

Of these Tutorial Classes, those at Bedford and Rugby have left the deepest imaginative impress. It so happened that when I went to Bedford I was fresh from my first reading of Mark Rutherford, and it was both exciting and moving to find myself in his very town, hitherto unvisited by me but familiar in my chambers of imagery as 'Cowfold' and 'Eastthorpe'. The grave, ironic realism of William Hale White; his Puritanism, emancipated yet nostalgic; his pure, unnoticed prose style; his deep melancholy, his moods of black dejection dispelled on occasion by Wordsworth, by sunshine, by mountains or the sea; his profound religiousness, surviving all the assaults of Apollyon — by all these tokens I recognized him as a kindred spirit, one who had been on my own pilgrimage before me. Not for years, if ever, had I been so stirred by this sense of recognition as I was in reading him. Imagine my emotions, therefore, on beholding the spire of Cowfold Church, Harpur Street, 'Tanner's Lane', and the Bunyan Meeting itself; on finding that the local Secretary was a member of that Meeting, and that in a sense the very ethos of my class was a product of the same provincial quest for liberation, for ampler air and wider horizons, which I knew so well as a theme in the novels.

The Rugby class was very different in tone and composition, and the place itself had as yet no meaning for me. Of my two sons, who both went to Rugby School later, the elder was only a year old when I began, and the other was born after the class was over. The School, for all its associations with the Arnolds, Rupert Brooke, etc. was just an extraneous presence to me then; my work did not bring me into its orbit, although I met the then Headmaster (Vaughan) and chatted pleasantly with him at Perceval House. I had already discovered at Bedford that the W.E.A. was not in the least 'Bolshy'; it was even largely bourgeois and nonconformist, and it was utterly non-political and free from class consciousness. No masked propaganda underlay its activities; all sprang from the pure desire for light and life, and there was no taint of envy, malice, or any uncharitableness. At Rugby we had, however, a wider social cross-section than at Bedford, and this produced some odd but not necessarily embarrassing conjunctions. At one end, for instance, there were some hard-headed, but very nice, artisans from the B.T.H. Works, of the kind who might, perhaps (if they hadn't been so nice and loyal), have aired rationalistic or atheistical opinions from time to time. At the other, there were one or two stragglers from the cultured world of Rugby School. One, in particular, the aged sister (unmarried) of a former Rugby master, came to play so prominent a part that I sometimes feared she would scare away the real 'working class' members, or make them feel they were in the wrong galley. She persisted in treating my lectures as edifying, semi-ecclesiastical occasions; and, in tones of incantation akin in timbre to the middle registers of the violoncello, she would unfailingly supply the responses, hallelujahs and amens. Her essays, which were numerous and voluminous, generally bore at their head a Greek motto from Plato or even one of the Alexandrian Fathers, in beautiful script, and complete with accents. Her voice in discussion, as she sat blinking heavy eyelids over an averted gaze, would often rise high above all competitors with something like: 'Aye erlways think Jurge Iliot must have been *Insparred* when she wrote that *won*derful passage in *Romola* when Tito — ' etc.; or 'But who is to be our *Padre Divino* now, Mr. Willey? Deah Dean Inge is perhaps a bit *too* waspish, don't you feel?' I sometimes suspected that she was casting me for that role. But she was a sweet and essentially lovable old dear, and her more plebeian classmates, feeling this, were tolerant and amused and patient, sympathising with my problem. At the end of the four years, she not only organised a presentation to me, but gave me as a personal gift a book I prize very highly: a first edition (1850) of *The Prelude*.

The other thing that made the Rugby Class memorable was the circumstance that it brought about my friendship with the late Rev. Dr. J. Cyril Flower, who was conducting a Philosophy class there on the same days, and with whom, accordingly, I used to travel on the long train-journeys from Cambridge. These journeys, including the change at Bletchley, took about 3½ hours, and we thus had ample time (except when revising our lectures, or 'regressing', as he called the afternoon naps to which we sometimes yielded) to discuss God, Nature and Human Life. Flower was the first trained Philosopher and psychologist I had met, and to my own untrained mind, with its amateurish but persistent philosophical leanings, his conversation was most bracing and salutary. Dear Cyril! so greatly-gifted, so penetrating, so patient, so sweet-tempered, such an admirable teacher! I had known of him before, as the Unitarian minister at Cambridge, and the Unitarian streak in my own early theology gave me some common ground with him. As an outcome of this friendship my wife and I started attending the Unitarian Church, not as a formal act of adhesion to that denomination, but in order to benefit by Cyril's admirable sermons and to experience the relief of worshipping without mental reservations and multiple meanings. I doubt if this phase could have lasted long; I found the atmosphere of a small separatist sect too suffocating, however noble, candid and honest its minister and members might be. When Cyril left (as he did in due course, to become a Tutor at Manchester college, Oxford), we left too.

2

As the much-misrepresented 'twenties drew near their close, and I had passed my thirtieth birthday, I came to a turning-point in my life. A wave of panic suddenly flowed through me, panic at the realisation of youth's departure. It is, I suppose, a feeling that comes to us all, sooner or later: a sense that ahead lie the hurrying rapids of middle age. How could one avoid being swept unresisting down-stream? Up to a certain stage – perhaps it is up to marriage? – we are supported, whether we know it or not, by the sense that 'This is not yet all; the best is yet to be; there is a glory to be revealed; there are higher peaks beyond'. And then, quite suddenly, we become aware that there is no more in reserve; the path lies before us straight and clear to the bottom of the hill. Life has done all it was going to do for us, and now it hands over to us the responsibility for what may remain. This, which had seemed only exordial to the expected rich unfolding, *was* life itself; we should none of us experience any dilation, any fulfilment; we should just go on with our jobs – I with my supervising, examining and lecturing – probably getting less and less efficient with increasing years, and that *will have been* our life. There will have been nothing else. How terrible! I felt trapped and scared. Was there any way of escape from the panic? Any way of arresting the flux and the acceleration?

It was at this time, and as a way of facing up to this crisis, that I began to write a few things other than lectures. It was probably a sound instinct that redirected me towards writing, for, after all, that had been for years my habitual solace. In those diaries and word-pictures, of which I made some use in *Spots of Time*, I had found, both before and during the war, a way of overcoming the world – not by evading it but by looking more intently at it and through it. And so now I thought to myself: 'if I can only manage to *delineate* the flux, both of thoughts and of experience, perhaps I shall feel that I have somehow mastered it, fixed it in some unchangeable medium?'

The first outcome of this impulse was a series of four prose eff-usions of varying lengths, three of which were published and the other never. The first was an essay accepted by L.P.Jacks and published by him in *The Hibbert Journal* (October 1930). The original title (altered by Jacks to 'The Worldmender and his Opposite') was 'Cosmic Toryism and the Religious Attitude'. Its main object was to contrast Cosmic Toryism, i.e. the acceptance of this world as the best of all possible worlds, with the religious estimate of it as fallen and evil-ridden, and to consider what sort of ethical outcome could logically be expected from each of these views. It had another motif running through it, the distinction (learnt from I.A. Richards) between factual and emotive

utterances; statement and pseudo-statement. This I indicated by app-
ending as a motto, at the head of the essay and just below the obvious
tag from *Candide*, the following from *Principles of Literary Criticism*:
'To mistake the incitement of an attitude for a statement of fact is a
practice which should be discouraged'. Many of the thoughts in this
essay, and some actual passages, later found their way into my *Background* books.

The second, the one never published, was called 'Mr.Aspinall's
Sunday Morning Service'. The idea was suggested to me, during one of
our early Norfolk holidays, by attending morning service at the Methodist Church of North Walsham, at which my grandfather had held his
first ministry. It was an attempt to re-enact both the service itself and
the undercurrent of thoughts, more or less digressive and unregenerate,
which ran in the mind of 'James', the narrator (myself, of course). I
give here an extract from it (the concluding passage), because it illus-
trates the mood I have been describing: the sharpened sense of 'time's
winged chariot hurrying near', and the accompanying desire for pause
and permanence:

'So that at the last', the preacher was perorating, and James
collected himself for the end of the service, 'so that at the last
we may be presented before the presence of his glory with great
joy, and enter into the life everlasting.'

The life everlasting! Ah, that came near the heart of the
matter: deliverance from the time-sequence, from the accelera-
ting wheel of middle life. James remembered that formerly he
had considered the question about the soul's immortality to be
an unimportant logomachy. So it was, until one got finally
trapped by life, caught in its wheel. Then one began to understand. Not 'personal survival'; oh no, the old phrase missed the
point.

In a country churchyard, some evenings before, for instance,
James had seemed to have an intimation, not of immortality, but
of the reason why this belief had for so long been taught as necessary to the religious life. In the still air many sounds were to be
heard: farmyard sounds of pigs and geese, cows munching, the
voiceless shriek of bats. There was a smell blended of corn and
stable-manure. A grey owl beat rapid wings and vanished. Inside
the church the death-watch beetle was riddling a grand fifteenth-
century roof. In the lane outside, there had been a hedgehog and
several toads flattened to the road by passing cars. And here were
the grave-stones, glimmering white, each with verses commending
its dead to the skies. Pathetic, yet somehow right and inevitable.
The human soul, driven by sheer panic to distinguish itself from
among the beasts that perish. Trying to link oneself to something that is not gut and bone and corruption. Losing one's life
to gain it — merging the perishable individual life in something

large and abstract: Church? or perhaps better *la sua voluntade?*
living *its* life, not one's own, and so sharing its immortality.
Certainly not preserving one's miserable little separate personality, unmerged, for ever and ever. No; but, in some sense, to
believe in the life everlasting, did seem a specific human necessity
. . . In *what* sense, James was prevented from more precisely
determining, just then, by the concluding hymn, which now sang
itself out with a brightening resonance, as of a train nearing the
escape from a tunnel. With the momentum thus gained, and with
the aid of excited chords from the organ (the train is now out in
broad sunshine, James thought), the congregation filed out, duty
done, dinner before them.

When I compare this (as I cannot help doing) with the extracts given in
Spots of Time, I am struck above all by the change of tempo; the
earlier ones were 'stills': this is 'cinema'. The change reflects the change
in life's own tempo between the ages of twenty and thirty; it reflects
also the acceleration of modern life in general. The reader will moreover not be surprised to learn that in my diary for July 1927 I find the
words 'discovered Virginia Woolf'. And let me here pay tribute to that
prose-poet, who at that time so greatly enriched my awareness of life's
complex inter-connectedness. What I was dimly groping after, she had
attained: the power to arrest the ever-shifting kaleidoscope of life; to
perceive relationships hitherto unapprehended, and to fix these in image or symbol; and to render and re-enact, not with mere photographic
realism, but with consummate imaginative beauty, the very texture and
diurnal movement of existence.

The third, and most considerable, of my compositions at this time
was another 'stream-of-consciousness' experiment called 'Suburban Prelude', which ran in two successive numbers of *The New Adelphi* (April
and May 1931). The choice of that title, prefiguring what I was to
attempt thirty years later in *Spots of Time*, shows with what persis-
tence the Wordsworthian *leit-motiv* has sounded throughout my life.
The piece itself was an autobiographical fragment under a thin and
very transparent fictional disguise.

The fourth and last of these trial-flights was an article called 'Wordsworth's Beliefs', which was written during the Christmas vacation of
1931-2, and was published in *The Criterion* (January 1934). It was
later incorporated with little change in *The Seventeenth Century Background.*

Chapter Three

Summer 1930

I Alfoxden

The summer vacation of 1930 was eventful enough (to me, at least) to deserve a chapter to itself. It all sprang from two simple things: a lunch-time conversation with 'Q' at Jesus College, and an invitation from the B.B.C. (then still at Savoy Hill, and known as "2/LO") to give a series of six Talks on Thomas Hardy. I was examining with 'Q' in Part II of the Tripos again that year, and had spent a May morning in his College room, then gorgeous with peonies, and with his own René André rose (planted by him) covering the old brick wall outside with blossoms. Never was a Tripos paper set in an atmosphere less academic; just as Sir Thomas Browne could be 'in England everywhere, and under any Meridian', so 'Q' could be in Fowey even when in Cambridge, and diffused an aura of the warm south around him. Even in May he had a coal-fire burning on the hearth. 'I'm not a particularly selfish man', he explained, as he padded across the room to fetch me a glass of Bristol Milk, 'but I do like a *fire*' (pronounced with a Cornish 'r'). At lunch afterwards I told him that one of my cherished daydreams had long been to retire some day to Alfoxden, if by some miracle it should ever come into the market. To my astonishment he turned to me and said 'Didn't you know? It's in the market now!'

I lost no time in writing to the estate-agents for particulars – not, I need hardly say, with any serious thought of acquiring a property as far beyond my means as it would have been beyond Wordsworth's (to *buy*) in 1797, but thinking that I might in this way at least see with my own eyes a house so charged for me with meaning and sentiment, but hitherto as remote and fabulous as the pleasure-dome of Kubla Khan.

So, the Tripos well over, and my wife fully preoccupied with the latest arrival (Peter, our third, born June 7th), I set out alone for Somerset. My plan was to follow this up with a visit to Hardy's Wessex, in preparation for my wireless Talks.

The estate-agent in Bridgwater, who gave me the 'Order to View', showed no surprise at the anomaly of a prospective purchaser of a £10,000 estate (as it then was) carrying a rucksack and travelling on to Nether Stowey in the 'Stowey Favourite' bus. When we reached Stowey I asked the driver-owner to recommend me a lodging for the night; he replied that his father had kept the 'Rose and Crown' for years, but that he would show me, if I liked, a 'nice private address, very clean'. 'Tweenways', calling itself 'Board Residence', proved better than I could have hoped. It stood in Castle Street, almost opposite where Tom Poole's house was. I was the only guest, and was made much of by the two elderly ladies who ran the establishment. Rain fell all the first night, and the sound of it blended with the brawling of the stream that ran down the centre of the village street.

Next morning I went first of all, as in duty bound, to Coleridge's cottage. I found that it had changed since his time; the thatch had been replaced by red tiles, and the front had been roughcasted. A new wing had been added at the back, in which the lady-caretaker lived. She was using Coleridge's living-room as her sitting-room; and in the evening I saw her looking out of the little side-window that commands the main street − doubtless a favourite look-out of Sara's. The right-hand room (S.T.C.'s kitchen) was used as a little museum: copies of works by Coleridge and about him lying on the tables; on the walls, portraits of the Coleridges, T.Poole, Charles Lamb, Wordsworth, Dorothy and others, also drawings of Alfoxden, the trysting-tree at Woodlands (now no more), Greta Hall, etc. There was also a framed autograph letter of S.T.C.'s − the one to his brother James about his discharge from the army in February 1794. My 1930 note-book adds: 'It is written in a vein of lachrymose and high-strained rhetoric. He bewails his mad folly in enlisting, his ingratitude to his family which cries to heaven in "tongues of thunder" etc., and implores James to make interest for his discharge. He is at Henley acting as sick-nurse to a fellow-trooper'. An anonymous pamphlet on the cottage (not ill-written) mentioned that 'under this beam' probably occurred − amongst many other passages − the well-known interchange between S.T.C. and Lamb:

S.T.C.   Did you ever hear me preach, Charles?
C.L.   I n-never heard you d-do anything else.

The 'Lime-Tree Bower' had disappeared, but in its place was a large bay-tree arbour. The brook that ran in the road in front of the cottage, singing its quiet tune, had also gone; so, too, had the gate through which Coleridge could walk from his garden to Poole's. But one could see the house which stood on the site of Poole's house: a grocer's shop in Castle Street almost opposite 'Tweenways'. The garden was well-kept as a kitchen-garden, and probably produced more than it ever did under Coleridge's husbandry. The two upper rooms in the front of the house were also shown (Coleridge had three upstair rooms): they were kept unfurnished, and the original floor-boards were visible in all their unevenness. In one of these rooms was a fireplace − the one mentioned in *Frost At Midnight?* I spent some time looking through the Visitors' Book, and found amongst other names Ernest Hartley Coleridge and several other Coleridges (including three great-grand-children); several Wordsworths; Rufus M.Jones; John Livingstone

Lowes (I think 1927), Winifred Hughes etc.

Warmed and elated by all this, I next walked up to the top of Stowey Castle — and there the *genius loci* suddenly had me in thrall. I caught my breath at the sight of the Severn Sea, the Welsh mountains beyond, Flat Holme and Steep Holme like giant stepping-stones across the Channel, and on the north-eastern horizon the long line of the Mendip Hills. Between this distant bounding-wall and the place where I stood, and from the sea to beyond the far-descried Glastonbury Tor to the east, lay the great plain of Somerset, Coleridge's 'huge amphitheatre'. The colouring was subdued. It was a day of cloud and intermittent rain, the wind having failed to veer after the wet night. Later on I watched the movements of the showers from the lane between Bincombe and Five Lords; the prevailing grey of the sky deepened to indigo here and there as a shower-cloud stooped upon a distant hill.

I now quote from my diary for Friday July 18, 1930. The entry is headed 'written at Alfoxden', and on the opposite page is a pencil-sketch of the house as seen from the top of the Park, near the Holford beeches:

'Mark Rutherford left a Quantock Diary, but I doubt whether he actually wrote any of it sitting in Alfoxden Park, as I am doing now. I am sheltering from a shower in the beech-spinney that crowns the hill to the south, looking down on to the very roof of the house below. There it stands, white-walled and grey-roofed, with an elaborate apse-like conservatory [now replaced by a loggia] projecting from a low wing at the western end. From my feet to the little patch of lawn in front of the house is a steep and rough bracken-slope — the base of Long Stone Hill — planted here and there with park trees. On the far side is beautifully timbered grazing-land, passing into fields which soon meet the sea. Far out on the horizon, almost directly over the house, is Steep Holme, with Flat Holme to the left. Through the fringe of beech-twigs to the right I can just see Gladstonbury Tor, miles away across the Somersetshire plain. No wonder Wordsworth and his 'exquisite sister' were happy here. I doubt if Wordsworth was ever really so happy again, even in the early years at Grasmere. Dorothy never spoke 'the language of the sense' more purely than in the Alfoxden journal.

The house is shuttered, and no smoke rises from the chimneys — in fact, all is just as it must have been in 1797 before the Wordsworths moved in. Very few changes can have taken place since then, either in the house or in the park and surroundings. Yet the memory of the *annus mirabilis* 1797-8 seems to have vanished from the neighbourhood itself. All readers of the Wordsworths, and of Coleridge, and of Hazlitt, know the name of Alfoxden (spelt Alfoxton locally now; I suspect that 'Alfoxden' was merely a spelling-by-ear on the part of the Wordsworths), and think of it as the place where Wordsworth's powers budded and expanded in the exhilarating companionship of Dorothy and of Coleridge. Yet no one comes to visit it. The postcard shops sell pictures of it, but they bear no mention of Wordsworth's name. The *Lyrical Ballads* were mostly conceived or written here, and here Wordsworth was at work on parts of what later became *The Excursion* and *The Prelude*. Dorothy's Journal, above all, made the place classic and holy ground, and her great holly-trees still stand along the lengthy drive from Holford. The little waterfall in the glen can just be seen by climbing down through an undergrowth of brambles. Just above this point a log stretches across the dell, perhaps all that remains of Wordsworth's rustic bridge. The dell itself is now impassable, I believe through recent neglect.

From time to time the walls of the house gleam white in a momentary ray of sunshine, but on the whole this is the sort of day when I think Dorothy, with her perfect directness, would have said that the 'landscape was uninteresting'. The sea is almost colourless, bluish-grey where the cloud-shadows lie, yellowish elsewhere. The fields, as usual in the late hay-season, are ochre or yellow-green according to whether they are cut or still in hay. Steep Holme is in dim sunshine at the moment, but it has little definition against the uniform greyness which hangs over Wales.'

I presented my 'Order to View', and was duly shown over the house by Rowe, the caretaker employed by the owner, Mr. Brereton, a descendant of the St. Albyn family who rented the place to Wordsworth. The rooms were furnished in refined but unpretentious country-house style; but, Mr. Rowe said, the family seldom came there and Mr. Brereton was at a loss what to do with it. There were family portraits in the dining-room, and on the staircase and landing, but no trace of any Wordsworth memorial. Mr. Rowe showed me a bedroom which, he thought, was traditionally supposed to have been the poet's. I could not help ardently wishing that the place could somehow be kept sacred to Wordsworth, and the memory of his connexion with it more effectively preserved. If the present owner, I thought, instead of asking £10,000 for the estate (which included 150 acres of park, woodland and Quantock slopes) would only rent it to *me* for £23 a year, I should know how to deal with it! It would make an ideal summer-hostel or reading centre for undergraduates, American visitors, or plain holiday-makers. I hinted this to Mr. Rowe, with what result will appear later. I even wrote to 'Q' and Tillyard from Nether Stowey, whimsically urging them to organise a fund and acquire it for English Tripos students. In this I was more serious than they probably thought.

My first sight of Alfoxden had in fact been gained on Wednesday July 16, at the end of a walk over the Quantocks by the track leading from Five Lords to the ridge over Danesborough. I was excited by my literary pilgrimage, and as I went I tried to think myself into the moods, feelings and reflections of those three ardent spirits, then exulting in the dayspring-light of youth and genius. Mounting 'smooth Quantock's airy ridge', I was encouraged by an occasional break in the clouds, revealing depths of blue beyond; but still more by the ineffable scent of the moor, made up of wet bracken, heather, peat, sea, woods and heaven knows what (heaven itself could smell no more ambrosial). Some of life's high moments are associated with that smell: the ride to Woody Bay from the station on the miniature railway, now closed (this was on our honeymoon in 1923); and the beginning of our Highland walking-tour at Callander in 1925. When I emerged on to the open ridge rain began, so I turned down for shelter into the wooded Holford Combe (Tannery or Butterfly Combe). Half-way down I found a miniature bog-garden containing cotton-grass, sundew, bog pimpernel, bog-asphodel and a diminutive pennywort which was new to me.

In the evening after supper I walked out again, towards Over Stowey. There was a fine stormy sunset: a long rack of dark cumulus, with gleaming upper-edges, was emerging slowly from behind Danesborough, across diagonal cirrus-strips of salmon-pink. Now, I thought, here is a good opportunity: how would those poets have responded to *that?* What would they have felt? Certainly that spectacle would have spoken to them remembering things,

> *Of ebb and flow, and ever-during power*
> *And central peace, subsisting at the heart*
> *Of endless agitation –*

in other words, it would have seemed to them a symbolic language, through which a hidden Presence was communicating assurances of love and of power. To gain an inkling of what Wordsworth's type of inspiration was like, I thought, one should take a mental gleam such as I (in miniature) have just had, and imagine it heightened very greatly and practised as an habitual mood of ecstatic vision. At the same time I strongly felt how *abnormal* this emotion must now seem to the mass of mankind, whether educated or otherwise; I even questioned its value except as a restorative to the nerves. Did the Wordsworths in their day, I wondered, also feel that their intense cultivation of it set them apart from 'the people', or 'people in general'? Probably they did, hence their fondness for Coleridge, with whom they could share it. But the sense of having *discovered* a new mode of exaltation must have produced in them an intense excitement and a deep satisfaction, which are inaccessible to us now.

I spent several more days walking on the Quantocks, exulting in their peace and freedom, and in the vast prospects stretching from Yes Tor to Glamorganshire, and from the Wiltshire Downs to Dunkery

D

Beacon and the Minehead North Hill, around whose rocky headland the Atlantic crisps white — 'Severn Sea' no more. This delectable country, whatever evil may have since been wrought upon it (I have not seen it for the past twenty years, years which have spoilt so many well-loved places), was then as it had been at the end of the 18th century, when those three pairs of visionary eyes had drawn inspiration from it.

On these Quantock walks I was reminded of my youthful attempts to fit words to things (especially scenes of natural beauty) and asked myself why so many of them now seemed to me 'false'. How can one avoid falsity in descriptive writing? To avoid cliché and stock epithets is only the first step. Even perfect accuracy, I reflected, can also produce the effect called 'falsity' if it remains purely objective; what is both interesting and 'true' is the union between the object and the observer's mood. Objects *as* objects are insignificant; it is as ingredients or symbols of the mind's processes that they take on importance. I used, when describing, to try to get outside myself to the thing described, and thus the thing that might have been worth saying remained unsaid.

2 Wessex

From Nether Stowey I wrote a note to Mrs. Hardy at Max Gate, telling her of my forthcoming B.B.C. talks and asking if I might call for ten minutes next week during my intended stay in Wessex. I enclosed a stamped envelope addressed to myself at Stowey. I scarcely expected ever to get a reply; Mrs. Hardy might think me a presumptuous intruder; she might not be living at Max Gate, etc. I had never before done any such thing, and could not believe that it would succeed — even if it were not, as I suspected, bad form. But such things cease to be bad form, I thought, and become laudable intrepidity, if they *do* succeed.

The evening after I arrived at Dorchester I walked out along the Wareham road and gazed at Max Gate (as my wife and I had done two years before, soon after Thomas Hardy's death). I heard a dog barking in the garden, and the voice of a child; a light showed in a bedroom window. There had been no letter from Mrs. Hardy. 'And so that', I said to myself, as I turned back in the dusk to go home to Casterbridge, 'is as near as I shall ever get to Max Gate.'

I hired a bicycle and spent several days identifying places in the Wessex novels: Cross-in-Hand (where I placed my hand on the stone in recollection of Tess), High Stoy, Blackmore Vale, Stinsford, Higher Bockhampton, Rainbarrow, 'Weatherbury', Waterston House (Bathsheba's farmstead), 'Kingsbere' Church with the Turberville chapel and tombs, Egdon Heath, 'Wellbridge' House and other places — the very heart, indeed, of Hardy's country-of-the-mind, in which his spirit

still seemed to stir. Then, early one morning, there came a telegram
from Mrs. Hardy (forwarded from Cambridge by my wife) inviting me
to tea the next day.

I spent the following morning and early afternoon in a state of
mounting agitation. When at length I found myself again on the Wareham road, I felt so hot and apprehensive that, were it not for the ignominy, I would gladly have given up the enterprise. Who was I, of all
the scores of Hardy admirers who visit Casterbridge every week, that I
should intrude thus upon his widow? I made up many provisional
speeches, designed to convince her both that I realised my insignifi-
cance and that yet I was not merely an inquisitive tuft-hunter; but I
suspected all the while that these speeches would never be made (and
they were not). As I approached Max Gate I saw a lady with a guide-
book under her arm looking timidly at the house from across the road.
I confess that in the weakness of my fallen nature I felt a momentary
exultation at the thought that I was going inside, while she must be
content to gaze longingly from afar. I hoped she would see me turn in
at the gate, but I fear she did not.

Mrs. Hardy received me in the sitting-room, in which there was a
cheerful log-fire burning (although it was July 24th). She at once began
to tell me how strange it was that while I had been in the Wordsworth
country in Somerset she had been in the Lake District (this accounting
for her delay in replying to my letter from Stowey). I explained how
my visit to Alfoxden had come about, and its sequel the visit to the
Hardy country. She said she had been in Dove Cottage, and had there
been surprised to find the many visitors being conducted round by a
'comparatively uneducated girl'. (Ah, Mrs. Hardy – if I may now, over
thirty years later, apostrophize your kindly ghost – how faulty was
your judgment here! For the 'uneducated girl' must have been Emily
Kirkbride (now no more), who lived to become the best of all guides,
known to Wordsworthians all over the world as the unique repository
of Dove Cottage lore, and exhibiting, in her shrewd and honest speech
and bearing, the very qualities which endeared the northern peasants
to the poet). This led on to the subject of Hardy's own dwelling-places.
She disliked the idea of turning Max Gate into a show-place or a Hardy
Museum; yet many people, such as 'their friend T.E. Lawrence', were
in favour of it. I remarked that if any house were to be thus made
public it should surely be the (birthplace) cottage at Higher Bockhampton; she agreed, because this best embodied the spirit of Hardy's life
and work. She had thought of buying it, but the landlords would not
then part with it. Max Gate, she added, was still exactly as it had been
in Hardy's lifetime.

I told her something of my recent explorations in Wessex, of how
my heart leapt up when I came suddenly upon 'Cross-in-Hand'; of my

visits to High Stoy, Egdon Heath, Kingsbere and the rest. I said that although one knew that Hardy's Wessex was something other than, and greater than, 'the thing itself', yet one was irresistibly led to try and find the 'originals', especially (in my own case) the main landscape features of the country, amongst which I had always felt the great ridge from Evershead to Bulbarrow to be the most sacred of all. I hoped that Hardy would not have disapproved of such pilgrimages? 'Oh no', she said; 'he would have started telling you a story at once – I can hear him doing it. He would have said: You ought to have taken such-and-such a path.' We continued talking of the places in the novels, and I said I had been surprised at the nearness of Egdon Heath to the cottage at Bockhampton. *Mrs. Hardy:* 'Yes, isn't it splendid? You can step straight out of the garden on to the heath. When my husband was writing *Far From the Madding Crowd* there, he used to run up to the heath for ten minutes each day before dinner, to stretch his legs. He often used to go out in the same way here too.' *B.W.:* 'I did not realise that Rainbarrow was so near Bockhampton; I had always fancied it to be further towards Wareham.' *Mrs. H.:* 'Oh, did you find Rainbarrow? I had lost it. By the way, the house called Duck Farm (the 'Quiet Woman' Inn of *The Return of the Native)* has been pulled down.' *B.W.:* 'Another point was about Sergeant Troy's door in the church-tower at Weatherbury. I always thought he had sneaked into the gallery by a back way, without entering the church, but I found there was no way through.' *Mrs. H.:* 'Perhaps Hardy combined that church with an-other; he often did that sort of thing.' *B.W.:* 'I found the inscription on the Turberville vault quite legible, in spite of the statement to the contrary in one of the guide-books. Are the Turberville portraits still visible at Wellbridge House?' *Mrs. H.:* 'No, they are quite obliterated. The last time we went there was when the Dorset Players performed the confession scene from *Tess* there. They thought it would be inter-esting to perform it in the house itself. There's a fine old ingle fire-place, but they have modernised the house and put up pink striped wallpaper. But perhaps it's better that these people (they're farm-people) should put in what they like, rather than deliberately try to make the place look antique. That kind of ugliness is not always out of place when it's what appeals to the country-people.' *B.W.:* 'Do they allow visitors to look in?' *Mrs. H.:* 'Sometimes they are very rude, but at other times quite pleasant and obliging.' *B.W.:* 'I felt myself to be really in the country of *The Return of the Native* when I was on the road from Kingsbere to Wellbridge.' *Mrs. H.:* 'There's a barrow over-looking the Froom valley, a little way down the road from here, on which my husband and I have often stood. He used to say that from there he could see almost all the inner part of the country he had written about. But I always feel his spirit brooding over everywhere this side of Salisbury. I have often cycled with him about Dorset.'

We discussed the subject of my B.B.C. talks. *Mrs. H.*: 'If I may ask, which books are you going to talk about?' I explained that it was to be *Far from the Madding Crowd*, dealt with in a series of six talks. *Mrs. H.*: 'I should have thought *The Return of the Native* the best to take for your purpose. Don't you think the elemental passions in it would be understood better by your simple audience [the talks were supposed to be for the rural W.E.A. type of listeners] than Bathsheba's coquetry? Country people *have* these deep feelings, you know, without understanding them.' I said I had felt *Far from the Madding Crowd* to be most suitable because its action was so closely linked up with the seasons and with country happenings, and because it contained so much rustic humour. She did not demur to this. *B.W.*: 'But of course if you feel strongly about it I could perhaps alter the syllabus.' *Mrs. H.*: 'Oh no, I didn't mean that. And Gabriel Oak is sure to be popular.' A friend who had known Gabriel Oak's 'original' had recently told her that he had died at the age of 30; she wished she had been able to mention this in her *Early Life*, but things like this were always cropping up, and she had had such a mass of material to cope with. *Mrs. H.*: '*The Return* seems to be generally regarded as his best work, but he himself had a special fondness for *The Woodlanders*. People sometimes discuss whether *The Dynasts* is his greatest achievement; he would himself have probably said — one or two of the lyrics.' She recommended me, in reading extracts from *Far from the Madding Crowd* for the B.B.C., to select as one passage the painful walk of Fanny Robin to Casterbridge Union, assisted by a friendly dog who is stoned away by an official when they arrive. I told her that I had been in Weymouth that day, watching the Jersey boats, and mentioned that my de Carteret ancestors, as well as the Le Hardy's, were Jerseymen. She said there was no doubt that the Hardy family came originally from Jersey. *B.W.*: 'He seems to have been much interested in the question of "spent" families. I wonder if he thought his own was an example of this?' *Mrs. H.*: 'Oh yes, I think he certainly did.'

I told her that I had noticed *Far from the Madding Crowd* and *The Return* in a cheap (2/-) edition in all the Dorchester bookshops, and that I didn't like the lurid dust-covers. She had not seen these, but supposed that the publisher had sent her complimentary copies. 'If you will just have a look at the pictures for a moment I'll go and find them', she added. I walked round the sitting-room, and noticed that most of the many pictures were water-colour sketches or etchings of places in the novels. Many of them were by H.J. Moule, and some by the first Mrs. Hardy. There was a little sketch of Highgate Hill by Hardy himself, and a fine oil-portrait of him by Strang, as well as etchings by the same artist and others by Alfred East. There was a good water-colour of Bulbarrow, I think by Moule. On the mantel-piece stood an antique hour-glass about a foot high. Presently Mrs. Hardy came in with a copy of *Far from the Madding Crowd* (in the cheap edition), and she agreed that the dust-cover was unsuitable. It represented what appeared to be an apocalyptic sunset; in the fore-ground, on the right, was a haystack surmounted by two small figures; and on the left, three or four cypress-shaped trees in a row like nine-pins. *Mrs. H.:* 'I shall write to the publisher and say that my attention has been drawn to the pictures, and ask whether they can possibly withdraw them. I don't suppose they will. I know what they'll say: "We have been advised that these designs are suitable and possess artistic merit, and we fear that no steps can now be taken in the matter." Still, I can try.' She then ran quickly upstairs again to fetch a copy (the first edition) of *Wessex Poems,* illustrated by Hardy. For a while she stood fluttering the pages, vainly trying to find what she wanted. At last she said, 'My husband always used to tell me — "Now it's no good, you know; you must just start at the beginning and go straight through." ' When she had found the page she said: 'If you'll come into the dining-room I can show you a little point of interest, if it gives you any pleasure.' She then showed me an old sofa with carved mahogany ends, which had been given to Hardy by his mother. This had been drawn as an illustration to one of the poems: it figured there as a bier, with a corpse lying on it.

In the dining-room hung two oil-portraits of Hardy, one by Herko-mer and one by Eves. The latter must have been the last portrait made of him. Mrs. Hardy said it was exactly like him in his last years, but that he had been sad and vexed with sitting to the painter, and this came out in the portrait. Once he even got up in disgust, and said he would not be painted — 'and he was not usually irritable like that'. But the picture faithfully reproduced all his traits: the lines on the forehead and between the eyebrows, the wisp of hair above the ears, and the triangular mark on the lower lip which he had particularly re-quested the artist not to omit. Mrs. Hardy gave me a lighted candle to hold up to this picture, which was in a dark corner.

In the entrance-hall, at the foot of the staircase, hung a large map of Wessex drawn by Hardy, showing all the places in the novels. It was an exquisite piece of penmanship (was it perhaps the model for the map given in some editions of the Wessex novels?). 'See how careful and accurate he was in everything he did', Mrs. Hardy said. She seemed anxious to show me everything she could think of which might in-terest me: 'it is my duty, as well as my pleasure', she said. So up she went again, and this time came back with a flat brown-paper parcel tied up with string. This contained the original pen-and-ink drawings of Tintagel Castle, made by Hardy for his *Queen of Cornwall* when he was about 83 years of age. The largest drawing, an imaginary re-construction of the castle at the time of the tragedy, was a remarkable enough piece of work for precision and clearness of detail, and quite astonishing as the production of so old a man. The parcel also con-tained an early water-colour sketch of his, which showed that his in-tent observation could express itself by brush as well as by pen.

Glancing through the volume of *Wessex Poems* I noticed a sketch of an hour-glass which resembled the one on the mantelpiece, and I asked whether they were connected. 'No', she said; 'I'll tell you how that came there. It was a present to me from my husband. Once we were listening to the Derby over the wireless, and although he hated racing and betting we amused ourselves by backing horses, the loser agreeing to give the other a present. Well, my horse happened to win, and I asked him to give me an hour-glass. He said "Yes, that *would* be a nice thing to give you". He picked that one up at an antique-shop.'

My time was drawing on; I had already been at Max Gate nearly an hour and a half. I will only refer briefly to one large section of the conversation, that in which Mrs. Hardy poured out, with much feeling and at considerable length, her grievances about Hardy's cremation and burial. She had wished Hardy's own desire (expressed in his will) to be complied with, namely that he should be buried in Stinsford church-yard with his first wife, parents and other relations. But she had been over-ruled in a way which she complained of bitterly. She knew that Hardy would have been horrified at the idea of cremation. On the other hand Miss Katherine Hardy (sister), whom she had consulted, had said: 'He would never have refused Westminster Abbey'.

As I rose to depart she told me that this Miss Hardy, the only sur-viving member of his own family, possessed a portrait of the Aunt ('Aunt Sharp') who was the original of Bathsheba Everdene. This was a sister of Hardy's mother, a beautiful woman, who had married a dash-ing soldier having some of the characteristics of Sergeant Troy without his profligacy. For instance, he was master of the wonderful sword-play with which Troy fascinated Bathsheba. 'Miss Hardy lives not far off, at Talbothays,' she said; 'would you like to see the picture at any time?' I replied that of course I should be most excited to see it, but that I had to return to Cambridge next morning. 'Could you go now? Have you a bicycle, or a car?' 'I can walk!' 'It's a beautiful walk, two and a half miles down the valley. I'll write a note to her and explain.' And down she sat at her desk (on which I saw my letter from Nether Stowey still lying), and scribbled a note to Talbothays. I went off with my note, thanking Mrs. Hardy profusely for all her kindnesses.

Half an hour's quick walking down the 'Valley of the Great Dairies', and through the picturesque village of West Stafford (the reputed marriage-place of Tess and Clare), brought me to a neat, modernish house, rather like a smaller Max Gate, with 'Talbothays Lodge' in clear letters on the gate. Several flower-beds ablaze with begonias brightened the lawn. A little grey-haired lady opened the door. 'I have just come from Max Gate, with a note from Mrs. Hardy', I explained, 'for Miss Hardy'. 'Oh yes. Is there any answer?' 'Well yes, I think there is, as a matter of fact.' She went indoors, and there was a longish pause during the deciphering of the note. Then she re-appeared, smiling and apologizing, and cordially asked me to come in. This was Miss Katherine Hardy. I scanned her carefully for any family likeness. It was not conspicuous, but she had the little bright-blue eyes, the diagonally-drawn upper lids, and perhaps the forehead; and, though not the great Roman nose, yet a suggestion of the curve about its tip; and certainly the sloping shoulders. She carried her seventy-four years very well.

The Bathsheba portrait hung on the staircase-wall, and we climbed to the landing to look at it. It had been painted by the other sister, Mary Hardy, from an old portrait or drawing. It was in oils, and showed a spirited young beauty in the mode of a hundred years ago, with brown hair partially concealed by a pretty lace cap, flashing brown or hazel eyes, a firm chin, and a general air of energy and exultant youthfulness. It corresponded well enough with one's notion of Bathsheba.

Downstairs there were many other interesting portraits, mostly the work of Mary Hardy, who was clearly a talented artist. I think the finest was one of old Mrs. Hardy, the mother. It showed her in profile, her grand old countenance bent forward in mingled light and shadow. There were also pictures of the father, the brother Henry, Mary Hardy herself, and some of the early portraits of Thomas Hardy which are reproduced in the *Life*. 'Now what else is there I can show you?' said Miss Hardy, in a tone of perfect simplicity and natural kindness. She went to a glass cabinet, and with infinite care took from it a blue-and-white porcelain jug. 'This was the cider-jug used by the Mellstock choir in *Under the Greenwood Tree*,' she said; 'you remember?'. To my mortification, I did *not* remember, not having read this book since boyhood, but to restore appearances I referred to the pewter jug used in Warren's Malthouse (in *Far from the Madding Crowd*). 'Oh yes,' she said, 'you mean the "God-Forgive-Me"!' Then, with equally tender care, she took from the cabinet a little porcelain house, so small that it stood on the palm of her hand. It was hollow inside, and had a chimney. 'This little house', she said, 'was a plaything of Tom's when he was a little boy. Father used to crumple up a piece of paper and set light to it, and then put the house over it — because Tom said 'twasn't a proper house without smoke coming from the chimney.'

On the half-landing stood an old grandfather clock. 'This old clock', said Miss Hardy, 'you might say, heard us all being born.' She opened its door, and disclosed a mass of pencil-writing on the inner side. This had been written by Tom as a youth, and was signed by him, with the date — I think 1858. It was verse, not of his own composition. 'You must have read it many a time,' she said; 'it begins "Somewhere beside a village street, There stands a something country seat." The signature has been varnished over, to preserve it.' I looked, but the varnish was over the date, and not on the name at all. I pointed this out to her. 'Well!' she said, 'how stupid of them! I'll do it myself.' Near by there hung an extraordinary toothed machine which might have been a man-trap or an instrument of torture. She explained that this was a cooking appliance, used at the old home. Across the open fire hung a bar, and this machine was fixed to the bar and held, on its hooked extremity, the various cooking vessels. The teeth were for regulating the distance of the pot from the fire. Near this, again, hung the family warming-pan.

The pictures which interested me most, however, were Mary Hardy's copies of the D'Urberville portraits in 'Wellbridge' House. 'I shall never forget the time when she did those,' said Miss Hardy. 'The house was untenanted then, and we were alone in it together. It was the ghost-liest house I have ever been in. There were little noises going on all the time — not loud sounds, but little quiet shuttings of doors. I said to Mary, oh do hurry up with your painting and let's get out of this!' The pictures accorded well with the haunted atmosphere of that house, and answered fully to the description of them in *Tess*. The faces, handsome in form, seemed to express every kind of evil passion, with mania superadded. What increased their horrid fascination was that it was not easy to identify the sex of either of the two people. One, the younger, looked a little like one of the portraits of Byron, but the poetic rage had become homicidal ferocity. The teeth showed white like those of a wild beast. The elder D'Urberville, man or woman, had the features of a vicious Roman Emperor; the face was that of an aristocrat steeped in pride, cruelty and sensuality. Even in quiet, mod-ern Talbothays these pictures were gruesome; in their original setting they must have 'thick'd the blood with cold'. The power of these copies proved Mary Hardy's artistic ability yet again.

I began to take my departure. Miss Katherine thanked me for my 'kindness' in calling upon her, and promised to listen to my wireless talks. Just before I left she said, 'I've got another treasure upstairs, that I value more than all the others. I've been told that if I sent it to London I could get untold money for it. But of course I don't want that. It's the little cap Tom wore when he was a baby.'

The next morning, when I was waiting for my train at Dorchester station, I saw Mrs. Hardy again, seeing off a friend. 'Did you see Miss Hardy?' she asked me. 'Yes, and she not only showed me Bathsheba, but lots of other wonderful things.' 'Good. Well, I've written to the

the publisher about those dust-covers!'

3 Alfoxden Revisited

At the risk of disproportion, I want to round off as briefly as I can the story of that 1930 Long Vacation, which for me was more than usually fruitful and diversified.

In August I revisited Alfoxton, this time accompanied by my friend the Vicar of Malvern, the late Rev. Hubert Bartleet. From our lodgings at Nether Stowey we took the bus to Holford and walked first to Rowe's cottage. Here we were told, to our amazement, that the Squire (Mr. Brereton) was in residence at Alfoxton, and would be pleased to see us. As we walked up the mile-long drive to the House, Mr. Bartleet, who had a wonderful gift for extemporising grandiose schemes, building cloud-capped towers and sky y-pointing pyramids on next to no foundations, rehearsed an imaginary conversation with the Squire in which we should acquire Alfoxton from him as a Wordsworth Centre, with myself as resident Warden, 'Q' and himself as long vacation lecturers, and with students pouring in from the world at large in response to a prospectus which he would immediately compose and distribute far and wide. But when the House came in sight it was at once apparent that something had happened: the chimneys were smoking; people were moving about. Rowe, instead of showing us round, merely grinned and led us to the front door, where we were received by a well-dressed and smiling young lady (a daughter of the Squire's, or some other scion of the St. Albyn line?). She offered to show us the house, and we began to follow her, not knowing for a while quite what was what. But it soon dawned upon us that the miracle had already happened; my July vision for Alfoxton had been realized. Mr. Brereton, either on his own initiative or — as I now think — encouraged by my suggestions as reported to him by Rowe after my first visit, had opened the place as a Guest House. The young lady was the manageress or the receptionist. It flashed upon us that this, our opportunity to be the first guests in Alfoxton, must on no account be lost, and we resolved to move in the very next day, Tweenways or no Tweenways. We met Mr. Brereton in the drive on our way back, and he promised with great cordiality to fetch us from Stowey in his car next morning.

Arrived in Alfoxton, the great problem arose: which of us should sleep in 'Wordsworth's room' (for I was due back at Croyde the day after)? Should we sleep in it by turns, the Vicar taking — say — from midnight to 3 a.m., and I from then onwards? Or should we cast lots for the whole night? The matter was settled by my decision to stay on for an extra night; Mr. Bartleet, as a reverend senior, was to have Wordsworth's room the first night, and I the second. The alternative, each night, was to be 'the Dorothy room', the more beautiful of the two and provided (as the other was not) with H. and C.

This was the first of many happy short holidays at Alfoxton throughout the middle 'thirties. Of course nothing came of the Wordsworth Centre scheme, though for a considerable time the Vicar's eloquence and enthusiasm beguiled Mr. Brereton into thinking there might be something in it − even some money, which was naturally his most pressing concern. At one time my father became seriously alarmed, fearing that I might throw up my Cambridge prospects and follow after the will-o'-the-wisp of an illusory 'Wardenship'. No practical moves were ever really made. The nearest I ever came to making one was when I persuaded 'Q' to invite Brereton to lunch in his rooms at Jesus; ostensibily to 'discuss' Alfoxton and the chance that 'Q' might come and lecture there. The lunch, which was attended by 'Q's' elderly and faithful votaries Miss Philpott and Miss Hutchinson, as well as by Mr. Brereton, my wife and myself, was skilfully steered by 'Q', with the aid of 'peach-fed' ham and the choicest wines, in the direction of genial anecdotage, and away from any serious business.

During the 1939-45 war, Alfoxton housed an 'evacuated' school, and units of the U.S. Army were quartered in the Park. After the war it was occupied for some years by a religious organization called the 'Christian Endeavour'. Of late years it has again, so I am told, become an hotel.

Chapter Four

The 1930's

It is no part of my present purpose to relate once again the outward events of this tragic decade. While crises racked our country, and the skies were darkening over Europe, my own thoughts — though far from being unaffected by the portents of the time — were preoccupied with my academic work, and above all by what seemed to me the overriding need to justify my existence. The same inward agitation which had driven me to write the short pieces I have mentioned, now impelled me to attempt something on a larger scale. Accordingly, in the June of 1932 I gave up my usual curative spell of mountain-walking, and plunged into reading and note-taking for a book on the seventeenth century. This continued, off and on, throughout the autumn, and in the Christmas vacation I wrote the first hundred pages of what became the book called *The Seventeenth Century Background*. This was a development from the lectures I had been giving for the English Tripos on 'Life and Thought' in that century, but it came to include much else besides.

It has been conjectured, I believe, that this book was inspired by T.S. Eliot's essays, particularly by the one on the Metaphysical Poets and above all by his theories about the 'inclusive sensibility' of Donne and his school and the 'dissociation of sensibility' which set in, according to him, after the Restoration. And I have no wish to underrate the debt which, like the rest of us at that time, I owed to him. But I can honestly say that if any one book suggested to me the leading idea of *The Seventeenth Century Background* it was Whitehead's *Science and The Modern World*. I can even remember the place and time when the flash of illumination came to me; it was, of all incongruous circumstances, while sitting reading Whitehead over a cup of morning coffee in Lyons's shop in Petty Cury. There and then it dawned on me that 'Truth' was not all of one kind; that 'scientific truth' was not the whole of truth; that poets and divines had access to regions of it which were closed to mathematics and physics; and that the intellectual history of the seventeenth century could be seen as the struggle of scientific truth to emancipate itself from religion and poetry and to claim for itself unique validity. In the light of that idea I wrote my book. When, in July 1933, the writing was nearly finished, I asked Chatto and Windus, who had already begun to publish works by my colleagues, if they would be likely to consider my manuscript. I did this without the slightest expectation that they, or anybody else, would accept it. I thought the book remote, severe and abstruse, and many of the writers and subjects treated therein so recondite as to put off any publisher at once. Moreover, I was of course an entirely unknown author, though Mr. Ian Parsons of Chatto's (ever since then the best of friends to me) had, I think, attended some of my lectures when he was at Cambridge. In reply to my enquiry, Chatto's said that they would at least consider the typescript if and when I sent it to them. In October 1933 I did send it, and to my unfeigned astonishment and joy they accepted it. It appeared in February 1934, and was so kindly treated by the reviewers that when Dr. G.G. Coulton's retirement created a vacancy I was appointed University Lecturer (as from October 1934).

I will here briefly record a few ensuing stages in my academic story. During the beautiful month of July 1934, I went to Oxford to work in the Bodleian, while our own University Library was closed for removal to the new building (it had hitherto, as some of my younger readers may or may not have heard, been housed in the Old Schools). I was then at a parting-of-the-ways: should I take the road backward into the Middle Ages, or forward — from the 17th century — into the 18th and 19th? Mistakenly as I now think, I took the mediaeval turning, and spent my Oxford weeks disconsolately struggling along the brambly and stony approaches to Aquinas, Wiclif, William of Ockham and the rest. My heart fainted within me as I gazed up at the North Walls of all those Eigers, and realized how guideless and ill-equipped I was for the ascent. Every evening, as I walked home to my lodgings in Manor Place in the glowing heat of July (such evenings as we used to have in those far-off summers!), and smelt the madonna lilies in the gardens, and heard the chafing of the crickets, I was saddened by their tale of the flying years. My instinct was telling me that I was on the wrong track, and must turn back while there was yet time. Oxford and its surrounding country, thirty years ago, had not yet lost all the loveliness which had enchanted me twenty years earlier still, and when I could forget my undertow of discontent I was happy to be there. Happier still when, as each fine warm Sunday was succeeded by another such, I went long cycling expeditions to the Cotswolds, the Berkshire Downs or the Chilterns — all 'countries in romance' to me, as the environs of Cambridge never were and have never become.

The following year (1935) was for us the most chequered and eventful of its decade, at any rate until the outbreak of the second war. The birth of our fourth and last child (Lucy), was preceded, accompanied and followed by mumps, tonsilitis and measles in the other three children, and extreme segregation was adopted to keep the baby from infection. In May-June I was examining in Part II of the Tripos with Aubrey Attwater, F.L. Lucas and Enid Welsford. I, who, through being in my own childhood more isolated than most children, had escaped most of the usual epidemics, caught measles from our own younger boy — developing it on the last possible day (the twenty-first) after exposure. I managed to finish my share of the Tripos scripts under the onset of what I thought at first was the worst of all colds or hay-fever attacks, but could not attend the final examiners' meeting. Measles at the age of thirty-eight was, I found, no joke at all, although admittedly absurd. In a life for the most part mercifully free from ill-nesses, this was the longest and most severe — except for that following my war-wound in 1918 — that I have ever had. The many days and nights of high fever were accompanied by lung-congestion, and follow-ed by weeks of lassitude during which the slightest exertion was un-bearable. Curiously, I made a sort of bogus recovery at the beginning of July, and rashly took my elder son Maurice, then a chorister at King's, for a trip to the Lakes during his annual school-break. We climbed Helvellyn, walked from Rosthwaite to Langdale by the Stake Pass, etc., and all seemed well. But when we returned, I relapsed into breathlessness and exhaustion, and was taken off by my father (who had nursed me all through) to recuperate at Sidmouth. There, the daily walk of a few yards from hotel to beach and back was all I could manage; an attempt to climb Peak Hill proved a failure.

It was while at Sidmouth that I heard the news of Aubrey Att-water's death. Aubrey's old war-injury, which had made him a lame man ever since, had begun to give serious trouble just before the Tripos, in which he and I had been examining until we both fell ill. But his lameness had for so long been victoriously combated by Aubrey's gay and gallant spirit that it had seemed a part of his person-ality: something with which he had managed to come to terms, and which he had conquered by turning it into high-pitched laughter. It was therefore strangely shocking to hear that, after being held under for twenty years, it had at last risen up and conquered him. His death was one of a series of losses which Pembroke suffered that year (Lawson, Comber), and which made 1935 a black year in College history. It had another and most unexpected consequence, which affected me vitally: it created a vacancy at the College for a Fellow-ship in English. And in October of that year my heart stood still as I read a letter from the Master, Professor Arthur Hutchinson, asking me whether I would accept a Fellowship at Pembroke College. I was admitted in November, 1935.

The Master had warned me that after dinner on the night of my admission I should have to make a speech in reply to the toast which he would propose. So I put together a few historical allusions which I hoped the Fellows might think appropriate, ending with a reference to another Peterhouse man who had crossed the Rivers Pot and Pem in an easterly direction: Thomas Gray. I noticed that during this peroration there was a stir of merriment amongst the Fellows, greater than seemed justified by anything I had said. I afterwards learnt that one of the Fellows had bet another that at some point during that evening's speeches — most likely in the Master's own speech — there would be a reference to Gray's migration from Peterhouse to Pembroke. The Master (a scientist) had *not* referred to it, so the joke was all the better when *I* did. Two other Fellows also elected in 1935, though a term before me, soon became, as they have ever remained, my very good friends; and both are now Heads of Houses: Sir William Hodge, Master of Pembroke itself; and Sir Gordon Sutherland, Master of Emmanuel.

My Fellowship at Pembroke was a turning-point in my life, and my gratitude to that beloved College is commensurate, I hope and think, with my debt to it. At last I had been received into the mainstream of Cambridge life; I *belonged* at last, and belonged to a community of friends and allies. I had a room in College — one of the greatest of my newly-gained privileges, for up till then I had for years taught my pupils in a bare and joyless room in the Norwich Union Building, Downing Street, where the English Faculty Library was then housed (of which I was Librarian). That room was papered in a depressing beetroot-red, and contained nothing but a table and some chairs. Moreover it was immediately below what was then the Club Room of the C.U.M.C. (Cambridge University Musical Club), and the supervisions were sometimes enlivened by 'music off'; sometimes, indeed, reduced to helpless hysteria, if the musician happened to be a trombonist practising arpeggios. I sometimes wonder now how my pupils and I put up with all this for so long; but there was really no alternative, and my own house was too far away for me to supervise at home. Moreover, in those days one did not think oneself ill-used if every University and College privilege and comfort was not immediately forthcoming. In that room a not inconsiderable portion of my life's work was done. I supervised there many people who have since become distinguished men and women, and many who, whether distinguished or not, seem never to have forgotten those days. One of my very earliest pupils, an Indian, has not once missed writing a new-year letter during the forty years and more since I last saw him.

But now — what contrast! — I found myself occupying (for my first year at Pembroke) what had been Aubrey Attwater's rooms, the finest set in the College; the rooms which had been Thomas Gray's and William Pitt's. This was only a temporary arrangement, as so fine a suite (it then comprised two bedrooms, a spacious sitting-room, a bathroom and a large library) had of course to be assigned to a bachelor Fellow living always in College. But to have the use of it even for one year, and especially to have the run of Aubrey's wonderful books, was a privilege indeed. While speaking of this, I wish to record that the first 'Gray Society' in Pembroke was founded in that room under my auspices during that year (1935-6). The founding members having been convened, they met there to hear me read Stonehewer's description of the room as it had looked immediately after Gray's death. The Society made a good start, but it was killed by the 1939-45 war. In the post-war era another Gray Society was set up, and still flourishes. But the curious thing (to me) is that the new Society seems never to have heard of the existence of its predecessor.

After this first year I moved to the rooms on C Staircase, next to the College Chapel, which remained mine for nearly thirty years. In 1936 I was appointed Praelector, and held that office for ten years. The Praelectorship, when I first took it on, was no light assignment. In those days there was no secretarial assistance, and I had personally to conduct the extensive correspondence with Pembroke men taking degrees, collect their fees, keep the accounts, and fill in with my own hand all the University forms and certificates relating to terms, degrees and examinations, as well as annually revising our section of the University Calendar. The Senate House ceremonies themselves, though perpetually recurring, were the least part of the duties.

It is extraordinary to reflect how recently, in the life of some Colleges at least, the modern secretarial apparatus (now taken for granted) has come into being. In the mid-'thirties, numbers, and the general tempo of life, had not increased beyond the point at which the gentlemanly, amateurish, 'with-my-own-fair-hand' approach becomes impossible. When I joined the Society, there were twelve Fellows; now, there are over forty. The effects of this big expansion, in all Colleges which were originally small enough to feel them, have been gradual but profound. A College Fellowship, now apparently almost regarded as a 'right' by every University teaching officer, is for that reason nothing like such a distinction as it used to be; nor is it such a privilege, for in many Colleges there are not enough rooms to supply every Fellow with a set — and the College room was one of the most valued, and indeed indispensable, of the former privileges. A College Society, once so closely-knit (and perhaps a little too 'in-bred' and exclusive), is now more like a Club, in which one may or may not recognize many of one's fellow-members.

Some younger readers of *Spots of Time* have already asked me to explain by what stages I evolved from the Puritanism of my youth into the comfort-loving and wine-bibbing individual they have known. I can gratefully attribute most of this to Pembroke. But for my gradual development from Liberalism to Toryism, Pembroke cannot be held solely or even chiefly accountable. It is quite true, and I am not ashamed to confess it, that I have in my old age become a Tory; but I can also see that I have only developed outwardly into what I always essentially was. By instinct and temperament I have always been a conservative, suspicious of change, loving old things and old ways and resenting innovation. But I had breathed so deeply, in my early years, the atmosphere of radicalism and non-conformity, that it was long before I gave up the habit of questioning and mocking all the dogmas of Conservatism — political, social and religious. Thus I was struck, and rather appalled, on entering the Pembroke circle, to notice there the almost unchallenged predominance of Tory principles, attitudes and assumptions. In those days I found this suffocating, and I dare say that by way of reaction to it I uttered, from time to time, sentiments which may have made my colleagues think me a subversive character. Thus, if someone was suggested for a Fellowship who was known to be a bit leftish, and therefore unsound, I would support his candidature, knowing how heavily the scales would be weighted against him. In all this I received moral support from a most unlikely quarter: the Master's Lodge itself. Not from the Master, but from his wife Mrs. Hutchinson, sister of Arthur Shipley (former Master of Christ's), a lady of advanced views. Bright-eyed, rose-cheeked and intense, she held 'emancipated' opinions on sex, on India, and especially on the Rights of Women. If anyone spoke to her of 'men', in the inclusive sense of humankind of both sexes, she would disconcert him by interposing '*and* gairls!' Though I held her in some awe, she was always very gracious to me, and once when I was sitting beside her at a Lodge dinner she whispered to me archly, *à propos* of politics, that she was glad to have in the College someone like me 'who was, perhaps, shall we say? ever so slightly *Pink*.' In fairness to the College, however, it must be added that one of the Fellows, and one of the most beloved, was actually a Communist — or if not a Party Member (to that I could not swear), certainly a strong Marxist. The College tolerated this man mainly, I think, because they could not help liking him personally for his sheer goodness, modesty, sweetness of temper and intellectual brilliance — however much they loathed his opinions.

It is of course well-known that the '30's were a time when Marxism was greatly in vogue amongst intellectuals. The economic slumps here and in America, the universal blight of unemployment, and the rise of Fascism in Italy and Germany, had all produced a general sense of frustration; and the opinion gained currency that the 'capitalist' order of society was grinding to a halt, and that these evils were the symptoms of its approaching end. The philosophy called 'Dialectical Materialism', applying an inverted Hegelianism to the explanation of history, was invoked by the malcontents to prove the inevitability of the present crises, and of the coming revolution which would put all to

E

rights (or rather lefts). As a student of the history of ideas I felt it my duty to try to understand dialectical materialism, and I did read a number of books on the subject, as well as the writings of some Marxian literary critics who explained all literature as a by-product of the class-struggle. At first I found all this rather new and exciting, and I attended one or two papers and discussions by initiate dons, which seemed to me very abstract and difficult. But I was aghast at the religiose solemnity of the initiates, and the more-than-Roman Catholic certainty with which they held and proclaimed their dogmas. I was not in need, as most of these people were, of a substitute for religion, and I soon found that their thoughts were not my thoughts, nor their ways my ways. In their interpretations of history, of poetry, and of religion, they seemed to me far too slick and schematic, distorting reality to make it fit their preconceived categories, and ignoring whole aspects of it altogether. In those days, when 'good' men lacked conviction, when many were losing confidence in the rightness of their own standards, and feeling guilty if they enjoyed any privileges of class, income or education, it was difficult to maintain a moderate, liberal standpoint, and conservatism appeared to have no *raison d'être* at all. It was indeed an unhappy time for liberal-conservatives, amongst whom I could then be numbered.

The Hitler-Stalin pact of 1939-40, involving as it did a cynical renunciation and reversal of all that Nazism and Communism were supposed to stand for, put a stop to most of this dilettante Marxism amongst the intellectuals. I remember confronting one of my pupils, a Marxist, with this hideous piece of political apostasy, and asking him what he thought of the Party Line now? 'Oh, surely it's *correct*?' he bleated; and disgust and contempt left me speechless. Hitler's invasion of Russia was a godsend to these people, as it enabled them to serve both God and Mammon, their country and their party, with a good conscience.

I had always been far too much of a lone bird ever to be 'dedicated' or 'committed' to any party, creed or cause, and politics only occupied my thoughts when they forced themselves in. One great, over-riding and passionately-held conviction, however, did dominate my mind and heart during the middle 'thirties: that War was the ultimate horror and must never be even conceived of as a thing which could possibly occur again. I hope the present generation, in judging of the 'thirties and of the behaviour both of its political leaders and its ordinary people, will try to remember how many of us had emerged from the 1914-18 war with precisely that conviction. That war, breaking in upon a long period of seemingly settled peace and steady amelioration, had shocked and appalled our generation in a way never before known; and we regarded it, not as a prelude to further horrors, but as a ghastly, abnormal incursion of evil — a thing never to be repeated in all future history. It was 'the war to end war'. Of course, in view of what has actually followed, it is easy to see, or to say, that we were deluded innocents, living in a fool's paradise, crying peace when there was no peace. We now see the force of the Churchill doctrine, anathema to most of us between the wars, that preparedness, military strength and determined statesmanship might have nipped Nazism in the bud and prevented the second disaster. But how could we ordinary folks be expected to see things in that light then? An armaments race had led up to the 1914 war; were we to begin another, which could lead only to the same result? No; to me, as to the vast majority of peaceable, idealistic Englishmen, it seemed that the only hope was to keep the very notion of war at a distance; never to admit, by word or even in thought, that a recurrence of it was conceivable. To do so, we felt, was to take the first step towards it.

In condemning the policies of the Baldwin era, as we are now forced to do, we must remember that Baldwin and the others were simply representatives of the powerful popular sentiment I have described; their influence depended upon giving effect to it. We underestimated the strength, and the potentiality for evil, of the Hitlerite movement in Germany; most of us even sympathised a good deal with German aspirations, and felt that at Versailles we had been too hard on a defeated foe. This was why I associated myself for a time with the 'New Peace Movement' started by G.F. Shove at King's, which held meetings and heard papers on the subject. (As a matter of fact, the only two papers I remember were a subtle harangue by C.D. Broad on the logical foundations of pacifism, which left me wondering which side he was really on; and a fiery exhortation by G.G. Coulton, urging immediate conscription, on the Swiss model, as the only hope.) In those days 'Peace' had not yet become a dirty word, equivalent to 'appeasement' or surrender to the dictators (whether Fascist or Communist). One could still believe in it and work for it, either from a Christian or a purely humanist standpoint, without being suspected of subversiveness. I was one of the many who thought we should take Hitler seriously when, in 1936, he offered peace for 25 years and general disarmament. Wishing to do *something* to help the only public cause I had at heart (the preservation of peace) I even wrote a letter to the *New Statesman* urging that we should take Hitler at his word. Folly! Blindness! — oh yes, I admit it; but was there no excuse for it? Again I beg the present generation to make the immense imaginative effort of putting themselves in the place of those who had been through 1914-18; to imagine with what passionate fervour we resisted all approaches to another such horror, and how obvious it seemed to us that re-armament would lead straight to it.

I might have learnt something of the vigilance of the Nazi regime from the circumstance, very surprising to me at the time, that soon after my letter appeared in the *New Statesman* I received a packet of glossy, illustrated leaflets from Germany, representing the new Germany in the most attractive light. So they had even thought an obscure, remote and ineffectual don like me worth cultivating! As time went on, of course, I began to experience, at each new act of Hitlerite aggression or atrocity, a steady recession of hope; and I still remember the sickening contraction of the heart which smote me when I read that the Führer had ordered conscription.

It will be said, and rightly, that everyone always wants peace; men only differ about the best means of procuring it. In the 'thirties, some thought that the best way was to prepare for war; others, that the best way was to *practise* peace. The latter group, of whom I was one, have been proved wrong; we are all Churchillians now. But our mistake was not an ignoble one; and, if the world had been only a little less wicked than it was, we might not have been proved wrong at all.

One thing I must add here, before I leave this subject. Some reviewers of my earlier book *Spots of Time*, in which my war experiences were described, seem to have received the impression that the war meant little to me. This is a strange misunderstanding. Either these readers have missed the point of the book, or I have most signally failed to convey it. I had thought it clear that the central theme of the book was the irruption of war into my early Eden (symbolised by the bugles heard from Mill Hill), a disaster which shattered the fabric of my existence and threatened with destruction all that I had lived for and by. If my descriptions of trench-life, for instance, seemed to say too much about clouds and sunsets, and not enough about blood and lice, that was due to two main causes — both of them evidences of my loathing for war: first, an attempt to fix my attention, amid the encircling gloom, upon whatever kindly light I could discern; and secondly, an attempt to give my parents (to whom, it should be remembered, nearly all my letters were written) as much reassurance, and as little shock or anxiety, as I could. It is quite true that, all through my army life, I tried (usually of course with total want of success) to live as though the war were an irrelevant interruption. But this was *because* I resented it so much; and the same feeling dominated my mind and soul for nearly twenty years afterwards. That book should be read as an impassioned repudiation of war, in which the passion was expressed not directly but by understatement, irony and obliquity.

Chapter Five

Cornwall

The decade of the 'thirties, the central decade of my life, was not all given up to academic work and political forebodings. It was diversified by a great deal of family happiness, and included much carefree travelling in the loveliest parts of England and Wales, on foot or by bicycle. I am glad that we made the most of our holidays then, for England's beauty was as yet almost intact, and one could move about without fear of crowds and traffic and without breathing everywhere the fumes of petrol and diesel-oil. Happy days! and we should have enjoyed them with even greater intensity, though with minds less tranquil, if we had known what England was soon to become: overcrowded, desecrated, and choked with traffic. 'Happy for the privileged classes!' the stock retort will come, 'for those who had long holidays and could afford to travel to the most delectable spots!' Yes, yes; let us humbly accept the rebuke, and bow our heads in routine contrition; we *did* have a better time than many were then able to have. Nevertheless, even then, the more enterprising and intelligent 'workers', were able, by wisely planning their short holidays, to derive more concentrated enjoyment from walking or cycling than their successors of today ever get from their bumber-to-bumper car-drives, their picnics in oily lay-by's, and their transistor-sessions on packed and littered beaches. Moreover, although we had longer holidays (especially we who were University teachers), we were in quite humble circumstances — far less affluent than most 'workers' of today. We did not dream of having a car until I was nearly forty, and many of our expeditions were walking or cycling tours, on which we were content with 'bed-and-breakfast' accommodation, often of the most primitive kind. It is a pity that the emancipation of the hordes, and the equipping of them with cars, has destroyed most of what they were supposed to lack, and to stand in need of: beauty, solitude, spiritual and mental refreshment. The whole process is symbolised by what has happened in an old town known to me, which used to boast a wonderful mediaeval bridge, worth going miles to see. This has been removed, because it was too narrow for the holiday traffic of today — traffic, going where? and for what purpose? to see some other disfigured town, with its interesting old buildings replaced by standardised supermarkets and car-parks? The logic of the process may be summarised as follows: a certain town possesses a building of historic beauty and interest. Therefore a lot of people come in cars to see it. Therefore there is an acute parking problem in this town. But there is nowhere to make a car-park except by pulling down the historic building. Therefore pull it down! The town will not suffer; it will be just as full of cars as before, for every parking space in every town, however uninteresting, is always full to capacity. The same thing is symbolised, also, by the fate of that beloved bay on the north coast of Devon, where for four successive summer vacations (1928-31) we had the happiness to rent a cottage. It stood on the sand-dunes bordering the bay, and looked across to Clovelly and Hartland Point. It was primitive, I suppose, for we had to pump the water from a well each day. There was only one village shop, about three-quarters of a mile away inland, where, although most things could be obtained, you had to be prepared for long sessions, the service being slow and conversational. But oh! the peace of those long days on the marrain-covered dunes, on the solitary beaches, or in the deep, narrow lanes innocent of all traffic but farm-carts! A year or two ago, my wife and I were drawn by nostalgic sentiment to revisit this place; and let me now warn all my fellow-creatures never to do any such thing. Never revisit a place you knew and loved on the far side of the watershed, thirty, twenty, or even ten years ago. We found our cottage converted into a junk, souvenir and ice-cream shop; the surrounding dunes flattened into a car-park holding hundreds of cars; the beach covered with swings, see-saws and ice-lolly shacks, with bungalows all round announcing tea-trays and barbecued chickens. The same thing is symbolised for us, still more vividly, by what has happened in the neighbourhood of our historic camp-site in Cornwall; and of this I want to discourse at some length.

Our Cornish camp forms a central theme in the family saga, and incredible as it may seem, although it was started thirty-two years ago, and although it is now encircled with all the horrors of today, it still exists. We were amongst the pioneers of the idea of family camping, beginning it long before communal caravan-sites and camp-sites were dreamed of, and when for the most part only soldiers, boy-scouts etc. ever lived under canvas. The idea was suggested to us by my cousin-by-marriage, T. Martin Lowry, then Professor of Physical Chemistry at Cambridge, whose camping history was already long, extending back even to his own father's time. The Lowrys, three generations of them, had been camping each summer for years and years in a certain Cornish valley by the sea which, lest it be still further profaned, I will not name. After our four holidays at the Devon cottage we had been compelled to resort once more to the east coast, as in earlier years. This was so little to our taste that in 1932 we began to cast our eyes westwards again. Hearing of this, Martin Lowry told us that there was space for another camp in his own sacred valley, and suggested that we might care to take it. We were at first rather hesitant, daunted by what to our inexperience seemed the hazards and discomforts of 'roughing-it'.

However, in our revulsion from the east coast, we resolved at least to see the Lowry camp-site; so, early in September (1932), my wife and I set out on a tramp round that part of the Cornish coast which included it. We went, in the manner of those happy years, without any pre-arrangement; walking from place to place, putting up each night where we could. There was never any difficulty then in finding lodgings (think of trying it now, in the height of the season!), and some of the cottages we stayed at were delightful. (One lodging was the reverse: a bed-and-breakfast at 4/6 in Penzance, where we had used sheets, and a toilet lit by a battery with a miniature bulb from an electric torch).

Never shall I forget the first sight of the sea on that expedition; it was peacock green-and-blue, and seemed, as it receded along miles of cliff and headland, to beckon us into untold regions of romance. The sight of it, palpitating there in the hot September sun, decided us at once; we knew that we had come to the right place. I had only seen Cornwall once, briefly, before; and that was in January 1919, when my father took me there for a short breather on my return from Germany. And I had forgotten that the sea could ever look like that: so blue, mysterious and alluring. Perhaps it was the Cornishman in me that felt the spell so strongly — for, as I omitted to mention in *Spots of Time,* my Willey ancestors were Cornish. Whether originally Cornish or not I do not know (the name hardly suggests it), but my forebears were there early enough to be amongst John Wesley's original converts, and my grandfather William Willey, the Wesleyan minister, was born in Camborne, the son of Peter Willey and Alice Trerice. The name is often found in churchyards between Falmouth and Penzance, and there are plenty of living as well as dead owners of it (though all unknown to me) in the district still. It is the only part of England in which, when I give my name to be written down, I know it will be spelt correctly (and not Wyllie or Willie).

One day we came to an exquisite sandy cove, backed on the land-ward side by a wild, wooded valley winding inland amongst bracken-covered hills. There were only two, lonely, human habitations to be seen, and there was nobody on the sands, but we knew from descrip-tion that this was the place we were in search of. A short walk up the valley, following the clues they had provided, brought us to the Lowrys' camp. Here, over a lavish tea, Martin Lowry and his wife and children gave us our first lesson in the art of camping. The spaciousness, order and comfort of their arrangements convinced us that camp-life need have no terrors for a young family, and the wonderful beauty, seclusion and convenience of our proposed site completed our con-version. Here, there was everything that could be desired: a stream and a clear spring; trees for firewood; steep ferny slopes to keep off the wind; a beautiful, almost impenetrable wood filling the romantic glen from which the stream descended; and a farm on the hill-top where milk, eggs, Cornish cream and vegetables were obtained, and where, during the winter months, all camp equipment was stored. It was from this farm that the camp-sites were hired (at a derisory rent of a few shillings a year).

Here, then, on this favoured spot, with the lamented exception of one or two years only, all our family summer-holidays were to be spent until this very day. That is to say, a camp of ours has existed there each year, though not, in later years, containing the whole family — for naturally, as our four children grew up and married, some of them have struck out on other lines of their own. But one of the younger families, with its own four children, has carried on the camp as its own (and is in fact there now as I write, in August 1965). My wife, youthful still in energy and spirit (the Lord be praised!) still loves to camp beside them; while I, for my part, visit the place each year at the start, and then disappear to my Lakeland retreat to write books like this one. Others of the younger generation visit it and stay there from time to time; and those who do not, all think nostalgically of it and wish they could be there. We were all there as a united family throughout most of the war summers, and well on into the post-war period. It was indeed a wonderful, an ideal way of spending the long summer holidays when our children were at school. They had complete and health-giving freedom, with none of the stuffy restrictions of hotel or lodging-house; spent all their time in the open air; and hardly had a day's illness throughout (until they returned to the less germ-free atmosphere of Cambridge, where they often had colds immediately). Moreover, of course, we could never have afforded such long holidays in an hotel; whereas camp-life was cheaper than living at home. But what, our friends have often asked us, happened when it rained? Well, what happens on a wet day in an hotel? You sit about disconsolately, or crowd into an ill-ventilated games-room. In camp, we had a large and cheerful mess-tent, where hilarious games were played by the hour. Or those who preferred privacy (myself, for instance) could retire to a separate tent and read or write. We had, it should be pointed out, seven or eight spacious tents; and gradually accumulated enough equipment (tables, beds, chairs etc.) to make the camp a veritable second home. For this reason, and because the camp could be expanded almost indefinitely, it became the frequent resort of friends of our own and of the children, so that in its most high and palmy days it sometimes assumed almost patriarchal proportions. In this and other ways it supplied a wonderful principle of cohesion, knitting the family together by virtue of a whole series of shared experiences, affections and private symbols.

There was, too, an element of ritual in the whole sequence, year by year repeated, which contributed greatly to the building up of a camp-legend. For the first four years of the camp, that is while we were still without a car, we used to travel down by night train from Paddington, occupying two third-class sleeping compartments. There was a fish-and-chip supper first at a Paddington Station restaurant (relished by the youngsters as one of the greatest holiday treats), and then the joyous climb into the sleeping-bunks, and off at 9.50 p.m. As the train slid silently out of the station we all relaxed from the first anxieties of travel from Cambridge, and went to sleep knowing that when we awoke we should be in Cornwall. Or if sleep came less easily to some of us, there were in compensation the muffled sounds of milk-cans, and other railway noises which concerned us not, at Reading or Swindon — all inexpressibly soothing to me; and, most loved of all, the nocturnal whistle of the old steam-locomotives (a sound almost unknown in these days of the blaring and importunate diesel-horn), which always came to me with a message from the 'fields of sleep'.

We were generally awake soon after crossing the Saltash bridge, and had glimpses of Cornish villages with lovely names (Menheniot, Doublebois, Liskeard, Lostwithiel), still sleeping in the grey haze of early morning. I tried never to miss the sight of Truro Cathedral, partly for the sake of its matutinal gracefulness, but chiefly as a reminder of my college friend Hubert Middleton, who had been organist there between leaving Peterhouse and going to Ely Cathedral. At about 7.30 there was the change at Gwinear Road (where it was often drizzling, so that 'gwinear' became a family adjective for that sort of weather) into the little local train to Helston. This branch line is one of the many, now closed by Dr. Beeching, which have been lamented with heartbreaking poignancy by Michael Flanders and Donald Swann in *At the Drop of Another Hat* (a piece I can never hear without a disposition to weep). The names of the stations along that little line, proclaimed by the guard in rich Cornish tones, and eagerly listened-for by us each year: 'PRAZE, Praze!' 'NANCEGOLLAN, Nancegollan!' 'TRUTHALL 'ALT, Truthall 'alt!' — would have been worthy additions to the Flanders-Swann collection of beautiful and evocative place-names. They were part of the ritual and the legend.

Breakfast at Helston was another indispensable stage in the sequence. This had to be celebrated, not at The Angel or any other hotel, but at the Dickensian 'Wills's Cafe' in Coinagehall Street (now no more), where we were greeted as old friends each year, and where, after paying our respects to 'Father', an infirm old man permanently seated in the back of the shop, we mounted a narrow creaking staircase to the breakfast-room above. From thence a bus or car ride took us to camp — but I have gone as far as (or further than) I had intended in geographical explicitness. Helston was then still the 'quaint old Cornish town' of the Floral Dance ('Furry'); and we loved it for its quiet cheerfulness, its flowering hydrangeas and fuchsias, its gutter-stream running rose-pink from a quarry, and its cosy, cushiony hill filling up the vista at the end of Coinagehall Street. What is Helston today? a mere adjunct to the vast and ever-growing R.N. Air Station "Sea-Hawk", which has ringed it round with densely-packed new brick houses, doubled its population, filled it with the din of aircraft and robbed it of all its charm.

It would be tiresome to the reader if I were to describe in detail the running of the camp. It is enough to say that, the more expert we grew each year, the more we observed a strict routine at every stage, from the opening of the wooden store-boxes to the erection of the last tent. It was a good lesson on the motto *respice finem*, for even while prizing open the tea-chests and orange boxes which contained all our things, we had to be mindful of the last day, when we should need all the nails and wooden 'slats' again for doing them up. Gradually we came to know every object in the camp-site: which willow-tree was most convenient for hanging one's face-cloth or shaving mirror; exactly where to clear the bracken and brambles to find the dipping pool in the stream, the particular tree-branch over the stream which was best for suspending the meat-safe, and so on and so forth. Every red-veined and polished serpentine boulder in the stream became a familiar friend. It was someone's first duty each morning to go up to the farm to get milk. At first I used to undertake this, but as the children got bigger one of them (generally Peter) would take it, and the camp-reveille each day would be the clanking of the metal can as it was brought down the hillside. There was the daily walk, by one or several, up to the one and only shop (about a mile and a half away) to get newspapers and groceries. The days would be spent according to the children's ages, in playing in the stream (the youngest), on the beach (all ages), or in walking on the cliffs and moors and along the lanes (parents and elder children). In those early years the beach was still pure and clean and lovely; one could spend every fine day there and wish for nothing better. A few families, several of them Cambridge people, the same each year, and all well known to each other, formed the only groups on the sands; nearly all were camping at widely-spaced sites, unseen by each other. At our own camp we had complete seclusion; no other human objects were visible, and no sounds reached us except the cries of sea-gulls, buzzards and curlews, the cooing of wood-pigeons, the mooing of our farmer's cows, and (on foggy days) the booming of the foghorn at a distant lighthouse.

The cliff-paths were wild and beautiful (as they still are), and our greatest delights were our walks along them to various fishing-villages, coves and cottages where cream- or crab-teas were to be had. We never tired of these walks and these places; we visited them each year, and every time they were as fresh and fascinating as ever. The rugged serpentine cliffs and rocks, the sea — in the main a deep sapphire, but glass-green over the sandy shallows, the lizards flickering off at our approach, the special heather (*erica vagans*) of the district, abundant here but nowhere else, the autumn squills and lady's tresses in due season, the liners and tankers passing all day out at sea — these and many other sights and sounds went to the making of that composite image 'Camp', which had such power over us all.

There were other ingredients in it too, less obviously enchanting but essential to the total impression and the tradition. My elder daughter Margaret (not a lover of the reptilian and insect worlds, but an irresistible attraction, it has always seemed, to members of both) could tell of the moths, spiders, slugs and toads discovered inside her tent, of marauding farm-dogs snuffling under the tent-flaps at dead of night, of grass-snakes and sometimes adders; and all could testify to the disturbing effect of an invasion by the cows, fortunately a rare occurrence, but one which seldom happened without the rupture of many guy-ropes and the deposit of excessive quantities of souvenir material. We had, of course, some terrible gales and rainy spells, and the valley-path to the sea has at times been waterlogged or even flodded. But, over a period of thirty years and more, how seldom have these misfortunes happened! Hardly ever have we had to put up the camp in rain, though once or twice we have had to leave it standing on departure, till a drier spell should allow the farmer to dismantle it for us. Only once do I remember a tent actually collapsing upon its occupants during a nocturnal tempest — alas! upon our younger daughter and her husband. The young wife was then expectant, and the drenching, the cold and the shock were not considered good for her. We administered hot coffee and bacon in the middle of the night, but she decided to depart next day. At dawn her husband went up the hill to their car, and found it would not start. He then walked the mile and a half across squelching fields to the nearest garage to get help, only to find the proprietor asleep in bed, having spent most of the night on lifeboat-duty during the storm. They got away safely in the end, and by noon on the same day the Cornish sun shone forth strongly and dried everything up in a few hours. (But it is to be remarked that that particular branch of the family has not revisited the camp since then.) This, as I say, was unique in our whole experience. Nearly always, the summer gales which battered other tents, on the hill-tops, left our sheltered encampment unharmed.

We made our own entertainment for ourselves, though a portable radio gave us the Proms when we cared to listen to them. Loud and long and hilarious were the card-games played round the big dining-table in the mess-tent after the evening meal: rummy, Rickety Anne, and above all Demon Patience — at which my wife and elder daughter showed a proficiency truly daemonic, easily outclassing all other players. The tent was warmed by a 'Valor' paraffin-stove, and lit by a hurricane lamp of the 'Primus' type. The heating was very welcome, for the cold air collected in the valley at nights, especially when the weather was fine and dry. At bedtime a shivering scuttle through the dew and the night air to the bedroom-tents, with the August meteorites swooping down from a velvet-black sky, was agonizing after the warmth of the mess-tent, but it generally meant a fine day tomorrow. A muggy, comfortable night meant rain, especially if it was accompanied by a hoarse murmuring of the sea.

The cooking was done either on primus-stoves, of which we had many, or on the camp-fire which burned continually at one end of the site, or on both. It was performed with superb efficiency by my wife, and it was universally agreed that no meals were ever enjoyed half so much anywhere else. They were varied, appetising, satisfying, and the hot dishes were served *piping* hot — even hotter than at home.

The farmer and his family were central figures in the camp drama and legend. They were always most kind, friendly and helpful; and, partly because of long acquaintance, and partly perhaps because one of the farm buildings bore a tablet saying that a certain Henry Willey built it in the eighteenth century, they came almost to regard us as 'one of we' — an honorary status rarely granted by the Cornish to any 'foreigner from up country' (i.e. beyond the Tamar). The farmer himself, though short of stature and bow-legged, was a handsome man, and his regular features and deep-set blue eyes were inherited by his sons and daughters — all (especially the daughters) very good-looking. One of his sons had a noble baritone voice, which used to re-echo across the valley as he drove the cows in to be milked, singing some operatic snatch as he went. This young man was thought gifted enough to be trained in London as a professional singer; however, he did not quite make the grade. And although a policeman's life is said to be not a happy one, he has no doubt been happier after adopting it than he would ever have been as an artiste. The farm itself was originally quite untouched by modern notions, and was run on lines doubtless traditional for centuries. The steep, stony lanes leading to it, and the farmyard itself, were never made up; the same holes, projecting rocks and mud-patches were there each year, and had to be avoided by our car when at last we added that item to our amenities. At the milking, the farmer has been seen to spit into his hands before starting, and rinse them from time to time in the milk-pail itself. The milking has been modernised of recent years, and I suppose the cows themselves and the milking process now conform to the standard tests. But no harm ever came of the old methods, either to the farm-family or to us.

The inside of the farmhouse had to be seen to be believed. Cats and kittens occupied every chair and ledge, to the endless delight of our children; dogs leapt and barked in and out, and all things were in great confusion. The table in the little back-kitchen, at which the farmer sat during his leisure hours, suggested the Mad Tea-Party in *Alice*: used plates, dishes and cups were shoved along to make room for the latest meal and remained there indefinitely; and bottles of H.P. and tomato sauce, bowls of eggs, jugs of milk, letters, and stacks of old news-papers, occupied every remaining square inch of space. At this same table, on this same chair, and (my wife avers) in the same collarless shirt and mud-stained clothes, the farmer, now over 80 and partly immob-ilised by infirmity, still sits, in this very year of grace 1965. I find this one of the most consoling and reassuring things to reflect upon, that amid all the winds of change, the wars and the revolutions, the rise and fall of dictatorships, and the collapse of our social order, 'old B.' should still be there as of yore. Long may he survive! — though now, every year when we bid him good-bye, there is a quaver in his voice and an unex-pressed anxiety in our own hearts.

Camp Sundays deserve a paragraph to themselves. Here our proceed-ings were greatly influenced by the example of Martin Lowry and his family. Martin was the son of a Methodist Chaplain to the Forces, and was himself a Local Preacher (the Methodist equivalent of Lay Reader) of great zeal. Cornwall was then (and I expect still is) a stronghold of Methodism, and Martin Lowry, a man of Cornish descent, and a famous Cambridge scientist, was much sought after to 'supply' the pulpit at neighbouring Chapels. When not so engaged, he and his family regularly set out at about 10.15 on Sunday mornings (leaving the Sunday dinner a-simmering against their return) to walk over the hills and valleys to the principal Methodist Church of the district, about two and a half miles away. Fascinated by their example, and impressed by the radiant glow of face and spirits with which they always returned (the joint effects of healthy exercise and of conscious virtue), we too got into the way of attending the same chapel. For me, with my Methodist ante-cedents and upbringing, this was of course a return to the fold, after a longish period during which my church-going had been erratic and somewhat eclectic. Apart altogether from deeper concerns, we found this routine of great value as a change from week-day preoccupations, and as a reminder that the cheerful animality of camp was not the whole of life. Having said so much, I may as well confess that the entertainment-value of some of these village services was of a high order, particularly when they were conducted by a really local Local Preacher (i.e. not Martin Lowry himself). We used especially to enjoy the occasions when Brother Trelawney was asked to 'lead us in prayer', at the end of a service. He would begin with an ascending bellow, such as the bull of Bashan might have uttered: 'O-oo-oo Lorrd! we 'ave 'eard thy Worrd; and we pray now that as oe'rr the tempestuous seas of loife we steer our fragile bark, we may ever be conscious of the steadyin' hinfluence of thine 'and. Give us the power to take courage, be strong and do ex-plo-its.' Religious readers will perhaps pardon this levity when I go on to say that to these Cornish Sundays I largely owe my resumption, never since intromitted, of church-going habits and regular membership. Naturally there is more to be said on such a subject, but I mean to say it at another time.

Year followed year with little change, except what resulted from the children's growing-up, their developing interests and powers, and the variety of the friends who came to stay. The very repetition of the pattern from year to year, as I have said, so far from producing boredom, was sought-for and cultivated as a principal charm. Even the outbreak of the 1939 war did not entirely suspend the camping; indeed, in the black summer of 1940 we 'evacuated' there instead of sending our family to America as many of our friends did. Of this extraordinary year I shall write separately. But I will round off the present chapter by mentioning two non-recurrent events which caused excitement at the time.

One year, the local authorities, doubtless spurred on by some directive from on high, but perhaps also becoming concerned about the steady increase of camping each year, decided to take matters firmly in hand. They announced that in future camping would be allowed by official permit only, and that such permission would only be granted to campers using the official sites, communal toilets and communal water-supply (the last two items to be provided by the Council in the large field adjoining the farm). It may be imagined, after what I have said about the long history and cherished traditions of the Lowry-Willey camps, how all this alarmed and horrified us. What? give up our seclusion and our proud independence, to join with the rabble in a communal field? Give up camping altogether, rather than this! (I should mention, in passing, that our observance of the laws of hygiene had always been most strictly conscientious; sanitation was far superior, we knew, to anything likely to be provided by the Council.) The farmer was very much of our own way of thinking. All this new-fangled nonsense! As for the proposed communal water-supply, he scorned it; 'Eem no good,' says he, 'eem river-waterr!' I wrote letter after letter to the Council, and even tried to influence its Chairman through his son, then an undergraduate at Pembroke. I deployed all the rhetoric at my command in pleading that our camp-sites were like hereditary demesnes, that they were ours by right of long usage, that over the years we had made them into second homes, that our sanitation was superb, etc. etc. Moved a little by all this eloquence, they sent an analyst to test specimens of the water from the stream and from the spring (the former we had originally drunk neat, but latterly only after boiling, and for washing; the latter we still used for drinking, storing it in large earthenware jars kept in the stream for coolness). In due course the report came that, after applying the 'McConkey two-way' process, they had found both stream and spring water to be contaminated with 'coliform organisms of excremental origin', and hence to be unfit for drinking. So great was the fuss and alarm at the time, that it is odd to reflect that we went on as before, unmolested. We merely used the farm tap-water more often, and always boiled the rest; but the Council contented themselves with our assurances, and with their communal toilets, which after a year or two were blown down by a gale and never re-erected (their ruins still lie *in situ*, more than twenty-five years after).

The other incident concerned our car — one of the very earliest we possessed. We were in the habit of parking this in the field near the farm, within easy reach of the camp, at the top of a steep path cut through the bracken. One year the month had been exceptionally wet, and when we came to depart, on an afternoon in early September, the field was so water-logged that the car would not move. The engine started, but the wheels just whizzed round in the mire. We thought of the idea of pushing the car gently backwards down the incline, hoping to strike firmer ground. Instead, we manoeuvred it into such a position that it became what climbers call 'crag-fast': stuck on a steep slope and unable to go either forwards or backwards. This was before the time of motor-tractors at this farm, so the honest farmer, when appealed to for aid, had to bring down a powerful cart-horse and attach it to the car by a metal chain. The horse pulled and tugged, but the car did not budge. Incited by shouts and imprecations from the farmer, the horse plunged and reared in ever more frightening contortions, but still to no purpose. ' 'E don' *like* the jarb, Mr. Wulley!' yelled the farmer to me from the scene of battle. Well, in the end the horse did succeed in pulling the car up to level and fairly dry ground. Even then the car was reluctant, so several of us pushed it from behind while my wife started the engine. One wheel whizzed, and it happened to be the one immediately in front of me. Instantly I was plastered with mud from head to foot, and entered the (at-last mobile) car looking like an actor in a slapstick film who has just been squirted with chocolate custard. And I was wearing my 'going-away' suit, for the benefit of the hotel where we were to have dinner that night.

Even in the earliest years I used often to return to Cambridge, during the middle weeks of camp, to do some writing or reading that could only be done there. During those spells I used to cycle over every evening for supper with my father at Shelford, where he had come to live in 1927 to be near us. By now he was in his seventies, and getting a little dim-sighted; but he was as vigorous as ever in mind and body. These evenings are pleasant to remember; they cheered us both, for both were quite alone in our respective houses. My father, ever generous and bountiful, and devoted to our children (who adored him), used to send to Cornwall a constant succession of huge parcels of produce from his beautiful garden and orchard: peas, beans, blue plums, greengages, early apples etc. etc. all of which were then difficult to come by in camp.

One of my returns to camp, after a period of work in Cambridge, I remember with a special glow of feeling. I had managed to finish the writing of *The Seventeenth Century Background* during the very first of these work-spells, and never did I re-enter the camp valley with a mind more at peace than I did that time. I had come late in the afternoon, and at Gwinear Road caught the last train of the day to Helston, the lights being put out at each of the little stations as we moved on. I lodged overnight at The Angel, and was back at camp, in bright sunshine, early next day.

I began by saying that what has happened to our part of Cornwall epitomises the changes which have devastated England since the 1939-45 war. True enough, it does. Where formerly there were hill-top meadows, hundreds of caravans and tents notch the sky in clusters like huge barnacles. Half a dozen immense caravan sites with fancy names (of the 'Golden Strand', 'Atlantic View' or 'Sun-Trap' type) shout self-commendation from painted placards, all advertising their own Shop, Deep-Freeze, Ice-cream and Snack-bar, shower-baths and toilets. From these, the hordes descend to the beach, where, joining forces with the crowds of day-trippers who come from all parts by car, they cover every square foot of the sands from end to end, mostly bringing their transistors, and leaving the beach every night carpeted with litter. I suppose they enjoy it, but the same body-to-body beach conditions, the same petrol-fumes and traffic-jams, could be had without driving anything like so far as Cornwall to find them. What they are *not* enjoying − what nobody can now enjoy − is what we enjoyed in the old days: silence, solitude, untrodden sands. Those who, like us, are old enough and lucky enough to remember what has gone for ever, can derive no pleasure from that congested and sullied beach, except at daybreak and after sundown. Then why do we still go there? It is because in our valley all is unchanged, and while we remain in it we can still fancy ourselves back in former times. The cliff-walks are still unspoilt; and once one has threaded one's way past the swarming and maladorous caravan-sites, the old magic gradually re-asserts itself.

Chapter Six

The Later Thirties

1 A Visit to Hitler's Germany

After 1935 the possession of a car altered the pattern of our lives, and widened our horizons. The car dispelled the fear that our devotion to camping might limit the family's outlook unduly. For we now undertook exciting trips, sometimes abroad, at other times of the year. The most memorable of these trips was our visit to Germany in the Easter vacation of 1937, at the invitation of Professor and Mrs. Karl Freudenberg of Heidelberg. We enjoyed, for nearly a week, the hospitality of this charming family at their newly-built and fascinating house in Posseltstrasse, beside the Neckar. With us were our two sons Maurice and Peter, aged thirteen and seven respectively.

We travelled by Harwich-Antwerp, and drove the first day to Cologne, via Malines, Lonvain, Liège and Aachen. At the German frontier the inspector commented with delight on the volume of *Sherlock Holmes* that was in our car; he knew it well. At Cologne we were received with almost excessive courtesy at the palatial Excelsior Hotel Ernst, where the meals and accommodation surpassed anything the boys had ever dreamed of. The same courtesy greeted us everywhere, as soon as we were known to be English; and I hope it is not uncharitable to suspect (as we did) that this was an aspect of the Nazi Government's deliberate policy at that time. However that may be, we had certainly chosen an auspicious moment for visiting Germany. I had not been there since December 1918, when I left the Kriegsgefangenenlager at Kamstigall-bei-Pillau. And we were far from admitting to ourselves, even then, despite the signs and omens, that another war was imminent.

The second day, after visiting Cologne cathedral, we drove first to Bonn to see the Beethoven House. Here Peter (the seven-year-old) horrified us by removing the glass strip from the keyboard of Beethoven's sacred piano, while we and the custodian were not looking, and playing some notes on it. From Bonn the route took us along the Rhine valley, past Godesberg (so soon to be famous as one of the Hitler-Chamberlain meeting-places) and the Lorelei to the new Autobahn and so to Heidelberg.

Who could fail to be enchanted with this romantic city and its surroundings? We saw it in the freshness of spring, with plum-trees flowering, and chestnuts budding; and we saw it from the riverside garden of our kindly hosts, in whose warm loggia or conservatory we used to have breakfast looking across the Neckar and watching the

F

lizards sunning themselves outside. Day by day they conducted us on sight-seeing tours, driving ahead in their own car to guide us, while we followed behind in ours. In this way we traversed the Rhenish Palatinate: Bad Durkheim, Limburg, Deidesheim, Worms and Lorsch; explored the Neckar valley up to Wimpfen (the most wonderful mediaeval town I have ever seen) and Maulbronn; visited Schwetzingen and Speyer (where Peter uttered the immortal remark 'I *hate* cathedrals'); and visiting, lastly, Frankfurt. At Goethe's House here Peter repeated his former offence by tinkling on Goethe's spinet. (It must not be inferred from these two incidents that we were the sort of parents who believe in letting children always do exactly as they like. Very far from it; we were both strict *and* friendly. It was just that Peter's movements, at this age, were lizard-like in their rapidity, and he was sometimes too quick for us.)

Karl Freudenberg was one of those peaceable scholars who put up with the Hitler regime as best they could, while loathing its worst excesses. He had reason to fear it, as one of his daughters had married a Jew; and it was embarrassing for us, when walking in the towns with him, to notice the many shop-windows marked *'Juden sind hier nicht erwünscht'*. When the Professor took me into the University, the janitor, as if to test Freudenberg's loyalty, raised his arm and snapped out *'Heil Hitler'*! with marked emphasis (possibly he was a Nazi informer), and I doubt if he was satisfied with the bored and impatient *'ja, ja'*, which was all the response he got. Behind the rostrum in every lecture-room a swastika of mammoth size was fixed to the wall, and this our Professor disliked. On the other hand he was a patriotic German, and if Hitler had been merely the noble leader of a German *risorgimento*, aiming only to recover lost provinces and revive the country's greatness, he would have supported him. Framed, on the wall of his entrance-hall, there hung a pictorial map inscribed 'Deutschlands blütende Grenze'; it showed the western frontiers bleeding from the amputation of Alsace-Lorraine, and the eastern from that of Silesia and the severance of Prussia by the Polish corridor. I remember how, speaking of Strasbourg, which we should pass on our way home, he said 'Oh, Strasbourg! Yes, it used to be such a nice old German city. But the French have messed it up terribly.'

Two small incidents of our stay at Heidelberg remain in my memory. The first was going with our host to a lecture at the University on Colour Photography, illustrated by slides. Never have I undergone a comparable ordeal, for the lecture was not only incomprehensible to me, but lasted for *over two hours*. Of course the pictures were enjoyable for the first half-hour or so; but the only words I could follow were the lecturer's repeated command to his operator *'Ich bitte das nächste Bild'*; and never, no never, it seemed, would *nächste* be turned into *letzte*. The other incident was simply seeing and hearing, one day, a march of Hitler Youth through the streets. Their look of radiant health and spirits, their exultant step, and their jubilant singing, all admirable in themselves, sent shivers down our spine as we thought of the possible objective of all this exuberance. The German newspapers, on the other hand, were still using a soft and conciliatory tone towards England. The favourite pose was injured innocence and starry-eyed surprise: what, does *England* think we are potential enemies? I remember a heading 'Wer ist Englands Feind? and the mock-incredulous remark that followed: 'Man sagt dass es sei Deutschland!'

On our return journey we drove, the first day, through Rastatt (which brought memories of 1918, but was now unrecognisable), and thence through the Black Forest and on to Strasbourg. Next day, after inspecting the famous *horloge* at the Cathedral, and the Guthenberg statue, we reached the mountain village of Gerardmer, which was all decorated with wild daffodils for the annual *Fête des Jonquilles*. Daffodils grew hereabouts in far more than Wordsworthian profusion; there were whole galaxies of them, and we thought it not a sin to pluck a few as a posy for the car-bonnet. Onwards through Epinal, Mirecourt, and Neufchateau to Domrémy – where we lit a candle to Joan of Arc in her Church; and on again through Bar-le-Duc, to Rheims, where we lodged at the comfortable Grand Hotel du Lion d'Or. Lastly – and this to me was the most interesting stage in our whole journey – we crossed the old battlefields of 1917-8: St. Quentin, Bapaume (passing near Moyenneville, the place of my capture in March 1918), to Arras, where – height of incongruity! – we had *lunch*. Villages like Roclincourt, once so familiar as ruins in the war-landscape, were tidily rebuilt and quite unrecognizable. Indeed, the only place which I could show to my wife and sons as a specimen of war scenery was that part of Vimy Ridge, near the Canadian War Memorial, where some trenches have been preserved as they were. On through Béthune, Lillers, Aire-sur-la-Lys (the first and last evocative of April-May 1917, as described in *Spots of Time)*, and St. Omer to Calais, where we spent a night before embarking.

We took the car to be serviced directly we got back to Cambridge, and, *as we drove into Herbert Robinson's,* a tyre went flat – from a nail picked up somewhere between Heidelberg and Cambridge.

2 Paris: at the Institut Britannique

Just before Christmas 1937 I went to Paris on an invitation from Granville-Barker to lecture at the Institut Britannique, of which he was then President. I stayed in great comfort at the Hotel Pont Royal, Rue Montalembert; and gave six evening lectures at the Institute on subjects connected with my forthcoming eighteenth century book. The classes were small, and rather of the W.E.A. type. By contrast, I ended with a tremendous flourish by giving a public lecture in the Theatre Richelieu at the Sorbonne. This lecture was one of a series organised by the Institute, of which the last had been recently given by Hilaire Belloc. My audience was by far the largest I had ever addressed, and the occasion realised the meaning and intention (as Jung might have thought) of a certain recurrent nightmare I had long suffered from. In that dream, I had always been appointed to lecture in one of Europe's most celebrated capitals. The evening had come, the destined hour was at hand, and the beauty and the chivalry of that famous city were thronging the streets in their limousines, and pouring steadily into the vast Hall to hear me. It was then that, with a sudden spasm of despair, I discovered that I had no lecture to give; I had not written it, not prepared it; it did not exist. True, this disaster did not befall me at the Sorbonne, but the occasion was sufficiently alarming in itself. My lecture was the piece about the idea of 'Nature' in the eighteenth century which was published soon afterwards as 'The Turn of the Century' in *Seventeenth Century Studies presented to Sir Herbert Grierson*, and later in my own second book *The Eighteenth Century Background*. The lecture was in English, of course, and the highly intelligent audience understood every word of it, with the exception of a few phrases which I quoted in French.

My spare time in Paris was all taken up with sightseeing and the social round. It was many years since I had been in Paris, so I revived my memories of the Louvre, the Sainte Chapelle, attended a Sunday service at the Madeleine, and visited Versailles (in a snowstorm). I lunched and dined with the Granville-Barkers at their princely flat, and heard there much brilliant and sophisticated society-talk. Both host and hostess had the manners, grace and condescension of royalty, and with perfect urbanity managed to make us all feel that we were at the social pinnacle. No ambassador, unless he had been as good an actor as Granville-Barker, could possibly have diffused such an air of easy magnificence. I was also invited to a Faculty tea-party given by the late Professor L. Cazamian and his wife and family; here I met several of the Paris University teachers of English. The Cazamians were charming and amiable, and of course great Anglophiles; and it saddened me to hear later that they entered a cloud for a while, after the liberation of Paris. I went to a Casals recital at the Salle Pleyel, taking with me a very intense English lady, *d'un certain age*, who was on the staff at the Institute. Casals played, amongst other things, that lovely work known as Haydn's Cello Concerto in D, and never have I heard it played more divinely. On the way back, in the Metro, my companion, stimulated perhaps by the music, tried to lift the conversation (in every sense) on to a very lofty plane. 'Don't you think', she yelled, raising her voice high above the roar of the train, 'don't you think, Mr. Willey, that the trouble with us all nowadays is our dualisms?'

3 'Once in Royal David's City'

That Christmas Eve, 1937, Boris Ord (then Organist of King's) chose our son Maurice, who had been one of his choristers for several years, to sing the solo verse of 'Once in Royal David's City' at the beginning of the Carol Service at King's Chapel. We heard the broadcast, and were actually present on the afternoon of Christmas Day itself, when he sang the solo in the traditional 'There were Shepherds'. I may anticipate a little to add here that at Easter the following year he also sang 'I know that my Redeemer liveth' at King's. After that his voice began to show signs of breaking, and was a little past its prime when we had an H.M.V. record made of the Easter solo. However, his services as chorister were still required till the end of 1938, so that he was rising fifteen before he could go on to Rugby. Although he had derived great benefit of all kinds from his time as chorister, and would not have missed it for worlds, we thought the late start at Rugby a handicap. So that, when our younger son Peter also won a choral scholarship at King's, it was decided that he should not accept it. Accordingly he reached Rugby at the usual age.

4 'Going Grand': the move to Adams Road

In the late winter, spring and early summer of 1938 we paid several visits to a house in Eastbourne. It was while we were away on one of these visits that we received a firm offer (from the late Dr. McCullagh of Queens') for our house, 282 Hills Road, Cambridge. For some years, since I had become fully immersed in University and College affairs, we had been meditating a move to some more central position; No. 282 was two and a half miles from the town centre, and quite outside what were then considered 'University' purlieus. In those days University people were more 'caste-conscious' than they are now, and only certain well-defined areas, enclaves and even streets were accepted as correct. So for some years our afternoon walks with the perambulator often took us towards 'Snobs' Alley' (Grange Road used to be so nicknamed) and its tributary-roads, where we scrutinised the mansions of the aristocracy, considered their styles of architecture, and speculated about possible sites. All this had been mostly day-dream. But now that we had had an actual offer for our house it suddenly became a practical issue, and we had to make up our minds quickly. We decided to accept McCullagh's offer, although we had nowhere else to go until a new house could be found or built. Luckily, on our return to Cambridge, we found a flat vacant at Pinehurst, No. 4 Grange Court; and here we installed ourselves from March to December, 1938. It cost us many a pang to leave No. 282, our first and only house, the scene of so much happiness for fifteen years. We all lamented it, and Peter (aged eight) heart-brokenly vowed that he would never forget it and never like any other place so much, or at all.

The next thing to be done was to find a house or a plot. None of the houses we considered was quite suitable, but we had had our eye for some time on a piece of ground in (or rather off) Adams Road. Just beyond the Trinity College playing field there was a grassy track or 'drift'-road leading to the Bird Sanctuary, and by exploring this we came upon a field full of cows and buttercups, lying behind the very few houses and gardens then existing on that side of Adams Road. Many a time, on our day-dreaming walks, we had peeped at this and built airy castles of imagination there. But now, real action was imperative. The buttercup field belonged to St. John's College, I knew; so I boldly went round to see their Bursar. Maps of the College lands were produced, and I pointed to the buttercup field and asked whether the College would be likely to consider letting me have part of it on a building lease (freehold being, of course, impossible). 'Oh yes, I think so', said the Bursar; 'how much would you like?' I gulped, and showed him how much — it was about an acre and a half. It is extraordinary to reflect, now thirty years afterwards, when building land has become so scarce that houses are springing up continually in other people's gardens, that in 1938 I could have asked for and obtained a plot double the size. In view of later developments I have sometimes wished I had; but no! It would have been too much to keep up.

The contract was signed, and Theodore Fyfe, then Head of the University School of Architecture, and a member of the Pembroke High Table, agreed to design a house for us. We were delighted to secure him as our architect, because of all the houses we had examined on our walks, the one we most admired was that then belonging to my Pembroke colleague, the late J. Trevor Spittle, in Herschel Road, and Fyfe had designed that. We asked him to produce something in the same general style, which was Queen Anne, and he agreed.

Mr. Fyfe was as good as his word. He produced for us what I think I can call without apology (for it is generally agreed to be so) the most beautiful house of its size in that part of Cambridge — I had almost said, in any part. It is lovely in its proportions, its details and its materials. It is built of old bricks from demolished houses, skilfully blended so that their blacks, reds, yellows and greys mingle to produce a pearly effect most grateful to the eye. The red-tiled roof is pitched high enough to give good balance (lack of this is the commonest defect in modern houses, even if they are not flat-topped), and also to provide a large box-room and three attic rooms, with dormer windows. The main windows are of the sash type, with panes divided into squares, and above each is a band of fine red bricks arranged key-stone-wise. The chimney-stacks are tall and graceful. The whole house lifts itself into the air most elegantly, but it also sits firmly and solidly within its own ground. I could go on for ever singing its praises, but it must suffice to say that never, through all the years we have lived there, have I ceased to look on it with admiration and love. I never even return from a daily routine errand in Cambridge without a glow of satisfaction at the sight of it. If I am sitting or working in the garden my eyes wander towards it often, to dwell fondly upon its lines. There it is: it was made for us, according to our own ideas; it has been ours now for nearly thirty years; it is bound up with all our middle and later years of family life; it is a thing of beauty, and it has added a daily beauty to our lives.

We were most fortunate in being able to build this house just when we did, for time was running short: the building was in progress between Munich and the outbreak of the war. We had dismal fears that it might not be finished in time, and that it might have to be left half-built for the duration. As luck or Providence would have it, however, we were in occupation by Christmas 1938. It was, indeed, the very last house of its kind to be built in Cambridge before the war; and that means that it was the last of its kind to be built at all, for no such house could have been built since the war except by a very rich man. In 1938, for instance, when labour and materials were plentiful and cheap, we were able to afford indoor luxuries such as oak floors, a truly beautiful (and much-admired) oak staircase, doors made of Canadian cedar-wood etc., and the whole project cost about half what it now costs to build the least distinguished little bungalow.

If we were self-indulgent in building ourselves so delectable a dwelling-place, we did ample penance for it in the following years. For naturally, a house with nine bedrooms soon attracted attention when evacuation and billeting began, and we did not have our home to ourselves for the first six years — indeed longer, for some of the students who had come to us during the last war years stayed on several years more to complete their courses.

The position of the house, too, was then unique; it stood in its own separate domain, far back from the road frontage, and we had to construct a long drive to give access to it. On three sides it had open spaces: the Trinity field; the Bird Sanctuary; and the rest of the buttercup field, with the countryside beyond. We suspected that the latter field might some day be built on, so we at once planted trees thickly along that side. Ultimately houses have been built there, but the war delayed this development for years, and by that time our trees had formed a good screen.

My final judgment is, then, that our beloved house has not been prejudicial to our souls' welfare; my original fears were needless. Any wordly pride it might have engendered has been purged away, first by the privations and self-denials of war-time, and afterwards by the tender associations, and the abundant hospitality, of which it has been and is still the centre.

There is one more observation to be made, one which bears upon the social history of the last decades. When we built our house, we seemed to be taking by storm a central stronghold of the Establishment; we were the new people, the interlopers (though the superiority of the house mitigated the harshness of the intrusion). Now, all this is reversed; we are not only amongst the oldest residents, but our house is one of the few in the road (of its age and size) which has not been honeycombed into flats and maisonettes. Moreover, since the 'thirties the old distinctions between 'correct' and 'incorrect' parts of Cambridge, like all the older hierarchies, privileges, castes, codes and standards, have collapsed into the grey uniformity of egalitarianism. Though Adams Road is still mainly a University quarter, we should now no longer have felt out of our proper milieu if we had still been at Hills Road. The housing shortage, the coming of the universal car, and the increase of numbers, have sent people farther and farther afield in search of houses so that not only Hills Road, but Fulbourn, Balsham, and even West Wratting, Meldreth or Kingston are approved areas for University folk. Within the town, too, roads which in my undergraduate days were regarded as 'working-class', if not slums, have acquired a *cachet* of their own. Their houses have been taken over, in many cases, by sophisticated dons or near-dons, painted blue, given brass door-knockers, and filled with objects of *virtu*; while their former type of inhabitant has either ceased to exist or has gone to live in a new housing estate where good plumbing, garages and all modern conveniences are to be found.

5 Three Great Men: Trevelyan, Keynes and Eliot

This chapter has become a conglomerate of pre-war material, so I shall not scruple to add here one or two disconnected memories belonging to that time.

The first of the great men of an older generation to take notice of my book on the Seventeenth Century was G.M. Trevelyan, by that time Master of Trinity. He read it, and at once asked me to lunch with him, alone, to talk it over. In those days I still had about me a great deal of the shyness, reserve and social ineptitude from which I had suffered so much in my youth, and such an invitation threw me into agonies of nervousness. I had an exaggerated respect for my elders and betters, and a terror of strangers and their houses, which made a call at the College room of a senior don or at the house of some distinguished person, a real ordeal, accompanied by cramp of the stomach and palpitations of the heart. In the case of so great a man as Trevelyan, my anxieties were increased by the desire to make a favourable impression upon one whom I admired so much, and whose good opinion I longed to win. This desire no doubt defeated itself by making me still more self-conscious, and by leading me to say stupid things in the effort to shine. As I afterwards discovered, when I came to know G.M.T. much better, I need not have worried; he himself found social contacts difficult, and suffered from shyness almost as much as I did. But then, he was a fully-fledged Olympian, while I was only just emerging from my chrysalis. We got on pretty well, however, even at this first meeting. His generous interest in my work, and his encouragement and kindliness, filled me with gratitude. Fortunately I had included in my book a concluding chapter on Wordsworth, and this, I think, was what had attracted his attention. Wordsworth, and the Lake District, were breath of life to Trevelyan; so they were to me, and this was the link between us.

From that time onwards Trevelyan never lost sight of me. He used to invite me to dine at Trinity, and in later years he often asked my wife and me to tea at West Road. Once he and Mrs. Trevelyan invited us to a grand luncheon at the Trinity Master's Lodge, at which we met Desmond McCarthy, who had just written a glowing review of my book in the *Sunday Times.* I cannot remember the conversation, which at first seemed to me constrained and frightening, but I do remember that what eventually melted the social ice, and made us all happy, was the irresistible charm and good-humour of Desmond McCarthy.

I have a number of letters and notes from G.M.T. amongst my archives. For instance, in one dated 16 January 1936 he invites me to the Trinity Candlemas Feast (1 February) as his guest; and then in another, written on 25 January, he regrets that 'Trinity has had to cancel the Feast on account of the King's death', and promises to 'try to secure' me for the next feast. Some years later, I had been asked to give a paper to the Trinity Historical Society, and he wrote:

24 February 1941

Dear Basil Willey,

I have arranged for the Meeting of the Trinity Historical Society on 6 March to be held in my Lodge here, partly because I am very anxious to hear your Paper. Could you dine with me in Hall before the meeting?

Yours sincerely,

G.M. Trevelyan

On another occasion I had been asked to preach on a Sunday evening in Trinity College Chapel, and in the course of my sermon (which began with an allusion to George Eliot's famous remark to F.W.H. Myers in the Fellows' Garden, 'on an evening of rainy May') I not unnaturally expressed some approval of Christianity and some wish that Christians might have more influence on the affairs of this naughty world. At dinner afterwards the Master (next to whom I had been placed) could not refrain from uttering some sardonic comments on the sort of thing that had happened in history when the Christians *had* been in control. 'Mind you', he added, remembering the duties of a host, and perhaps seeing my embarrassment, 'I'm not trying to jack your sermon!'

In succeeding years, each time anything of mine was published, I always sent him an early copy; and sometimes I found that he had already procured one and had read it 'overnight' — for until his sight failed he was an omnivorous and rapid reader. In return, he afterwards inscribed for me a copy of his Clark Lectures, *A Layman's Love of Letters*. I had attended these lectures with the greatest enjoyment, and was sorry to have to miss one of them on account of some unavoidable engagement. I told him of this beforehand, whereupon he sent me a typed copy of the lecture-script so that I might not lose the thread. I was glad to be able to requite this kindness by making one small correction in the script, which he gratefully acknowledged and adopted.

I append another letter of his, because it refers to one of the most widely-known of his own books:

14 October 1941

Dear Basil Willey,

May I quote the last dozen lines of p. 264 of your *17th Cent. Background* in a book on social history which I wrote before the war and am now preparing for press at Longman's demand, tho' I much doubt if war conditions will really permit its publication.

Yrs. very sincerely

G.M. Trevelyan

At those West Road teas, in his declining years after his retirement from the Mastership, G.M.T.'s age and deafness made communication rather difficult. But his mind was alert to the end, and it was always possible to rouse him by steering the conversation towards topics dear to us both: Wordsworth, Matthew Arnold, the Lakes, the National Trust (Meredith, alas! was never one of my heroes, so I had to skirt that holy ground with circumspection). He would often tell stories about departed Cambridge characters, amongst which I recall this of A.W. Verrall (the first holder of the Chair I then occupied): 'Verrall once asked an undergraduate, who had come to a party at his house, who was his favourite novelist. The undergraduate said "Ouida". Verrall was momentarily nonplussed, but after a short pause came out with "Well, if that's what you think, I suppose you may as well AVOW it" ' (pronounced with exaggerated emphasis, and followed by one of G.M.T.'s loud cackles).

I will anticipate here in order to describe how I paid a last tribute to G.M. Trevelyan. Through the courtesy of his daughter, my friend Mary Moorman, I was able to attend the little ceremony, held in Langdale (25 August 1965), when a tablet to his memory was unveiled at Side House. Langdale is that portion of English ground which, as the inscription on the tablet rightly says, 'he loved more than any other place'; the head of the valley was bought by him, farm by farm, and given to the National Trust; his holiday home was there, and there his ashes now repose. No more fitting memorial to him, therefore, could have been conceived than the gift to the Trust of Side House, which rounds off and completes the work he had himself done for the nation. A small group stood in the open, listening to Lord Chorley and Mrs. Moorman speaking of him, and though the day was blustery, and the sky black over the Crinkles, the sun shone throughout the ceremony. I had attended the memorial service at Great St. Mary's in Cambridge, soon after his death (1962), but this day's observance, in a temple not made with hands, seemed a thing more after his own heart. The sun shone full upon Harrison Stickle and Pavey Ark, lighting up the white streaks of the Mill Ghyll torrent; and that majestic mountain mass, aloof yet close at hand, seemed not only to watch our proceedings but to symbolise, and indeed to identify itself with, the spirit of Trevelyan himself. Lord Chorley, amongst the many good and appropriate things he said, made an allusion to something which had been uppermost in my own mind — the tribute to Christopher Wren beneath the dome of St. Paul's: *si monumentum requiris, circumspice.* He did not refer to it as such, or quote the Latin; but what he did say was 'If you want a memorial to George Trevelyan, all you have to do is to look around you!'

One day in 1936 I received the following postcard:

King's, 21.5.36

Can you come to lunch with me on Sunday at 1.30 to meet T.S. Eliot?

J.M. Keynes

The reader of this book, especially if he should have also read its predecessor, will conceive my alarm. To brace myself for a meeting with anyone far less exalted would have cost me much effort, but now I was summoned into the presence of two of the most famous men of the time. To one like myself, so unused to mingling with the great, so apt to worship them from afar as beings of a higher order, it was unnerving indeed. I lost sleep, and weight, in preparing myself for the ordeal. I could not read *The Economic Consequences of the Peace,* but I could, and did, read or re-read some of the works of Mr. Eliot. The dreaded day came, and I had to present myself at Keynes's rooms with all the ignominy of a razor-cut, doubtless caused by my agitation.

My fears, which were momentarily increased, on entry, by Roger Fry's frescoes, were soon dispelled (of course) by Keynes's exuberant conversation. I had been asked 'to meet T.S. Eliot', and Eliot was indeed there; but it was with our host that real contact was made. Eliot was immaculate, impenetrable, inscrutable; uttering little, but looking very handsome, melancholy and wise. Keynes, on the other hand, poured forth words with a virtuosity I had never yet heard approached. No matter what the topic might be — and several of them were connected with my recent book, which he had been reading — he talked victoriously on, as much at his ease with Hobbes or Cudworth as with finance or ballet. Neither Eliot nor I needed to do much more than eat the superfine lunch that Keynes provided, drink his excellent wine, and listen to his improvisations. I deliberately use this musical term, because when I left him I felt exactly as if I had been hearing a recital by a virtuoso musician. The ease with which he handled difficult ideas, the slickness and speed of his transitions, the sureness of his touch, his pace and his momentum — all these things warmed and quickened my more torpid circulation, and sent me away feeling momentarily much cleverer than I really was; just as, after hearing Cortot or Schnabel, I have sometimes (for the ensuing half hour or so) enjoyed a slightly enhanced facility on the piano.

I never met J.M. Keynes again socially (it would not have occurred to me then to *return* his invitation, which I had accepted as one accepts a royal command); though later, when I had become a Trustee of the Arts Theatre, I constantly met Lydia Lopokova, by then Lady Keynes, at the meetings. But Eliot I did meet once or twice more. One of these meetings was in the rooms of a young don who had recently been my pupil (how soon he had outsoared his former teacher's limited sphere, to be able to offer him such company!). This was a much less alarming occasion than the other, but even so I had done a little anxious homework beforehand. Unnecessary, again! for the conversation never for a moment approached seriousness. It will hardly be believed, but even then I was still so ignorant of men and the world as to suppose that a poet, if actually encountered in the flesh, would talk about poetry, and especially his own poetry. In fact, most of the time not devoted to readings from P.G. Wodehouse by our host, was spent in discussing 'make-up'. 'Personally', said Eliot, 'I always used to prefer green; it's so much more striking and cadaverous, don't you agree?' I very soon lost my foothold in this torrent of frivolity, and was rather shocked to find Eliot admitting that he had given thought to such trifles. No doubt he was talking nonsense for the very purpose of shocking his juniors, but even this jesting brought him no nearer as a human being; on the

contrary it kept others at a distance, and added another layer of thick-
ness to the impenetrable shell within which he chose to live.

Chapter Seven

Munich and Hitler's War

I

Our sixth Cornish camp (1938) was overshadowed by the Sudeten-land crisis, though the more acute phases of it came just after we had left. We were alarmed, of course, at the monstrous growth of Hitler's power in Europe; horrified by his anti-semitism, by his concentration-camps and all the abominations of the gestapo; and appalled when we occasionally heard on the radio his frenzied voice working up his hearers to hysterical enthusiasm. Yet still, the vast majority of people in this country felt that there was some justice in the *Anschluss* of Germans to the German Reich, whether in the Rhineland, in Austria, or in Czecho-Slovakia. We could not approve the violence with which these re-unions were achieved, or the crimes which accompanied them. But, in themselves, *could* they justify us in going to war over them? Mr. Neville Chamberlain was the embodiment of that sentiment; his function and duty, he believed, were to give effect to it. That is why he received such overwhelming support, praise and admiration for his eleventh-hour efforts to avert war. True, there was a minority, and an increasing minority, which followed the Churchill line. And now that we have been through the second Great War, energized, exalted and guided by Churchill's inspired leadership; now that we have read his books and accepted his interpretation of inter-war history, we are compelled to look back upon ourselves and our leaders as deluded, foolish, and miserably inadequate to the historical moment we were in fact approaching. I suppose we should now be entitled to plume ourselves for political prescience if, instead of welcoming Chamberlain on his return from Munich as our deliverer, we had been amongst the few who scorned and derided him. But it is a comfort to remember how numerous, and how respectable, were the misguided hosts to which we belonged. Only a day or two ago I heard Lady Violet Bonham-Carter describe, in a broadcast talk, the way in which society was divided on this issue. She said that her step-mother, the famous Margot Asquith, was so passionate a believer in Chamberlain that she dared not meet Lady Violet at a luncheon, in case the latter should say something derogatory to her hero, saint and redeemer.

The very day we left Cornwall the newspaper-posters (in those days still properly printed and displayed every morning and evening), were saying 'WAR UNLESS —' We stayed for a week, on the way home, at my father's Eastbourne house, where we tried vainly to enjoy the

Sussex Downs with a sense of imminent disaster growing upon us each day. It was there that we heard the news of Mr. Chamberlain's first flight, that to Berchtesgaden; and we thought it a brave and noble action. We attended an intercession service at Jevington Church, where we had prayers for peace, and for the success of Mr. Chamberlain's mission; we had a sermon on the text 'in quietness and confidence shall be your strength'; and we suffered once again, as in 1914, the misery of singing that ill-omened hymn 'O God our help in ages past'. Ages past? No! it was only 'yesterday'! and must it be invoked again, so soon? And would our sons be dragged in, at any rate the elder one, as I was myself a generation ago?

We were back at our temporary abode, the Pinehurst flat, by the beginning of September, and there followed a week of miserable anxieties and dreads. Although I now pass Pinehurst and Selwyn College every day of my life, and have done for years, I sometimes feel a faint distaste for them, traceable to the emotions of that September. For, in no time, sand-bags were being filled and piled against the walls of both buildings. The sort of characters who always emerge from their lairs at the scent of war duly appeared once again, after nearly twenty years' quiescence, and began directing the digging of trenches and the distribution of gas-masks. May I be forgiven if I speak of all this with passion, and seeming ingratitude. Of course we must be grateful to those who were ready, at the first hint of danger, to do their best for the country's safety. But it is not the least of the miseries of war that it forces us to rely upon, and be grateful to, the last people towards whom we should wish to feel any obligation; people who too often seem to exult in the return of war, and to leap towards it like hounds unleashed from long confinement.

Well, the second Chamberlain flight (that to Godesberg) took place. It was a failure, like the first; France mobilised; so did our own Fleet; hope was virtually abandoned. We were dejectedly digging a trench in my father's garden at Shelford, when suddenly there came news of the third (Munich) flight – news of a settlement! With unspeakable joy and relief, and in a glow of feeling like that of a condemned man to whom reprieve comes just as he mounts the scaffold, we all rushed straight off to Southwold, with my father, there to drink deep draughts of contentment and thankfulness, and to adjust our minds to the prospect of continued life. On the way, while we were having tea at Bury St. Edmunds, the news came through of Mr. Chamberlain's landing at Heston; of how he had said 'When I was a little boy, they used to repeat to me this verse

> *"If at first you don't succeed*
> *Try, try, try again" ';*

and how he had waved in his hand a piece of paper, signed by Hitler and himself, vowing that there should be no more wars between Germany and England; and how he had added the words 'I think it is peace for our time'. Pathetic? Childish? Absurd? – or perhaps some stronger and darker word? So it may seem to our hindsight, our wisdom after the event. So it did seem to a few wise people then. But to most of us it seemed something very different. Mr. Chamberlain's courage and determination, his threefold attempt in spite of every discouragement and at the risk of humiliation, had proved to the world the reality of his own and his country's love of peace. He had succeeded, and he was acclaimed as the deliverer who alone had known how 'to give light to them that sat in darkness, and to guide our feet into the way of peace'.

2

The Michaelmas Term of 1938 began a few days late, perhaps to give us time to recover our breath and poise after the emotional strain of the past weeks. I remember beginning my first lecture with a short preamble referring to the dazed and stunned condition of us all. It was not long, of course, before reaction and disillusion set in; reaction from the mood of Munich, and disillusion about the prospects of 'peace for our time' – the first shock coming with the November Pogroms in Germany. One of our bitterest private anxieties during the crisis had been lest war should interrupt the building of our half-completed house. Munich did dispel that fear, and in the event we were able to move in on 3rd December. The mood of that term was well expressed in the remark, interchanged by many at that time: 'Well, at least we shall have another Christmas.'

The Christmas Eve service at King's that year was Maurice's last as chorister. His voice had broken too much for any more solo work, but he was still considered valuable in the choir. Boris Ord wrote us a very nice letter, describing him as the best all-round chorister. In January 1939 Maurice began at Rugby.

During that Michaelmas Term I began writing my second book, *The Eighteenth Century Background*.

3

In the Easter holidays of 1939 we had recovered enough confidence to take the three elder children on a car-trip in France. We went by Newhaven-Dieppe, because our objective was Normandy. The sea was excessively rough, the boat was crowded, and we were all (except Margaret) very ill indeed.

For the rest of the time the weather was April at its best. Little did we guess, as we drove along the primrose lanes of Normandy, what scenes they would witness after a few years, or what a last-minute chance we were then enjoying, of seeing places soon to be in ruins — Caen, in particular. We visited Versailles, spending a day in the Palace and grounds; we drove to Paris, and found all the Parisians sunning themselves in the Tuileries in innocence and security. On the other hand we heard that the stained glass was being removed from the Sainte Chapelle, 'as a precaution'. And the Paris newspapers were announcing the invasion of Albania by Italy, and the capture of Tirana (a place I for one had never heard of). On the way back we went to Chartres, Falaise, Caen, Bayeux and Lisieux. We shall remember the ferry at Quillebeuf, because before embarking on it we rashly went into a cafe which said 'Tea Room', no doubt to attract the English. The very stout proprietress agreed most affably to give us tea. When we poured out the contents of the teapot, we noticed that the brew was extremely weak, even for French tea; and that such very slight taste as it had was peculiar. We looked inside the pot, and found that the black deposit at the bottom consisted almost entirely of dead ants. Of course, not a word was said to upset the *entente,* on which we had found all the French people understandably keen at the time.

The return voyage was as calm as the outward one had been stormy. After breakfasting on board, we had a delicious early-morning drive through the primrose-studded Sussex lanes, and heard the first cuckoo.

4

During the early summer of 1939 I received invitations to lecture at Baltimore and Princeton in the following spring (1940). These I accepted all the more readily because by this time I had written most of my eighteenth century book and had material mobilised. In June, after I had finished my duties as Chairman of the Preliminary Examination in English, we took Peter to Grasmere for his ten-day break. It was on this occasion that he amazed us by the exuberance with which, at the age of nine, he climbed Helvellyn, returning via Patterdale and Grisedale, with no sign of fatigue but with a tremendous appetite for dinner at The Swan, for which we were two and a half hours late. This was the last of our Lakes visits on which my father accompanied us; and it was on one of those June evenings of 1939, after sunset, that he leant with me over the Wishing Gate and pronounced the words with which *Spots of Time* closes.

Undeterred by rumours of war, we set up our Cornish camp in August as usual, for the seventh year in succession. This time I went ahead by train with Margaret and her school-friend Faith Fisher (now Mrs John Broadbent) — then both about thirteen years old — and Lucy (four and a half), to prepare the camp-site. Once again, following the usual routine, I went back to Cambridge to finish my book; finished

G

it, and returned to camp at the beginning of September. The weather was glorious, but this was September 1939, and this time war really did seem inevitable. And so it was in our valley, sitting in the September sunshine with a portable wireless set beside us, that on Sunday 3 September we heard Mr. Chamberlain's voice announcing – not peace for our time, but – war with Germany.

5

Our eldest son was fifteen: surely he would never be called up? We could not know that the war would last six years, though Hitler said 'Germany would fight with hard determination'. But the immediate problem was what to do next? We all expected disastrous air-raids immediately, and it seemed madness to go straight back to East Anglia. On the other hand we heard that petrol would very soon be rationed, and we might never be able to get home at all; also, that children and others might be evacuated from London, and our house might be needed. Moreover, our gas-masks were at home, and we thought we ought to be within reach of them. Lastly the black-out, which began at once, was difficult to manage in tents.

Accordingly we left camp on Monday 4 September, breaking the journey at Exeter. In all the towns and villages we passed through, we saw crowds of evacuees, all carrying gas-masks; there was no lack of preparedness in that respect. Roads were already marked down the middle with white lines, to guide traffic in the black-out; public buildings were sandbagged. We heard of the R.A.F's leaflet raid on Germany; and this I thought a fine and imaginative stroke, beyond what I should have supposed any government capable of. At Frome, my wife had the foresight to buy as many candles as possible; there was already a shortage. All the way back we scanned the skies for hostile aircraft, but saw none. We were home just before black-out time, and found our house still empty.

The very next morning we were awakened by an air-raid warning at 6.45. We hastily rigged up one of the bedrooms as a 'gas-room'. The All Clear went at 7.30, and we began breakfast, only to hear the siren again at 7.45 (All Clear at 9.0). Well! if the first days of the war were going to be like this, what of the rest? But of course it did not turn out like that for a long time; we had first about eight months of 'phoney war' – totally unexpected by us ordinary people and puzzling in the extreme. My father had billeted upon him at Shelford a mother with a fortnight-old baby, together with another child of nine. But after the first scare had died down they soon returned to London.

In due course we, too, began to return to ordinary routine. Maurice went back to Rugby, and the Cambridge Michaelmas Term started. I took my gas-mask with me to Mill Lane for the first lecture, but did not do so again. We had four visits from air-raid wardens before we succeeded in making our black-out perfect. My wife and I made our wills, appointing guardians for the children; and I cancelled my projected American tour. We began planting fruit trees in the garden, and preparing a large potato-patch (this was called 'Digging for Victory'). Later, and for years, we also kept hens; and though I found the feeding and care of these, year in year out, a most irksome tie, the abundant supply of nest-fresh eggs throughout the years of austerity made up for it, and proved one of the few good things the war brought us. For a time we even kept a pair of Chinese geese, and had a prodigious number of their huge eggs as well.

What first began to change our way of life was the arrival of two Bedford College (London) students to be billeted with us, their College having been evacuated to Cambridge. From that time on, right through the war, we had a continuous succession of these girls, in pairs. As time went on others came as well: two Polish officers (who fortunately had their meals at their own mess elsewhere); one or two Cambridge undergraduates; and finally, when the doodlebug and V2 attacks on London began, a whole family, consisting of mother and baby, grandmother and (at weekends) husband. Most of the Bedford College girls were very nice, though some were a bit spoilt and demanding. The Polish officers were mainly a joke, though in some ways a great nuisance. They had, of course, nothing whatever to do, and used to foregather in the bedroom of one of them, talking loudly, and listening to ear-splitting Polish broadcasts. The boys called them Pole *Ma* and Pole *Mi* respectively. Pole *Ma*, who spoke hardly any English, appeared to be something of a rake. Almost the only thing he ever said to us – and he said it very often – was 'Too-day, I go too Lowndon!' – and we were glad to see him go, without enquiring into his motive for these frequent expeditions. Pole *Mi* was much more of a bourgeois type, precise and opinionated, but inclined to try and share our family life a little. He used to play tennis with us, but would only return a service if he thought it a fair and sporting one. If by some rare chance one of us got in a really stinging service ball to him, he would stand aside and watch it pass by, exclaiming 'Oh pleece! Impwossible!' He would spend hours patiently practising return-strokes with Peter, and if Peter made a good return he would shout 'Oh! Well!' (which meant 'good shot!').

Of the London family, perhaps the less said the better; liberation from them was the first and most obvious boon which, for us in our little world, resulted from the allied victory.

We got accustomed to the full house and the constant clamour of voices, as one gets accustomed to everything perforce. It was a trifling affliction indeed, when compared with the monstrous horrors in the world outside. Unfortunately one can hardly avoid measuring good and evil by the standards readiest to hand, namely one's own preconceptions and expectations, in the context of one's normal life. Measured by any absolute standard, these things were nought; measured relatively, they were afflictions in their way.

6

On 8 January 1940, food rationing began — with bacon, butter and sugar. It was soon, of course, extended to include bread, meat, all fats, chocolate and sweets, and clothing, etc. etc. The weekly butter ration was the size of a domino, and the sugar was about as much as some (such as I) would normally have used up in one day. It is strange to reflect that only people of about thirty years old and upwards can now remember any of this. Yet to older folks it still seems all too recent; after all, it went on for ten years (till 1950) — longer, I believe, than in any other of the ex-belligerent countries, including the 'defeated' ones. We as a family certainly benefited by having so many strangers within our gates; the pooling of all the coupons produced, or seemed to produce, greater plenty than a smaller group would have enjoyed.

7

My special 'war-job' began in the Lent Term of 1940. This was the Secretaryship of the Faculty Board of English. Faculty Secretaryships, since the great expansions of late years and the growth of a vast central bureaucracy in the University, have by now become very onerous; and my task from 1940 to 1945 was doubtless light by comparison. On the other hand, the Secretaries of today have well-equipped offices and highly efficient clerical assistance: clerk-typists so intelligent that they could easily administer any Faculty's affairs singlehanded. Whereas I had no assistance whatsoever. All the minutes, reports, agenda, returns, letters and what-not were written by me in my own study at home; and, since I was always a miserable typist, mostly in my own handwriting. All this took up a great deal of time. I never considered that I had any real aptitude for administration. If I got through my five-year spell of duty without any major blunder, it was by what Sir Isaac Newton called 'always intending the mind'. By keeping on the stretch, I was able to achieve what others could doubtless have done effortlessly. I was greatly helped by serving under Chairmen who were not only excellent men of affairs but also my very good friends: Stanley Bennett and Brian Downs.

8

In April 1940, lulled into false security by the continuance of the 'phoney' war, my wife and I took the two youngest children for a short holiday to Sidmouth, one of the places I had loved in my own childhood. I recall this little excursion mainly because it was while we were there that the 'phoney' stage of the war ended. My first intimation of this was a conversation overheard on the esplanade one morning: Hitler, I heard, had invaded Denmark and Norway. I suppose I was more innocent of world-politics and military strategy than most people of my age and education, for I received this news with blank astonishment. Denmark! and *Norway*! My amazement and horror were mingled with a touch of admiration for the audacity, the scope and the brilliance of our common enemy; the Devil himself could not have played the game, I thought, with more skill and foresight. Well, this revealed to me, and, I suppose, to the rest of my poor, purblind fellow-countrymen (except the few who were in the know, and were not only expecting this but preparing other and even more imaginative counterstrokes elsewhere) the true nature of the conflict which lay ahead.

May and June 1940 were months of miserable foreboding. Holland, Belgium, and finally France collapsed; what next? What could be left except the invasion of Britain itself? The awful fate of Rotterdam would soon overtake our own cities; and we lived in moment-to-moment expectation of devastating air-raids. Fifth-columnists were assumed to be everywhere at work, preparing the way for the parachutists who would drop from the sky like locusts. It happened that all through May an east wind blew remorselessly, bringing down a continual and unusually heavy fall of elm-pods. To our overwrought nerves this seemed portentous: our diabolical foe had cast a spell over nature itself, compelling the winds to obey him and to scatter upon us tokens and harbingers of his evil purpose. One sunny day, just before the fall of Paris, when we were innocently at tea with the Hodges in Barrow Road, the sky gradually darkened to purple-black. It was not the darkness of a thunder-cloud; it was more like what one might expect of the *Dies Irae* itself. On going out into the garden we found that all the flowers, the lawn, the garden-seats etc. were coated with a film of something soot-black. The wind was from the south-east: could this have blown across from some smoke-screen put up by the retreating French? The accepted explanation, however, was that it came from a petrol-store blown-up somewhere on the Dutch coast. The same south-east wind also brought distinctly to our ears the gunfire of the Dunkirk battle.

It was at this critical moment that many of our friends (the F.P. Wilsons, the Tillyards, the Henns, the Hugh Macdonalds and the J.W.C. Turners, etc.) decided, like so many other parents, to send all or some of their families to the United States or Canada to save them from death or the horrors of invasion — or if they escaped destruction, from being brought up under a Nazi regime. Open-armed and open-hearted invitations poured in from generous American households, and it was not easy to decide where our duty lay. But we did not hesitate long. We decided to stick together, and share, as a united family, whatever fate had in store for our country. But before long we heard rumours that the authorities of the Eastern Region were expecting invasion from the east coast, and a colleague of mine who knew more than most people said to me 'If you're clearing out, you'd better do it pretty damned quick'. The University cancelled its General Admission, and King's College School was closed. So we removed Maurice from Rugby (not without heartsearchings, for he had only been there since January 1939), and decided to 'evacuate' to our Cornish camp. Although Paris had already fallen, Cornwall still seemed a safe distance away from any probable scene of invasion and subsequent fighting. We had not as yet fully grasped all the implications of the fall of France, or realised how soon the whole French coast would be over-run and brought into 'fearful proximity' to our own southern shores.

The very night Maurice arrived back from Rugby, 18 June, there was an air-raid on Cambridge (11 p.m. to 3.30 a.m.), in which a good many people were killed and a row of small houses destroyed on the east side of the town. This naturally led us to think that Cambridge, since it was one of the first towns to suffer, would be a principal target thereafter. Fortunately this proved not to be so, though of course we could not know it until the war was over. Cambridge lay so much on the track of enemy air-raids that it had a prodigious number of air-raid warnings all through the periods of attack. We could never be sure that any one of these might not mean the real thing, though admittedly we became so used to the sirens that we took very little notice of them. Our excellent 'daily help', Mary Stokes (the last of her kind we ever had, from then to this present day), lived in the very road which had been hit, yet she turned up as usual, early next morning – for that was the morning fixed for our departure. We set forth, all six of us in the car, at 7.30 a.m. on 19 June, prepared for an absence of we knew not how long. Lucy's kitten Didymus we gave (ah! woe and heartbreak) to Mary Stokes.

How did we manage to drive 350 miles in time of petrol-rationing? Only by the help of kind friends who, for one reason or another, had extra coupons to spare. The family legend expresses it concisely; we got our first 'boost' at a Lunatic Asylum and our second at a Bishop's Palace. And this is true, except that we also had help at the outset from my good friend and ex-pupil Gordon Fraser (later, of Christmas card fame), who was then doing something 'official' on a motor-bicycle; and that the first establishment mentioned would now be known as a Mental Hospital (we knew two of the doctors in charge there). The Bishop's Palace was 'Lis Escop', at Truro; we knew the late Bishop Hunkin and his family because one of the sons, Oliver, had been my pupil at Cambridge.

9

That midsummer-journey to Cornwall was a strange and unforgettable experience. Because Cambridge had been the scene of all our pre-war and war-time anxieties, we had the illusion, as we sped westwards through the fragrant June hayfields, of release and relief. The weather was heavenly, and the deeper we went into the west, the more we seemed to be snatching a wonderful and unprecedented sort of holiday, one taken not in drab and dusty August, but in the very sweet of the year. We had a picnic breakfast, in solitude undisturbed, on the grass verge between Stony Stratford and Buckingham; and lunched at Deller's Cafe in Exeter. Here we read, in a local newspaper, an account of our air-raid of the previous night; and we felt like warriors returned from the front line (alas! how soon the South West was to suffer far worse disasters than East Anglia ever did). Nor was this the only reminder that our journey was no ordinary, carefree summer frolic. At the threat of invasion all the signposts throughout the country had been taken down, and all the mile-stones either removed or defaced. This had not mattered to us much at first, for up to a point we knew the roads by heart. But at a later stage, somewhere between Shepton Mallet and Taunton, we took a wrong turning, and at length realised with a spasm of panic that we were wasting precious petrol on an infuriating and needless detour. In the end we could only find our way out of the maze of obscure roads and villages by asking some of the rustics, who stared at us as though they thought we were spies.

We reached camp at 10 p.m., and paused for a moment to let the silence and peace of the valley sink in, and to savour the sweet smell of fresh-cut grass in June – a delight that we August migrants had never yet experienced there. Enough midsummer after-glow remained for rapid camp-preliminaries, and then – bed and deep sleep.

10

This was the eighth of our successive Cornish camps, and by far the longest. We had no idea how long we should have to remain there. We went prepared, if need be, to winter in Cornwall (not necessarily under canvas), sending the children to school in Redruth, where St. Marylebone's, of which my friend Philip Wayne was Headmaster, had been evacuated. But in any case we were determined not to treat this camp as 'holidays'. I bought school text-books of all kinds in Helston, and each morning was regularly devoted to lessons in the mess-tent.

This was not quite simple, as the eldest was sixteen and the youngest five; moreover, there were certain subjects, such as mathematics, at which I was no great shakes. However, I did my best to make up for this with history, geography, French, Latin, English etc.

The elder children used to 'help' on the farm in the afternoons, mostly by hoeing the vegetable-fields. I don't think the farmer relished this much, but tolerated it because he knew it made us feel virtuous. I thought it my duty to join the local 'L.D.V.' – Local Defence Volunteers – as the Home Guard was originally called. So, wearing a blue armlet with gold lettering, I used to walk two and a half miles every afternoon to the look-out post (a little turret, with windows on four sides, above a garage) for several hours' duty. I took with me a book to read and a 'Milky Way' to eat, and could have forgotten the war very happily if I had been alone all the time. Unhappily this was seldom the case; I nearly always had the company of a certain local resident of no occupation but much conversation. On other days we practised musketry at selected lonely places on the coast, using antiquated carbines brought back, I believe, from Dunkirk. One night I was detailed, with others, for night-guard duty in the tower of a neighbouring church, which being on a hilltop commanded a very wide prospect of land and sea. We took the watch in shifts, which meant alternately standing in the open on the top of the tower, and 'sleeping' amid the bats, spiders and owls in the belfry below. This was worth while, I thought, if only for the intense pleasure of the walk home at daybreak on a fresh midsummer morning, with the low sun striking the hills at an unusual angle, and the rabbits still scuttling about in the dew.

By the end of June or the beginning of July we had realised that, with the occupation of the whole of Northern France and the Channel Islands by the Germans, Cornwall was no more immune from air-attack than any other part of England, in fact far less so than many others. On 5 July we heard that Falmouth had been bombed; and at 7 o'clock the next morning, after being awakened by the noise of bombs dropping not far off, we saw a German aeroplane flying high towards the sea. Others were heard during the morning; and in some villages, on the false alarm of a German landing, church-bells were rung. All the following week Falmouth was bombed every day and sometimes at night as well. The sounds of German aeroplanes and of falling bombs became a daily occurrence; and once a destroyer in the bay fired an A.A. gun. A little later we began to hear, regularly each night, the distinctive hum of the German bombers flying north-ward towards Bristol, South Wales and beyond. In reply to this new threat, A.A. guns were placed on the hills behind us; and the noise of these, and their flashes lighting up our tents, made the camp feel uncomfortably like a battlefield. And this was not all; it came over us that our camp, consisting of five or six old Army-tents in a straight line, would look from the air uncommonly like a military post guarding the bay, and might well attract bombs or machine-gun fire. The same idea evidently occurred to the more responsible local inhabitants, for a policeman (or rather, 'the' policeman, for there was only one in our whole big peninsula) called one day and genially suggested that we should camouflage our tents. Accordingly, we went to Truro and bought some camouflage paints, a pot of brown and one of green; and I tried, not with conspicuous success, to daub one of the tents with irregular patterns of these colours. The tent still looked too much like a tent. So we fell back instead upon festoons of bracken, tied to the tents with string. These made a tolerable camouflage when fresh, but they were constantly getting blown aside, or off altogether; or else shrivelling and needing renewal. The difficulty of blacking-out the tents at night was also a great worry.

And so, day by day, we pondered and discussed what we ought to do: should we return to Cambridge after all? if so, when? in August? September? Or should we take a firm line and stay in Cornwall for the winter? There was a general expectation that England would be invaded in the near future — or at least that an attempt would be made at invasion; in that case, would Cornwall be a likely landing-point? and should we, at that or some other stage of the affair, find ourselves cut off from Cambridge — which meant, remember, not only from College, University and livelihood, but from my father, now in his seventy-sixth year and still living alone in his house at Shelford.

One night, after the usual attack on Falmouth, we heard the enemy planes zooming away, and prepared ourselves for some sleep. All at once, something swished through the air above our tent, sounding like a rocket. Ah! the rocket-signal, to be let off in case of a landing? So we got up, and got the children up, put on our long Dutch trousers, and stood there on the wet grass, listening intently. I then walked down alone to the sand-dunes beside the bay, to reconnoitre. The moon was shining brightly, and I could clearly see the beach, the cliffs and the sea. What were those dark patches, a lot of them too, out there at sea? Flat-bottomed barges! — no, cloud-shadows cast by the moon. Finding myself a rather conspicuous object in the moonlight I walked back towards the darkness of our valley, and just as I turned, a rifle-shot rang out from the cliff. I found the family anxious for my return, and rather shivery with cold and scare. We got back into bed, but lay awake a long time listening. All the innocent night-sounds — the tinkling of the stream over its boulders, the rustling of the wind in the trees, or the plop of a water-rat — seemed like the stealthy footfalls of invading Nazis.

Next day we learnt that a German flare over Falmouth had been mistaken by a coastguard for an invasion-signal. He and several of his colleagues, highly agitated, had then rushed down towards the cove, 'seeing things' as they went. One of them had fired at a bullock or a shadow (the swish over our tents); another, after challenging – a bullock or shadow? – three times, had also fired (the rifle-shot that might have been at me). Through my having related this adventure to one of our farmer-friends, the story got about that I was the object intentionally aimed at. And eventually an old fisherman at a neighbouring village on the coast was heard to say, in the course of an afternoon gossip: 'You know that *clergyman* [italics mine] who camps down to the cove over there? Well, 'e were shot on the beach that night'. The story in this, its final version, was relayed to us by Pauline Marrian, * a lady-novelist then staying at the aforesaid fishing-village.

11

Events such as these began to make our presence in Cornwall seem meaningless, even absurd; Cambridge appeared to be having a much quieter time. The expected invasion did not come: 'normal' life, then, must be resumed by us all? We by no means understood the full meaning of the great air-battles now beginning over southern England, nor did we realise by how slender a thread our fate still hung. The phrase 'Battle of Britain' was as yet uncoined, and the great blitzes on London had not yet begun.

On 22 August, 1940, then, we packed up and began our return journey to Cambridge, breaking the journey overnight at The George, Trowbridge. Here, at dead of night, we heard gunfire, and the now-familiar buzz of German bombers making for Bristol. The very day we got back to Cambridge there was a siren, followed quickly by the dropping of a stick of bombs across the Shelford road near the Gogmagog golf-links.

From then, and onwards throughout the autumn, air-raid warnings sounded almost every day and night, often several times within the twenty-four hours. Sometimes these were followed by the noise of exploding bombs, sometimes by the whine of a falling bomb which proved a dud (one such fell very near us, in a field beside the Coton footpath); occasionally there would be a rush of air which shook the windows, and at first there were several raids without the warning siren. A few bombs fell within, as well as around, Cambridge; near the Station, near Fenner's, at Lyndwode Road, at Grantchester Meadows and near the Union building. And there were, inevitably, some tragic casualties. But – to anticipate for a moment – if one considers Cambridge's war-history as a whole, one must agree that it got off

---

* After the lapse of a quarter of a century, Pauline has offered me another, and a still more apocryphal version, in which I myself am said to have challenged a cow. A good illustration of the development of oral tradition.

very lightly — though not as lightly as Oxford, which (I believe) was untouched throughout. The only damage done to University or College buildings, I think, was the burning of part of the Union, and the pitting of the Sidney Street walls of Whewell's Court. I believe that a bomb fell in the Cavendish Laboratory, but was a dud. Perhaps the most spectacular raid we had was on a night when the 'Baedeker' raids had begun (raids on cathedral towns and other places of historic interest), and when we had been given official warning that Cambridge was to expect retaliation for an allied raid on Heidelberg. We were all on tiptoe with expectation, and the siren duly went. But all that happened was the dropping of innumerable incendiary bombs in the fields round the town. The lights and fires flared and flapped, and swept the white walls and pinnacles of Cambridge in a stormy chiaroscuro of shifting illumination and blackness; but that was all. Some of the most disturbing moments came after D Day, when the flying-bombs began. A fair number of these passed over us, and several (those that came at night) were visible as large meteorites. One, which crossed our house, made a noise in the chimney like an express train. It was surprising to us that this menace continued right up to April 1945, though with long gaps of immunity. We could not imagine where the flying-bombs were launched, as by that time the emplacements in northern France and Belgium had been captured by the allies.

When the great blitzes on London were at their height we could hear the distant cannonades; and we watched with solemn forebodings the glare in the southern sky and the sparkling of innumerable A.A. shells. But I think our most heart-quelling experience came on the night of the attack on Coventry (14 November 1940). The enemy bombers, whose peculiar throbbing buzz we knew so well, passed over us in what seemed an endless procession, making for the Midlands. We did not know their objective till the next day — but, Maurice was at Rugby. At a later stage in the war the procession was in the reverse direction, and on a vastly greater scale. Every fine night, soon after dark, it began, and it seemed to go on till dawn. We hoped it meant that victory was nearer, but it was none the less terrible.

I took the Civil Defence course, and became an Air Raid Warden. The post for our district was at Desertlyn, Grange Road, the home of Sir Gerald Lenox-Conyngham, who was our chief. Being a Warden meant that every time the siren went, except during the day-time when normal duties prevented it, we repaired to the post as quickly as possible. Many a vigil have I passed in that house, attired in navy-blue siren-suit. Sometimes the 'alerts' lasted for hours; sometimes there were several in the course of one night, and no sooner had we got to bed after one of them, than we were up again and out to the post for the next, and so on. It was a minor hardship (good heavens! when one thinks of what Wardens underwent in the blitzed towns), and the worst consequence was broken nights – sometimes many in succession. Nothing ever happened which called for action by our own personnel. The kindness and patience and unvarying good humour of Sir Gerald and his daughter were exemplary. Miss Lenox-Conyngham used to bring us tea and light refreshments at intervals, to keep us awake (alas! it meant that she too was kept awake). After a time I got into the habit of taking a book with me for these sessions, and in that way did some preparation for my own next book (*Nineteenth Century Studies*). My second book, *The Eighteenth Century Background*, had been published – most inauspicious of times for launching such a thing upon the world – in 1940.

12

The University was never paralysed by the second great war as it was by the first. The Government's system of deferments for students meant that numbers, though of course reduced, were fairly well maintained throughout the war years, and lectures and supervisions went on as usual. On the other hand there was a shortage of dons, many of whom had gone off to do expert work of all kinds or to serve in the forces. At Pembroke there was a period of years when not more than two dons, and for a while only one, actually lived in College. That 'one' was the Chaplain, Wilfrid Knox, and it was he above all who, on the personal and spiritual side, kept the College together. On the administrative side the adroit management and experience of the Master, Sir Montagu Butler, meant a great deal to the College. Those of us who were left in Cambridge had to 'double-up' our College duties; thus, in addition to being Praelector I became Tutorial Bursar and (for a time) a sort of deputy-assistant Tutor.

Wilfrid Knox can never be forgotten by those who knew him. He had all the intellectual brilliance, much of the wit, and more than the eccentricity, of his remarkable family. Slight in build, he had a face whose expression of childlike innocence was belied by the massive forehead and bulging cranium which told another tale. Either through asceticism, carelessness or sheer poverty (I think, something of all three), his ordinary garb was very shabby: a worn-out suit, threadbare and green with age, concertina trousers, and (in the winter) woollen mittens with frayed edges. He had a faint, dry and unmusical voice, which often made his remarks hard to catch through the conversational din in Hall, but which one strained to hear for the sake of the witticisms which, with his high-pitched whinnying laughter, would pour forth in rapid succession. He was seldom serious in his talk at High Table or in Parlour; what he loved best was to defend some outrageous paradox or exploded opinion (as, for instance, that piano-playing by boys at Rugby meant decadence) with mock gravity and irony. It was generally believed that he was tone-deaf, and could not tell the difference between God Save the King and Pop goes the Weasel. Certainly his voice, when he was saying Evensong in Chapel, was beyond his own control, and would fly off at tangents most unexpectedly. His expression in repose was solemn and owlish, but directly he was addressed his face would light up, and his blue eyes swim with merriment. He was indeed a saintly and learned man, with the heart of a child. Many stories are told of him, of which I give one related by Father Denis Marsh. Knox was once asked to conduct a service at the Church of St. Edward the King in Cambridge. When he arrived at the porch he was met by a younger man — whether priest, server or verger I know not — who approached him politely, and the following interchange ensued:

'Will you take the North side, sir, please?'

'Young man, you will have to guide me: I have left my compass at home.'

13

There are a few war-time moments I want to record: moments of escape from the monotony of Cambridge during those years when the house was full of strangers, the nights full of alarms, the diet scanty yet stuffing, and the car virtually immobilised. After their defeat in the Battle of Britain, and their failure to break the morale of London and the big provincial cities and ports, Hitler and Goering switched their attention elsewhere, and this country, especially London, enjoyed a period of comparative immunity from raids (1941-2). During this period, in the June of 1941, my wife and I seized the opportunity of visiting her brother Hubert Ricks, a Master at Mill Hill School which had been evacuated to St. Bees in Cumberland. We had to go by Euston, and this, our first visit to London since the blitzes, gave us a glimpse of sights all-too familiar to Londoners, such as the underground railway-stations lined with bunk-beds for shelterers. Even in June 1941 nobody knew what might happen next, and I remember wondering, as we waited at Euston for our train to depart, what a blitz on a great terminus would be like; and hoping not to be given an ocular demonstration.

I remember that visit to St. Bees chiefly for two things. The first was the news of Hitler's attack on Russia, which began while we were there. We received this (to us) amazing news with a great surge of hope, almost incredulity: could Hitler, who had always seemed so astute, really be mad enough to repeat the folly of Napoleon, and bring down upon himself the whole weight of that mighty power, whose real strength none could guess? Yet so it was; there was now a continental Front, and we rightly felt that while Hitler was fully engaged in pressing eastwards he would have to leave the west comparatively alone. After our terrible isolation in 1940-1 it was an immense relief to know that Hitler, by invading Russia had turned that vast country overnight into an ally of ours. Six months had yet to pass before Pearl Harbour brought America in as well (December 1941); and thereafter the final issue seemed hardly to be in doubt, however far off the end might still be.

The other thing was a climb to the top of High Stile, accompanied by Bertie and his Mill Hill colleague John Morison with his wife and family. We went up from the Ennerdale side by Scarth Gap, and thence struck up to the ridge to the left. As we were approaching the summit a violent hail-storm suddenly broke upon us, and within seconds we were groping about in dense vapour trying to find each other. There was a flutter of anxiety lest the children should get lost, but it did not last long. A general move in the Ennerdale direction soon brought us out below the cloud-level, and all that remained was a steep but direct slither down to Gillerthwaite through the wettest bracken and grass I can ever remember. We were all, of course, soaked to the skin; but how refreshing it all was, and how restorative!

There was also, at some point during the war years (I cannot remember exactly when), a short, very short, escape to Grasmere. It must have been after a long spell of nocturnal sirens, for what I remember best is the luxury of going to bed at the Swan *knowing* that the night would be undisturbed. It's still true, I thought to myself then — and again when I stood on the top of Helm Crag gazing at the familiar Vale and marvelling at the richness of its green — that though unholy deeds ravage the world, tranquillity is here.

Another time, my wife and I snatched a few nights of the same blissful immunity at Church Stretton on Shropshire — which also gave me another sight of hills beloved before I had known Lakeland: Longmynd and Caer Caradoc. The utter rest of those few nights, at Grasmere and Church Stretton, taught me what blessings, before the war, we had taken nightly for granted.

Even during the war years we managed more than once to get down to Cornwall, one year staying in an hotel at the Lizard, and another year actually camping — but on another site, not so much exposed to enemy view as our own. Actually all was quiet again on the Cornish coast by then, but until we should return to our own site, and until we could do so as a united family (Maurice was now in the Army) the spell was broken.

The moment the flying-bombs finally ceased, we celebrated our deliverance by an Easter week (April 1945) in Sussex: Eastbourne and the South Downs. We just sat in the sun on the cliffs, or at Birling Gap, and tried to realise that ordinary life was beginning again. Afterwards I went up alone to the Lakes, there to breathe the more restorative air of the Fells. Some of my best and longest walks were done that week; I wanted to steep myself very thoroughly in mountain influences before beginning a new Term. It was while I was in Grasmere that news came of President Roosevelt's death. Morning Prayer at Grasmere Church on Sunday (15 April) was turned into a memorial service for him. I found it very moving to hear 'The Star-Spangled Banner' played in that setting.

Chapter Eight

After the War

1 Switzerland

The inhabitants of the British Isles, however much they love their native land, do not care to be forcibly confined within it. Had they ever before been imprisoned inside their own coasts for as long as six years? I doubt it. The re-opening of Europe after 1945, then, naturally brought with it a great revival of continental travel — a mere trickle for the first few years, but increasing thereafter to a mighty flood. For my own family it meant above all the discovery of Switzerland, which, incredible as it may seem, none of us had yet visited.

This discovery was speeded by the arrival on the scene of a new friend, Heinrich Straumann, Professor of English in the University of Zürich. Heinrich, like all his fellow-countrymen, had suffered acute claustrophobia during the war years, when Switzerland was completely hemmed in amid the warring giants, and he could hardly wait for the official peace-day before rushing over to England again. I first met him at the Pembroke High Table one evening, when he was dining there as a guest of Frank Norman-Butler (some of whose kinsmen, residing in Switzerland, he had known during the war). I took to him immediately, and we have been close friends ever since. If he could come to England, why should I not come to Switzerland? he argued. If lack of travel-currency were an obstacle, he could help me out with hospitality, and fees for lectures. I confess that I am constitutionally sluggish and froward when such suggestions come my way; but this time I accepted, and next summer I went. Heinrich kindly put me up at his own flat in Zürich, which was in Mühlebachstrasse.

After six years of war-time austerity in England, what struck me first about Switzerland was the abundance of good things everywhere displayed: shop-windows stuffed with fruits, chocolate, sweets, clothing — in a word, all the things which we had formerly taken for granted but which for years past had become rare luxuries, only to be obtained in minute quantities by coupons or queuing. My first glimpse of this marvellous Aladdin's palace was at Basel station, where I changed trains and had breakfast. The food-trolleys on the platform were piled high with bananas and oranges and boxes of Lindt chocolates, and one could actually *buy* them, buy as much as one liked! The delicious coffee was served with bowls of sugar (each bowl containing the equivalent, say, of three persons' weekly sugar-ration); and the rolls with unlimited butter and unlimited cherry-jam. I hope I shall be pardoned for these childish raptures, but sugar and butter had always been the two substances on which, to the exclusion of all others, I could gladly have supported life; and for six years we had been virtually deprived of them. (The discovery of a farm near Cambridge where one could buy unrationed honey in bulk had been one of our big triumphs on the home front. But even the taste of honey palled in the end, after it had long been used to sweeten everything, including porridge, tea, coffee, stewed fruit etc. etc.)

Zürich impressed me as representing the old pre-war European civilization, still whole, fresh-painted, opulent, glittering, and without scar or blemish. It surprised and touched me, coming from my battered, impoverished and hungry land, to find myself treated everywhere, by the delightfully civilised and prosperous Swiss people, almost as a hero — simply because I was English. Never did the prestige of England stand higher abroad than it did in Switzerland at that time. I think, too, that the Swiss had felt uncomfortable at living so long in an oasis of luxury at the heart of devastated Europe; and it pleased them, and relieved their conscience, to be kind to anything that had blown in from the outer darkness.

But there were other memorable things about Zürich; there was, above all, that breath-taking distant view of the Alps at the far end of the Lake — seen to special advantage from the garden of a country inn to which Heinrich took me, beyond the town on the northern side of the water. It was not 'my first view of the Alps', for I had visited the French Alps in 1920 on a vacation walking-tour with a Cambridge undergraduate friend; nor, in this year of grace 1965, would it be appropriate to indulge in Ruskinian ecstasies. But it was a moving spectacle all the same — surpassed, however, by the famous view from the Terrace at Berne, which I saw a week later.

Another was the evening spent in the company of Bertrand Russell, who was lecturing at the University. Heinrich, representing English studies at Zürich, was his host, and invited him and me to a dinner *a trois*. Afterwards several other Zürich dons came in to meet the great man. Bertrand Russell was urbane and charming, but his mind was obsessed with one thing: the Atomic Bomb. Hiroshima and Nagasaki were then horrors of recent date (August 1945), and Russell only differed from the rest of us in the rapidity and completeness with which he had foreseen what this meant for the future of mankind, and the impassioned zeal with which he had already set himself to try and prevent it. Whatever view one may have taken, or may now take, about the nuclear 'deterrent', and about nuclear disarmament, one cannot but reverence the pure flame of Russell's disinterested passion for saving humanity — a flame already kindled, and burning brightly, on that evening in Zurich in 1946. Since I shall not be referring to Bertrand Russell again. I will mention here the only other occasion when I met him. I was at Trinity College some years later, when I took the Chair for him at a meeting of the English Club. Of his lecture, I can only remember that it was about Byron. But I liked and remembered the human touch after the meeting. It was universally known that Russell despised titles, and insisted on being described and addressed as plain Bertrand Russell. Very good: but when the meeting was over he wanted a taxi to take him the two and a half or three miles to his house, then on Hills Road near the Gogs. So he came up to me and asked me to arrange this with the Trinity porter: 'If you tell him it's for Lord Russell it will be all right'.

From Zürich I went on alone, and discovered Grindelwald. I was one of the first of the British post-war *revenants*, and one could still get in at any hotel, as I did, without previous booking. I could not remember which one had been recommended to me by someone, so went by chance — and what a lucky chance! — to The Belvedere. I fell in love with the place at once, and it has been a favourite resort of ours ever since. The friendly courtesy of old Mr. Hauser (now no more) and his son and daughter; the wonderful balcony looking towards the Eiger; the breakfasts in the open front-courtyard, where one sat in the sun and ate croissants with butter and black cherry jam; and, sometimes, the pause and hush during the evening dinner when one of the Hausers would invite us to go and look at the *alpengluh* on the Eiger and Wetterhorn snowfields — these were some of the special delights of the hotel itself. But the village and its surrounding valleys, mountains and glaciers were full of joys and marvels. Old Hauser used to issue his guests with a programme of suggested walks and climbs, graded so as to lead up by easy stages from the simplest to the most exhausting. The last and crowning expedition was the ascent of the Faulhorn (7000 ft.), and he specially advised me not to attempt that until I was in good training and fettle. He did not reckon with the muscle and wind of a seasoned fell-walker. I went up the Faulhorn on the first fine day, which happened to be the day after I arrived; and I was rewarded with the most stupendous mountain panorama I had ever beheld: to the south and east, all the peaks and glaciers of the Bernese Oberland — Wetterhorn, Schreckhorn, Finsteraarhorn, Eiger, Monch, Jungfrau; and to the north the Brienzersee and Thunersee, and infinite blue distance beyond. I humbly confessed my transgression to Mr. Hauser in the evening; he shook his head as if pained at this violation of his testimonies, but of course with these English — well, you had to take them as they were.

I returned by Zürich again, once more enjoying Heinrich's hospitality for a few days. Zürich was nothing like so crowded and trafficky as it has now become, and I enjoyed its liveliness and glitter. Heinrich took me to many delightful cafes and restaurants, including one where he had often seen James Joyce sitting alone. He saw me off into my Paris train at the Enge Station, and on boarding it I found myself sharing a sleeper with a Prince of Afghanistan, he on the upper berth and I on the lower. The Prince, who had been educated at the Sorbonne, was most amiable, and spoke fluent French. I did my best to reply in kind, allowing myself, before each remark, a few seconds in which to compose my sentences. I called him Votre Altesse, which seemed to please him, as also did the information that we English had a tremendous respect for all royalty.

My accounts of this trip so worked upon the feelings of my family that late in September I actually went to Switzerland again, this time with my wife and our elder daughter Margaret (aged 20). We went to Lucerne, and stayed at the Schweitzerhof, where we had wonderful rooms with balconies overlooking the lake. The first breakfast on the balcony, in the hot sun after the night journey, with the lake and the mountains spread out before us, is one of the rememberable things. For me, the chief joy of this heavenly week was to see Switzerland through the eyes of my dear companions, and to share their transports at all the abundance which had delighted me before — especially their joy, after six years of austerity (almost a life-time for a girl of twenty), at being able to go into shops and buy things to their hearts' content. One of our pleasant difficulties was coping with the immense meals, to which we had long been unaccustomed. At one restaurant we ordered trout for three, and soon the waitress brought a hot dish bearing three very large and succulent specimens. To our consternation, she placed all three on my wife's plate, and hastened away to get the second, and the third dish, also bearing three each. Seeing our embarrassment, the waitress mistook it for displeasure and nearly wept to think that the English family, who deserved the best she could provide, did not like what she had set before them. At last I made her understand that, being English, we were out of practice at eating, and that one each of these delicious trout would have more than satisfied us.

2 Denmark

Another of my post-war experiences was an October visit to Denmark, as the guest of the Danish association of teachers of English. I attended the Teachers' Conference in Copenhagen, lectured to them and enjoyed many social meetings and meals with them. They spoke impeccable English, meticulously observing phonetic subtleties and niceties of intonation which I had never thought of as things one could teach or learn. Also, by the kind invitation of Professor Carl Bodelsen, I gave a lecture at the University. Excursions took me to Frederiksborg, where the first object that met my eye in the Museum was a statue of King Knut, doubtless placed there conspicuously for the edification of English visitors; and to Elsinore, where an English company had recently been playing *Hamlet*. I noticed how very conscious the people all were of the *Danish* nationality of Hamlet, an aspect of him which I for my part tend to ignore almost entirely, as I do the various Italian cities and states of Shakespeare's comedies. It was exciting to look across the straits from Elsinore and see the far-off coast of Sweden beyond it; and to remember my voyage home from Germany in 1918, through those same narrow seas, in the Danish S.S. Russ.

The return voyage was rough and made me very ill. At the height of the pitching and rolling, a bottle of whisky (not my property) fell off a rack in my cabin and smashed to pieces, filling the air with an aroma which, however acceptable in happier conditions, was then sickly in the extreme. When at last I saw the slender grey line of the English east coast, scarcely upraised above the weltering ocean, I thought how precariously my country seemed to float there, so far from the solid mainland of Europe. Usually, on returning from abroad, I had been greeted by Dover Castle, which, with its neighbouring cliffs, gave one the idea of a massive solidity far surpassing anything on the French side. Still more reassuring, in its rocky and mountainous permanence, had been the circle of heights round the Firth of Forth, seen from that other Danish ship in 1918.

Chapter Nine

The Professorship

On 12 May 1944, 'Q' died at Fowey, in his eightieth year. I think his passing would have attracted more notice if it had not happened just when it did – a few weeks before D Day.

I will not speak further of 'Q' here. I have already paid some tribute to him in an earlier chapter of this book, as also in my Introduction to the Centenary edition of *Troy Town* (Everyman, 1964). The vacancy in the King Edward VII Chair of English at Cambridge was not immediately filled. It is a Crown appointment, and in 1944 the Prime Minister had some rather more pressing concerns to attend to. So he had in 1945, not to mention his dismissal by a grateful electorate that year. I believe also that the Chair was declined by one or two persons to whom it was at first offered. At all events, it was not until February 1946, when Mr. Atlee was Prime Minister, that 'Q's' successor was appointed.

I was in my rooms at Pembroke talking to my former pupil Matthew Hodgart, not long returned from distinguished military service in the Far East, when a letter was brought to me marked 'Prime Minister'. I opened it in wonderment, and was dumbfounded to read that the Prime Minister wished to know whether I would allow him to recommend me to His Majesty for appointment to the Chair. I could not refrain from reading this out to Matthew, not without emotion; he was thus the first to hear the news.

I cannot exaggerate my own surprise at this extraordinary event. I had never thought of myself as a conceivable successor to 'Q', nor had the slightest hint ever reached me that my name might have been considered. I shall probably never know now on whose advice the Prime Minister's Patronage Secretary acted, though I had and still have a suspicion, quite unsupported by evidence, that G.M. Trevelyan may have had a hand in it. The news was received at home with jubilation, and my daughter Margaret, not usually very demonstrative, so far forgot the dignity of her twenty years as to dance round the dining-room table. The communication of the news to the Faculty Board of English was embarrassing to me, for on that Board sat several colleagues who were senior to me, and who might very well consider themselves, or be considered, to have superior claims. I thought so myself. The announcement was made by my old and dear friend Stanley Bennett (himself about eight years my senior), who, tactfully waiting till the Board meeting was about to disperse, said 'My colleagues will be glad to hear that someone has at last been appointed to the King Edward VII

Professorship, and that it is Basil Willey'. There was a moment's hush of astonishment, and then good breeding triumphed over other possible feelings and they gave me a hearty round of applause. Let me not be misunderstood here: I was never, either then or afterwards, made to feel that my appointment had disgruntled any colleagues. All of them were loyal and friendly throughout, and my embarrassment was mostly caused by my own diffidence. Still, quite apart from this, I think that as a general principle it is much easier for everybody if a new professor can be appointed from outside. There is then much less invidiousness.

· This appointment changed my way of life in one very important respect: I could no longer do College 'supervision', this being forbidden by Statute to University professors at Cambridge. I was then little short of fifty years old, and had been doing College teaching, for several Colleges besides my own, during nearly half that time. This work, though very well worth while, and richly rewarding – in terms of the gratitude and friendliness received from many pupils, and retained for years afterwards (however undeservedly) – was always fatiguing to me, and I was glad and relieved to be able to give it up. I had never discovered the art of letting the supervisions run themselves, or making my pupils share the burden. Instead, I kept all the controls in my own hands, and was giving out nervous energy the whole time. I found that it was only by driving on in this way at my own pace that I could at once overcome my own nervous reluctance, and keep the discussion from wandering into inanity or chaos. But at the end of two successive supervisions I was dreadfully tired, and if – as sometimes happened – I could not avoid three on end, I was virtually done for. These sessions left me with dry, immovable lips and a sense of having been excavated within.

Nevertheless, I did from thenceforth inevitably lose touch with the young people, and I fear that I was not the sort of professor who manages to make up for this in other ways. 'Q', in the early days, used to hold evening classes on Aristotle's *Poetics* in his large room at the Divinity School. Coffee was served, and the great man, pipe in mouth, would walk slowly up and down the room scattering pearls of wit and wisdom, and occasionally engaging in a dialogue with some bold spirit. Most of the time we were content just to sit silently and enjoy the fun of listening. But how many people were reading English then? 75 all told, perhaps? Now, after the second war, when I began my reign, the numbers shot up into the hundreds; and adding all three years together there might, I suppose, be nearly 500. It was thus no longer possible to do what 'Q' did; the Professor *could* not meet and know all the people reading his subject. I could, I suppose, by embarking on a big schedule of piecemeal invitations (in the style of some Masters of Colleges, or

Senior Tutors), have contrived to meet most of them each year in a constant round of parties or sessions. But this was just the kind of thing for which I was least fitted, either by temperament or qualification; moreover, I doubted its value – even socially. So in the end we limited ourselves to an occasional sherry party, musical evening, or garden party for research students, and it was thanks far more to my wife's initiative than to my own that we did even this. Gradually, as years went by, the type of undergraduate changed, and the gap between the generations widened steadily. This process of estrangement was accentuated in my case by the specialised nature of my own reading and interests, which led me further and further away from the main beaten-tracks of 'Eng. Lit.' I came to realise that I was not much interested in the kind of books the young (and most of my colleagues, for that matter) thought important, and that their thoughts were not my thoughts, nor their ways my ways. Rightly or wrongly, I felt pretty sure that the best manner in which I could fulfil my function was by giving my lectures, and by research and writing. I put the best of my powers and energies especially into writing, and after my appointment wrote five books at intervals: *Nineteenth Century Studies, More Nineteenth Century Studies, Christianity Past and Present, Darwin and Butler (*the Hibbert Lectures for 1959) and *The English Moralists.* Of course, as a Fellow of a Cambridge College I could not entirely lose touch with the young, and each year there were always some, both in College and in my lecture-classes, whom I liked and got to know. In this I owe more than I can say to my wife (a far more sociable being than I), who, as Chorus Secretary of the C.U. Musical Society for many years, always had troops of young friends and used to bring some of them round to our house regularly to sing Gilbert and Sullivan, Purcell's Fairy Queen, Haydn's Creation and other suitable works – the piano part being taken by Ethel Whitby or myself. I could make contact with younger people much more easily through music, which was native to me, than through literature, which was only acquired.

Sometimes now, when I see some of the undergraduates of today in the streets of Cambridge, with their dirty unsightly jeans, beards and hair-mops, and often with their arms round equally dirty and unsightly but often shorter-haired girls, I ask myself 'are *these* the people I used to teach?' They seem to me almost a different race of beings; and if today is their day, then it is time for me to depart.

The Professorship quickly brought with it an increase in outside activities. The British Academy invited me to give the Warton Lecture in 1946,* and elected me to a Fellowship the following year. Manchester University did me the great honour of conferring upon me the Honorary Degree of Litt.D. in 1948.** I was often asked to give broadcast talks. I allowed myself, misguidedly as I now think, to become a

* *Coleridge on Imagination and Fancy*
**The others who received Hon.Degrees at the same time were Lord Halifax, Lord Kemsley, Lord Woolton, Professor C.E. Raven, Professor Galbraith and Sir J. Stopford.

governor of three Schools: Rydal (Colwyn Bay), Culford (Bury St. Edmunds) and my own old School, University College School (London). At Rydal School I was not only a governor but Chairman of the governors, for about ten years. These appointments meant a good deal of rail-travel, as each school had about three Governors' Meetings a year, as well as Speech Days. In addition to all this, I was for a number of years a Trustee of Wesley House, Cambridge, the meetings being held in Central Hall, Westminster. I hope I may proffer those years of service on governing bodies in extenuation of a life for the most part insufficiently dedicated to public ends and interests. If one could measure a man's moral excellence by the amount of reluctance he has to overcome to do good deeds, then I think my governorships would qualify me for canonization. Though I never could bring myself to feel genuinely interested in the details and problems of school administration, and though the continual meetings bored me inexpressibly, I went on manfully with them as long as I could. But, of course, as all moralists from Aristotle to Bernard Shaw have known and taught, one cannot measure virtue in that way; he who acts virtuously against his will, says the Stagyrite, betrays his real adherence to lower standards. However, I continued to do penance of this kind, thereby partially, perhaps, justifying my existence, for a great many years after I had resigned from my schools. As Professor, I was *ex officio* a member of the Faculty Board of English, and thus had to attend their meetings — which steadily gained in length and intensity year by year — for a continuous period of eighteen years in that capacity (I had been an ordinary member long before that); whereas most other Board members had occasional spells off. As Fellow of a College I had also for nearly thirty years to attend the fortnightly College Meetings in term time, and these frequently followed immediately after a Faculty Board. When this happened, one was sitting at tables from 2.15 to 7.15 p.m. with little break.

To complete this particular tale, or shall we say to complete my case as defendant against the charge of having lived too much to myself, I will add that for a time, admittedly a very short time, I was actually a member of that august body the General Board of the Faculties. This may be read with incredulity by those who know me, but a reference to the records for 1946 will confirm it. I accepted this only on the understanding that it was a temporary, 'caretaking' appointment; as soon as Brigadier Tom Henn returned from the army I would step down (as I did, with thankfulness). One incident alone remains with me from that strange interlude. It was the time when the efforts of the Music Faculty to establish an independent Music Tripos, efforts long and valiantly repeated under the inspiration and guidance of Hubert Middleton, had at last issued in a Report to the University. I am happy and proud to say that when the Vice-Chancellor, at a meeting of the

General Board, asked for some proposal about this Report, it was I who moved its adoption. It was carried, but not without the dissentient and carping voices which are always heard when anything new is being done. One such voice (I will not specify whose) spoke these immortal words: 'Mr. Vice-Chancellor, may I ask what Professor Willey knows about music?' It will serve to give piquancy to that anecdote, and also to round off this whole subject, if I add that less than ten years after this I became a member of the Faculty Board of Music, that I remained on it till my retirement and that I ended by being its Chairman. If I can ever be said to have 'enjoyed' any Board meetings, it was these; I liked the people, the subject, the ethos. Though there were periods of tension, as must happen in all human groups, the remark I once made in comparing the English Board with the Music Board remained broadly true, that whereas one was Counterpoint, the other was Harmony.

Chapter Ten

My First Visit to America

1 A Holiday in New England

By far the most important, to me, of the Academic Consequences of
the Peace – and of my professorship – was my American journey in
1948. This was not in fact a renewal of the original invitation (see
above, p.97) which had been frustrated by the war. It was a new
invitation, to go to Columbia University, New York, for a 'semester' or
half-year (September to January) as Visiting Professor. I accepted, not
without trepidation, for I knew the experience would tax my energies
to the uttermost. I had not been away from England and my own
people for as long as six months since 1918, and the task of assembling
all the necessary books, lecture-notes etc. etc. was formidable. And
there were some lengthy sessions at the U.S. Embassy to be gone
through. At length, however, I succeeded in convincing the officials
that I was not a criminal, nor a lunatic, nor a Communist, and that I
had no intention of trying to overthrow the U.S. Government by force
of arms. One other necessary preliminary, of quite a different kind, had
to be endured: I had suffered severely, all through my early and middle
life, from toothache and dentistry, and foreseeing that American hospitality would exact from me an almost unbroken succession of smiles I
resolved to have all my remaining teeth out. So I went off to the Evelyn
Nursing Home, and came back the next day completely equipped with
all that art could supply to remedy the defects of nature. I had said
good-bye for ever to one of the worst banes of my earlier life; and if
this meant also a partial farewell to some forms of mastication, it was
a price well worth paying.

I sailed in the *Queen Elizabeth* on 14th August 1948, and had as a
companion all the way from Cambridge to New York my friend and
colleague Gordon Sutherland, whose company at meals, at ping-pong,
deck-tennis etc. was a great piece of good fortune to me. Although the
war had been over for three years, rationing in England had not been
relaxed one jot or tittle (nor was it to be till 1950); my amazement at
the Menus in the restaurant of the 'Q.E.' can therefore be imagined
(but I was sensible enough to eat warily and by careful gradations).
Remembering the meagre fare on which we had been living in England
for eight years and were still living, I think it was unkind of me to
write home that the lunches and dinners consisted of about twelve
courses (if one cared to sample them all); and that one began with
cantaloupe or honeydew melon, then followed on with soup or smoked

salmon (or both), then halibut or salmon, then duck or turkey or sweet-breads or chicken or beef or lamb or ham-and-tongue, with about six kinds of salads and vegetables, eight or nine kinds of fruit or coupes or ices, an equal choice of cheeses, plates of oranges, plums or grapes, and finally petits fours, and coffee with cream and unlimited sugar. But I did try to atone for this later by sending home a constant stream of food-parcels from New York.

The first three days of the voyage were windy and rough, and al-though the great ship was extraordinarily steady compared with any I had ever been in before, I think her long, deliberate rolling from side to side would have undone me if I had not taken some excellent pills. In fact, I only missed one of the fabulous meals, and was not actually ill at all.

The greatest moment of the voyage was the first sight of the New York skyscrapers, at first dim-descried, blue and misty, sprouting from the horizon like a close-packed mountain group. Another sight, amazing to a war-time Englishman's eyes, became visible as we approached the American shores: an unending stream of cars — hundreds, thousands — moving along the coast roads. I had never seen so many all at once in my life before (would that I had not now become familiar with the like, or worse, at home). We entered the great estuary in brilliant sun-shine and docked at about 6 p.m. Then followed the worst part of the whole expedition: the customs examination. I had to wait, in a pande-monium of voices and clattering trucks, for nearly two hours before my luggage was even disembarked. The baggage all came helter-skelter down from the ship in a sort of escalator, and I watched and watched for my own cases till my eyes nearly dropped out. Two of the three cases at last hurtled down, but not the important third — which con-tained my lectures. Finally the noise and shouting stopped, but still it had not appeared. I found all three at last, a long way up the vast platform, piled under the letter M (instead of W). Even then, there was an hour of queuing for an inspector, followed by queuing again for a porter. At last I got out, and found poor Storer Lunt, my American friend, patiently waiting for me at the barrier. How long he had been there, I prefer not to imagine; but Storer is not the man, in matters of friendship, to think of the 'nicely-calculated less or more'. On the waterfront we found a huge mob struggling for taxis, but Storer man-aged to grab one and took me straight to his apartment, where he had prepared for me a comfortable camp-bed in the sitting-room of his bachelor flat. Before we retired for the night, he took me out to supper at a Fifth Avenue restaurant, under an awning on the pavement in the Paris style, with the Empire State Building, ablaze with lights, rising literally into the clouds close by. Storer wanted to take me to the top of it then and there to see the wonder of New York at night, but the elevator man said that owing to cloud there was no visibility; so we postponed that till later. Looking up at this mighty tower from the pavement below made my feet tingle; it is, of course, practically sheer from top to bottom, and about the height of Wansfell Pike.

But before I go on I must pause to say a word about this same Storer Lunt. It was Columbia University who had invited me to America, but it was Storer who introduced me to the country and kept a friendly eye on me throughout. I suppose I should have gone to Columbia if he had not existed, but I should have had far less inducement to go, and should have missed much of what was most valuable in the visit. How shall I, how can I, speak of Storer now that he publishes my books in America and will probably be the first of his countrymen to read the typescript of this one? If I say what I think of him (viz., the world), will he not blue-pencil the passage? Well, I must chance it. Storer is my oldest and best American friend. It was he who, far back in 1923-4, attended my first lectures in Cambridge, and, pleased to hear me lecture on Thoreau, came up after the lecture and told me so. He was then, as he always has been, an admirer and disciple of Thoreau, and was both surprised and delighted to find him included in a Cambridge lecture-course. That was the beginning of our friendship, and in spite of my having also been his Cambridge 'supervisor' for a while (it still pleases him to call me jokingly his 'old Tooter', although I am his junior by seventeen days) the friendship has endured and grown ever firmer with the years. Between 1924 and 1948 we only met occasionally, when he happened to be in England, though we always kept in touch by letter. But when, after the war, he heard that I was coming to America, he set himself to do the honours and to ensure that I had the best of possible times. To the many who know and love him on both sides of the Atlantic it will seem merely re-stating the *quod semper, quod ubique, quod ab omnibus* when I say that in generosity, in good-will and benevolence, and in all the aspects and offices of friendship, he has few equals in this world. I have never known anyone who more genuinely loves his fellow-men, more habitually sees the best that is in them and more infallibly elicits it from them.

But I must spare his blushes. It will sufficiently illustrate what I have said if I describe a little of what he did for me in 1948-9. To begin with, he gave up to me his whole summer holiday that year, and planned an elaborate itinerary to include the greatest possible number of interesting places and people between my arrival and the beginning of the Columbia term. To this end he hired a luxurious 25 h.p. Oldsmobile car, *at his own expense,* for a month. It is unnecessary to add that in those days, and for many succeeding years, an Englishman in America was almost penniless until and unless he could earn his keep. It was agreed that when my Columbia salary started I should share the expenses of the tour, but Storer insisted that the hire of the car (a costly item I fear) should fall on him alone.

The trip he had planned for me was to take us through his own New England (he is a native of Portland, Maine), as far north as Mount Desert and Sourdnahunk Lake, not far from the Canadian border. We stayed sometimes at hotels, but more often at the hospitable homes of Storer's friends. I thus had the advantage, not enjoyed by every tourist, of immediate personal contact with some of the nicest possible Americans in their own domestic setting. Because I was Storer's friend, they all received me as if I were already their friend too. By way of example, I will describe the first of these households. It was at East Jaffrey, New Hampshire, in the heart of a great pine-forest. The house was an old, white-painted wooden structure of the original New England type, formerly a farm house but now converted into a modern country dwelling. The grounds consisted of about 100 acres of forest, cleared around it to form a garden. A road passed beside it, but one had here a refreshing sense of real remoteness. One of the first things I saw was a humming-bird, hovering in front of a row of scarlet bean flowers: an exquisite creature not much bigger than a dragon-fly, but of course a bird in miniature. I spent my first morning sitting against a pine-tree writing letters, in full view of Mount Monadnock (Thoreau's sacred mountain); and in picking 'blueberries' (the American bilberry, but larger) for dinner. There was a mountain stream running through the woods, which in one sequestered spot widened into a pool full of cardinal-flowers — a water lobelia bearing spikes of scarlet blossom, very showy and exotic.

The delightful and cultured family who made this their summer residence lived in a manner new to me. The grandfather (a noble, patriarchal figure, formerly a Harvard Professor) and his wife occupied the old white house, while their daughters and grandchildren were disposed by families in log-cabins spaced about 200 yards from each other and from the house. Storer and I shared one of these cabins with an undergraduate grandson. But let no ignorant Britisher misunderstand that word 'cabin'. Each one was a building of great size, containing an immense sitting-room, numerous bedrooms, kitchen, bathroom, refrigerator, hot-water system etc. etc. One of the largest, a converted barn (I think) was equipped as a music room, complete with Steinway Grand piano, and an electric record-player with an amplifier artfully wired into the rafters and concealed there. By day I used to be summoned from time to time to play piano duets there with one of the daughters, while her husband (a Chicago University Professor) played tennis with Storer and others. After supper we used to sit on the lawn outside this barn and listen to Brandenburg Concertos, or Schnabel playing

Beethoven Sonatas; and the amplifying was so good that one could half-imagine the music to be 'live'. The nights were intensely hot and still, and the moon rose from behind the pine-trees as we sat there.

My first sight of the American Sunday papers astonished me. Since those days our own have begun to emulate them, though without approaching their massive proportions. But to an Englishman accustomed for years to war-time issues of four to six skimpy sheets, it was something new to find that although one *could* just lift a complete Sunday newspaper from the ground, it weighed about as much as — say — a fortnight's pile of ours. One does not necessarily, even in America, believe everything one is told, but I found no difficulty in accepting a friend's assurance that the country's Sunday papers used up every week fifty acres of timber.

It was some time before I could adjust myself to being in a country where every one of life's comforts, amenities and luxuries was taken for granted; a country, too, so vast as to seem to its inhabitants the whole world (or, at least, the centre and norm of the civilized world), so that little outlying places like France or England, with their hardships and privations (and their wars, described by one American friend as 'brawls'), seemed to be just pathetic aberrations. But all the Americans I met were full of concern and horror about our sufferings: 'it isn't *fair*!', they kept saying.

I was astonished at the capacity everyone seemed to have for talking — slowly, deliberately, nasally and endlessly — without wearying; everyone had an inexhaustible stock of stories about certain local worthies (Linc, Sam, Gus, etc. etc. etc.), the mere mention of whose names at once produced a hearty sense of good-fellowship. On maturer reflection, however, I do not now think I ought to have remarked this as a specially American *trait*. It is surely common to all mankind; but my instinctive and lifelong evasion of this kind of talk had made it less familiar to me than it is to many: and in a foreign setting it was still more difficult to absorb. I may say that I now enjoy 'gossip' much more than I used to — another sign, perhaps I may hope? that I have been becoming a slightly more sociable being in later life.

As we travelled on through Connecticut, Massachusetts and New Hampshire, I began to be familiar with many aspects of the New England scene, especially the villages and small towns. Any Englishman who expects to find nothing in America but what is raw and new will be pleasantly surprised by the antique and settled air of the New England villages, many of which are full of eighteenth- or even seventeenth-century houses. These houses, all wooden and white-painted, and many of them having classical porticoes, are widely-spaced and set deeply back behind noble avenues of old elms growing out of wide grass-verges. The houses stand surrounded by lawns and gardens which are entirely unfenced. At the heart of each village is the Wren-like church or meeting-house, expressing in its whiteness, austerity and classic proportions the very spirit of the Puritanism which built it and New England itself; a spirit whose decline, in these degenerate days, is sometimes marked by the conversion of these churches into cinemas or dance-halls. In certain favoured residential neighbourhoods, however, I saw 'causes' which were evidently flourishing. One in particular, where Storer and I attended a morning service, remains clearly in memory. Half an hour before the service the precincts were thronged with rich-looking cars, and a long queue of intending worshippers had formed in front of the entrance-door. We joined this and waited. At last the parson arrived with the choir, and stationed themselves at the head of the queue. Then, after ushering in the choir, the parson turned to us and shouted 'Well, folks, I guess it's time to get the show on the road!' Whereupon the queue began to file in; but Storer and I were so far behind that we might not have found room had not the well-known actor, Raymond Massey (churchwarden), spotted Storer as an old college-friend, and beckoned to us 'friends, come up higher'.

At Concord, Massachusetts, we visited the houses of Emerson and Thoreau, heroes of my youth; and we made a pious pilgrimage to Walden Pond. Alas! the Pond, with its public swimming-pool and lido, and its ice-cream shops with attendant litter, had lost the auroral holiness which invested it in Thoreau's day, and in my own youthful imagination. I can still, with an effort, make a mental image of Walden as Thoreau had shown it to me, but only by resolutely excluding the profanations of the twentieth century.

On we went, in temperatures that mounted daily through the upper 90°'s to 100° in the shade. For this great heat my kind hosts apologised profusely, explaining that for the end of August it was quite exceptional. In a way I enjoyed it (warmth being such a rare commodity at home), and in the day-time the motion of the car kept one cool. But the nights! The lovely wooden houses in which we stayed never cooled off. And the towns, when we stopped for a meal, hit us like a blast from a furnace. At home I perspire hardly at all, but here I could watch the beads forming on my hands and trickling gently down wrist or arm according to position. My clothes were always soaked, and the only remedy while on the move ('drip-dry' was a concept not yet known, or not to me) was to have baths twice a day, and to buy new shirts and pants at every possible opportunity. I began to understand why it was that every house had a refrigerator the size of a wardrobe, why ice-water was served with every meal at home and in restaurants, and why public buildings contain machines like huge radiograms which produce, on pressing one button, a carton-cup, and on pressing another, a stream of ice-water. It was on afternoons like these that I suffered when tea was forgotten, or deferred till 6 p.m.

But I owe it to my American friends to add that they did all they could to pamper their English guest and minister to his eccentric needs. For instance, one day when we were driving round the sea-coast of Massachusetts in quest of cool breezes, a special visit was arranged to the 'House of Seven Gables' in Salem, not because of Hawthorne, but because tea was served there. (And how was it served? in a glass decanter full of hot water, in which three or four little canvas tea-bags were suspended like drowned mice.) We found a few patches of life-giving coolness down by the sea, but I for my part, not being yet accustomed to the phenomenon of a nation on wheels, was appalled by the crowds and the cars. There seemed to be no attempt to control the traffic, and the narrow lanes leading to the beaches were in that chaotic state of congestion which we now think normal here twenty years later.

At Scarborough Beach, Maine, a delicious breeze out of the north broke the heat-wave for a few days, but it soon returned in a modified form, and the endless pinewoods of Maine, as we drove northwards, were all 'tinder-dry' and smelt of turpentine. We preferred not to imagine what one cigarette-end thoughtlessly thrown could have done (and *had* done the year before).

The coast of Maine is a 2,500 mile-long series of creeks, estuaries and islands separated by long peninsulas, say 30-40 miles in length. It thus takes a considerable time to get from one place to another, and each place looks exactly like the last one. There are many fine sandy beaches, and the creeks and estuaries are a yachtsman's paradise; but I saw no stretches of cliff to compare with the Cornish coast. The coast-line is the edge of a vast pine-forest running down almost to the sea, and separated from it by low, granite rocks. There seemed to be no cliff-paths as in England; if you wanted to get to the sea-edge you had to force your way through the forest-jungle (avoiding the poison-ivy if possible) and then scramble along the rocks. A further obstacle was that many of the peninsulas were the private preserves of communities of rich people, who had built houses along the sea, and owned the whole place, including the beaches.

After staying at one or two delightful hotels (the most memorable being the Club at Small Point, to which Storer belonged), and after visiting two celebrities at their holiday homes (a privilege I owed, once again, to Storer's influence and wide connexions), namely E.B. White of *The New Yorker* and the late Edith Hamilton, we began to approach our northern destination: Sourdnahunk Lake. This, the remotest spot I have ever visited, lies 35 miles from Millinocket (the nearest town); and away beyond it, to the N. and N.W., an almost uninhabited forest stretches for about 150 miles towards the St. Lawrence River. Of that 35 miles from the town, about 15 were traversed along a narrow, twisting earth-track, crossing dry water-courses on planks (a few boards for each pair of wheels), and running through pinewoods so dense that if by mischance you met an approaching car it was always a sudden crisis, ended only by backing into ditches and rocks. Five miles short of the Lake the road became admittedly impassable for ordinary cars, and we were met by a vehicle called a 'station-wagon', which rattled and jolted us over boulders, and through holes and pools, till I was reduced to quivering jelly. The lad who drove us had done 150,000 miles to and fro along this road, and was of course quite unmoved. He grinned at me, and said 'You wanna sit right bayack an' ree-layax!' At a sudden bend he pointed out to me the hind-quarters of a moose which was lurking in a thicket by the lakeside; I was lucky to see this, for it is, I gather, a rare sight nowadays.

Arrived at Sourdnahunk itself, we at once found ourselves in an oasis of civilisation. It was a camp consisting of log-cabins: a large central one for the kitchen and dining-room, and about twenty smaller ones for the visitors. Each cabin was like a prefabricated house of Swiss-chalet design, and contained a couple or more beds, running water and wash-basin, and a stove (burning logs). The one which Storer and I shared had a verandah overlooking the lake — a mere pond by American standards, but about the size of Crummock. On three sides the banks were low, rounded slopes covered by impenetrable primeval forest, but on the fourth ran the Katahdin mountain-range (about 5,000 ft.) which headed the lake with a skyline rather like that of Great Gable — Scafell seen above Wastwater. But this was no walkers' country; to climb Katahdin would have meant first a five-mile trip in the bone-shaker, then a five-hour climb through mosquito-ridden forest, then a three-hour descent through the same, and lastly the bone-shaker again in reverse. The universal occupation was fishing for lake-trout. Storer used to take a canoe and spend long restful days on the lake, generally returning with a fine catch; and while he was out I would sit on the verandah in the warm sun, watching the light, summery clouds, listening for the eerie cry of the 'loons', and desul-torily editing the typescript of J.B. Leishman's *Monarch of Wit* for Hutchinson's. The meals in the common dining-room were lavish, and it was here that I was first surprised by the American habit of mixing foods which we, in our more conventional and hidebound way, regard as incompatibles. For instance, at breakfast Storer had ham, eggs and trout all together on one plate, adding two heaping spoonfuls of marmalade to the mixture.

Sourdnahunk was so inaccessible that some of the visitors used to come and go by hydroplane. I enjoyed the remoteness and novelty of it all, but I learnt here once again (as elsewhere in America) the old lesson taught by Coleridge in his letters from the Hartz mountains, that

I

appreciation of natural beauty depends far more than we think upon heartfelt associations and human sympathies. My first lesson on this subject had in fact been impressed upon me thirty years before, when, as a prisoner of war in Germany, I had looked out upon those same Hartz mountains through the windows of a (4th Class) railway-carriage. How alien, sullen and dismal they looked! symbols, merely, of the 'fremd' and hostile land in which I had been trapped. At the sight of *any* hill, from the lowly Box Hill, Ivinghoe Beacon, Leith Hill or Chanctonbury Ring to the more lordly Malverns, Yes Tor, Longmynd, Caer Caradoc or Arthur's Seat and on finally to the Delectable Mountains of Lakeland – my heart had always leapt up. But here, in the middle of enemy Germany, the mountains merely scowled at me; they spoke to me no rememberable things. And even in beautiful free America, surrounded by comforts and kindness and friendship, and without any of the former reasons for imaginative numbness, I yet felt something of the same disability. To respond fully to scenery, I discovered, I needed to see it as the embodiment (or 'projection') of former states of feeling, as the reminder and token of former passages of life, historical, national, domestic and personal, of joys and fears and loves deeply felt and long cherished, as the expression of ancient, slow-moving and traditional ways of life. Our native mountains touch me so deeply because they raise into the upper air, above the region clouds, the whole panorama of (what used to be) England's green and pleasant land, imparting to its history-laden plains a celestial touch they would otherwise lack. The bold outline and serrated edges of the Langdale Pikes tell of skyey influences, but at their base, and running far into the heart of the rugged Crinkles and Bow Fell, are the flat, green, elysian meadows and white farmsteads of Westmorland. The mountains are affecting because they link 'the kindred points of Heaven and home'. I suppose my imagination and sensibilities are of the sluggish, home-keeping, conservative kind; had I possessed the alert, mercurial responsiveness of the born traveller or journalist I should have been able to supply from within, or from fresh knowledge quickly and eagerly acquired, the emotional colouring needed to give life to these new scenes. As it is, they had little message for my heart. Of all places I saw in America, I think Walden Pond would have moved me most; and that was because I had lived there in imagination with Thoreau, sharing his lonely, withdrawn life, his ecstasies and his communings with the infinite. I say 'would have', because (as I mentioned above) the Walden of today is not Thoreau's.

Our motor-tour ended with a night in Vermont, where we were most kindly welcomed at the house of my former pupil Charles T. Prouty and his wife Ruth. Charles, who was full of Cambridge memories and anecdotes – many of them shouted from the kitchen while he was frying the breakfast — told me one about our daughter Margaret (which I suspected of being apocryphal). He remembered that once when playing darts with us at our Cambridge home, in 1938-9, he was so successful that Margaret (then aged 12 or 13) exclaimed 'Ha! obvious where *you* spend your time — at "The Still and Sugar-Loaf"!' Margaret was very sharp and knowing at that age (as at all ages), but I confess that this shook me; I, of course, had never even heard of such a place.

Storer and I parted company at Fort Ticonderoga, where I took train to Montreal to visit my Aunt Connie. She was the widow of my scientist-uncle Arthur Willey, who had been Strathcona Professor of Zoology at McGill University till his retirement in 1937. He had died in 1942, but his widow lived on in a Montreal apartment.

I have always been a lover of my native land, but I have more than once been surprised, when abroad, to discover the depth and intensity of this passion. For instance, on my arrival in Canada, although I had only been away about a month, the sight of the Union Jack, and the King's head on the coins, nearly moved me to tears. The sense of being on British soil again, and the family link, made Montreal seem homelike. It relieved the home-sickness which was already gathering inside me, though mostly just below the conscious surface. I was affectionately received by my Aunt, and various parties were arranged by McGill friends in honour of 'Professor Willey the Second'. The climax of this Canadian visit was a pilgrimage to Mille Isles in the Laurentian hill-country, where my uncle had built a vacation-bungalow. Readers of my previous book, who remember how fond I had been of Uncle Arthur, and how much I had admired him, will understand what it meant to see, in that remote and rugged garden-plot, the place where his ashes had been scattered, and the memorial tablet bearing his name.

2 Visiting Professor at Columbia

Back in New York on the 14th September, I was met and given a night's lodging by the faithful and indefatigable Storer. And now it was goodbye to holidays, for the Columbia University term was about to begin, and with it the very exacting routine, academic and social, of a visiting Professor's life. My apartment was on the fifteenth floor of Butler Hall, in Morningside Drive, adjoining the campus. Here I had two large rooms (a sitting-room and a bedroom), a kitchenette, bathroom and cupboards. Daily 'maid-service' was provided by a good-natured if slightly dense, and (as it later appeared) a devoutly religious, elderly soul of part-negro extraction. The view from my bedroom window took my breath away: it stretched for four miles over roofs and streets to the famous New York skyline. It was most spectacular at night, when the city best deserved its name of the 'Modern Baghdad'.

It then looked, indeed, like some enchanted city raised from nothing by the Geni of Aladdin's Lamp: a dark, nightmarish welter studded with innumerable lights — gold, green and red — out of which sprouted those strange, frail-looking stalagmites the Empire State Building, the Rockefeller Center, the Chrysler and Woolworth Buildings and the rest of the cluster. At night, when these Babel-towers were lit, they seemed from a distance like fragile structures of black cardboard fretted with squares of gold paper. To the left, below the 'Heights' on which Butler Hall and the University stood, lay a region of grim-looking brick-built blocks known locally as 'The City of Dreadful Night'; this was Harlem, the negro quarter. It was separated, like a hell, from this white-man's academic heaven, by a narrow strip of park and a steep flight of steps. I was warned not to venture thither; the park especially, which looked pretty enough, was said to be dangerous at nights. As it chanced, one night much later when I was returning from a concert down town, I boarded the wrong 'Subway' train, and found myself at midnight in the very centre of Harlem instead of at West 119th Street. I walked peacefully home, through the terrible park and up the steps, having seen nothing (except the complexion of the thronging and well-behaved crowds) which would have attracted attention in Oxford Street or Tottenham Court Road.

Eggs being my staple diet when housekeeping on my own, I at once tried to buy an egg-cup, which was not included in my kitchen outfit. I found that such a thing was unobtainable and unheard-of; the way to eat a boiled egg was to peel off the shell and eat it from a soup-bowl. There were no normal shoe-cleaning arrangements in any American hotel, however posh; the Englishman, following the invariable practice at home, puts his shoes outside his bedroom door and finds them untouched in the morning. I was so astonished at this when I first experienced it (not caring to go down to breakfast in muddy shoes) that I protested feebly. It was at once clear that I had said the wrong thing: 'get a shoe-shine in any barber shop' was the only comfort I was offered. One evening as I was walking along the Hudson Riverside enjoying the sunset, a nice-looking little boy of about twelve, carrying a shoe-cleaning outfit, accosted me with 'Shoe-shine, sir?' I said 'No, thanks', but he persisted with 'Sure you won't have a shoe-shine, sir? *You need one!*' This was very true; so I gave in, and we had a chat while the operation was in progress. I found that social values were as mixed up in this country as their menus: this boy said that both his parents were school-teachers, that they were now taking courses at Columbia, that they taught him at home, and that he had brothers and sisters at boarding-schools — one of the brothers at the 'swell' school (looking like Marlborough) which Storer attended as a boy. He told me he made a dollar and a half a day by shoe-cleaning, which went towards the family expenses.

I had been warned by a Cambridge friend who knew America that politeness on the part of customers in shops or restaurants was not expected, and that if used it would be derided. And I did notice that orders were often given in sharp tones, without please or thank-you. However, I kept to the habitual courtesies and was certainly not laughed at for so doing, though occasionally the salesman or waitress would look at me with a twinkle and say 'You're vurry welcome', which I thought was rather pretty (I think it usually meant 'nice of you, but you needn't have bothered'). In general, the informal, breezy, kindly man-to-man (or rather guy-to-guy) approach, which everywhere prevailed, and which I took to be an expression of American egalitarianism, seemed to me a pleasant change from our own more starchy and inhibited social style. It amused me, when travelling with Storer and Howard Wilson, to hear a roadside cafe-proprietor say to us 'Sorry, men, I'm out of soup!' Or, when negotiating a terrible road-crossing in New York (and evidently wearing a panic-stricken look) to be comforted by a lorry-driver with 'Take it easy, Pop; you'll make it!'

Some of the arrangements in New York City seemed to me admirable; others, less so. Speed and efficiency were highly regarded. No parking was allowed in the City, and consequently many citizens simply owned no car, or none for town use. Fast traffic hurtled along special speedways on the water-fronts. On the buses and tubes New York managed much better than London (why can't we follow them when they set us a *good* example?); you paid a dime (10 cents) for any and every journey, long or short. There were no bus-conductors, ticket-clerks or tickets. On a bus, you put your dime in a slot as you got in, and this rang a bell informing the driver that you had paid. In the subway, your dime opened a turnstile and let you through. What a saving of time and irritation! On the other hand, I was surprised at the almost total absence in New York of what we call 'public conveniences' — or what the Americans, with their different taste in euphemisms, call 'rest rooms', 'wash rooms', or 'comfort stations'. I asked Storer if there were any to be found, and he said 'There are; but there are darned few'. How right he was.

Turning to affairs of greater importance, one of the first things that struck me was the great difference between the ways of American and English undergraduates both in term and in vacations. Storer's nephew for example, had just gone up to Yale, and directly he arrived there his first duty and care had been to look for a job which would support him while at College. This sort of thing, I found, was quite normal at American Universities: the students drive lorries or taxis, wait in restaurants, or operate lifts even in term-time. The English idea that an undergraduate's studies are his whole-time job was — when I described it to this young man's parents and others — almost incomprehensible to them; just an aspect, they supposed, of our effete old class-system. I found, of course, that in the United States hundreds of thousands of young people go to a University who would never dream of such a thing in England; I believe that at that time almost one in every four Americans were graduates of some kind, even if it were only in journalism, hotel-management or apiculture. Today (1965) these differences, like all others, have become much less marked; the English undergraduate, though he still sticks to his proper work in term-time, is now almost as likely as his American counterpart to be your porter, waiter or page-boy at your holiday hotel.

I soon fell into the weekly routine at Columbia. The duties were light for an American Visiting Professorship, and I fortunately had plenty of material with me and was not forced to compose lectures *de novo* (as happened, alas! at Cornell five years later). I lectured every Tuesday and Thursday, and took classes on the afternoons of the same days; the rest of the days were my own. Hardly a week passed, however, without some invitation to dinner with Storer or to the Faculty Club, or to lecture at Amherst, Connecticut College, Syracuse, Rutgers, Smith College, Johns Hopkins, Charlottesville, Cornell, Princeton, Yale and Toronto — all of which I visited and lectured at from my base at Columbia. There were also papers and after-dinner speeches to prepare, and receptions, parties, plays and concerts to attend; and at most weekends Storer took me on long expeditions into the country. My time was thus very fully taken-up.

Columbia, I found, was a vast impersonal academic power-station, rather like the University of London, to which some 50,000 students made their way each day, mostly by train, or subway; or in the evenings only, if their days were already taken up by their jobs. My lectures were on my usual lines: 17th, 18th and 19th century studies in the mornings, and 'moralists' topics at the seminars. All the students who attended were in their third, fourth or fifth years, and their academic quality was high; I could expect, and received, as good a response as in Cambridge — in some ways a better and more lively one. My colleagues at Philosophy Hall and Hamilton — Oscar J. Campbell, Marjorie Nicolson, Andrew Chiappe, Bennett, Tindall, D.L. Clark, Lionel Trilling and many others — were all as kind and friendly as could be,

My main purpose, in this as in the previous volume, is not to discuss ideas or recommend opinions, but rather to try and convey what it felt like to be living through the various phases of my life. And so now, instead of describing the state of English Studies in American Universities, or comparing American and British undergraduates, or estimating the respective merits and demerits of their Universities (fascinating yet potentially boring subjects on which I have said quite enough in conversation, and on which others are far better fitted to write than I), I shall attempt simply to re-capture the ethos and savour of my day-to-day living in America.

My lectures were given in a ground-floor room which abutted on the busy and noisy Amsterdam Avenue. The lecture-room was overheated, so the windows had to be kept open, letting in the noise. There was thus a dilemma: was it to be apoplexy or inaudibility? At the beginning of the Term the weather was still as warm as in the hottest English August, and I soon found that my English three-piece tweed suit would never do. I ordered a suit of 'tropical worsted', and while this was being made I lectured in an extraordinary sports jacket I had bought in Concord — double-breasted, white with grey stripes — apologising to my audience, and adding that I thought they might prefer a professor in unorthodox garb to a mere pool of grease on the floor. This eased the temperature-problem; but I often feared that my voice would not stand the strain of being raised above the din of traffic.

I do not like living in a great city. Nor do I care for living in an 'apartment'. My flat at Butler Hall, fifteen floors up from the ground, often seemed to me dead and meaningless. Whenever I returned there, everything was exactly as I had left it; nobody was sitting knitting by the fireside — there was, of course, no fireside, only an over-hot steam radiator smelling of paint and metal. Not even any letters on the door-mat, all letters being kept in the janitor's office on the ground-level. At intervals the thermostat in the refrigerator gave a click, and then for about half a minute there followed a mechanical noise like a coffee-grinder at work. It was no excess of *quiet* which depressed my spirits in this flat; very far from it! The windows had to be kept wide open to avoid suffocation by the heat, and through them came an incessant and complex shindy from the streets and houses below. I could only compare it to the sound of a tank corps moving continuously into action: grindings, scrapings, thumpings and screamings; and all this intermingled with human cries and shouts, megaphonic loud-speakers, and the reiterated wailings of police and ambulance cars. Sometimes there would be a confused clamour of haranguing voices, as if some desperate revolution were being staged on the Campus; with one loud, vehement voice — the voice of some student Danton? — rising above the general murmur. I have heard this din swell, sometimes, to such a climax of bangs, thuds and shrieks that a murder might just have been enacted. And to judge from the number of sirens, there might be a crime or a street-accident occurring every quarter of an hour. I found all this baleful and foreboding, especially at nights. No one ever seemed to go to bed in New York; the sky-scrapers were lit up far into the night, and if I were sleepless I could hear the frantic rush and hooting of taxis at 3 a.m. almost as much as by day. How heartrending, at such times, was the thought of any 'wet, bird-haunted English lawn', especially my own! No doubt I should have felt much the same if I had been in the heart of London or any other great metropolis (though as a Londoner born I must assert that I have never heard anything approaching such noises in my native city). The trouble was not so much New York, as the fact of being cut off from all natural sights and sounds. Never before had I realised how immensely privileged I was to live, at Cambridge, in a house surrounded by tranquil fields, yet within ten minutes' cycle-ride of the University. I once showed Lionel Trilling, a snapshot of our Cambridge house and garden; he covered his eyes, with a gesture eloquent of yearning and envy.

Like every other visitor to New York, I found it, at first, thrilling and stimulating. My breath was taken away each time when, looking up towards the cornice of an average sixteen-storey block, I beheld, in the zenith far above it, a Himalayan skyscraper. The surge and exuberance of the population, the magnificence of the Fifth Avenue shops and restaurants, the beauty of Central Park, of the Hudson riverside at sundown, of the George Washington Bridge, of the Grand Central Station, of the Manhattan skyline seen from the ferry to Staten Island – to all these things and much else I responded warmly. But I had soon had enough of it – of the interminable avenues all as straight as a die; of the sidewalks which I tramped till the soles of my feet burned; of the crowds and the traffic pressing on and on – whither? What, after all, was the *raison d'être* of such a place? Apart from the piling up of wealth, what was the aim of human existence? There seemed to me to be no soul in it all; nothing but a restless, febrile determination to be 'happy'; to be successful in competition with other people and other nations; to pile up still more wealth, and to use it – at best – in philanthropy, in hectic weekends in the country (intended for 'relaxation' and pseudo-religious nature-worship), and lastly in voyages to Europe and especially England. The hunger felt by all the most cultivated Americans for what is old and stable, what can touch the imagination by the pathos or sublimity of its history, or soften the heart by its witness to spiritual reality – this I met continually, and with this I most cordially sympathised. But it meant, I thought, that American life itself is a vacuum, filled indeed with many *simulacra* of happiness, but essentially a place where the soul is perishing of cold. Of course the same is now true of most industrialised countries everywhere. I merely noticed it more in America twenty years ago, because the disease was further advanced there, and because I saw it undisguised by mitigating associations.

More than all the pomps and glories of New York City, more than all its tumult and shouting, I valued two quiet retreats: first, the Women's Graduate Club at Philosophy Hall; and secondly, Storer's

apartment near the top of No. 35 Fifth Avenue. I forget how I got
introduced to the former; it seems, I admit, anomalous. But the presid-
ing genius of this club was 'Dean' Margaret Pickel, who, as a Canadian
by birth, perhaps had special compassionate feelings towards an exiled
Britisher, and who in any case had introduced the custom of afternoon
tea at Philosophy Hall. To this she invited me to come any afternoon I
was free. I need not say how gladly I accepted. The Women's Club
became for me the true centre of civilised living in up-town New York,
and I turned up there at tea-time frequently, meeting, generally,
Margaret herself and one or two other ladies. Over the tea-cups I would
give them all the news of my latest doings and impressions. Margaret
used to pose as my monitress, warning me against over-work and over-
excitement. 'What have you been up to now?' she would ask; 'What
time did you go to bed last night? and what are you planning next?
Lecturing at three different Universities in one week, reading a paper
at the Faculty Club and lunching with Alistair Cooke? I give you up —
you're hopeless! But don't say I didn't warn you.' Poor Margaret
Pickel! Though not beautiful, she was kind; and when she died, not
many years later, I am sure she went straight to heaven.

Storer's apartment was a holy-of-holies for many reasons. It was, to
begin with, the home of my best American friend, and in every point
expressed his personality. It was here that I was welcomed on arrival;
here that I many times stayed as guest; here that I found sprays of
flowers or autumn-leaves (from the gardens of friends in New Hampshire, Virginia or Delaware) displayed for my delight; here that I
breathed the air of true friendship, honesty, and laughter. This apartment, which was in the Hotel Grosvenor (recently taken over by New
York University, and so no longer Storer's home), was situated so far
down-town as to be in a quiet enclave between the uproar of 45th
Street at one end, and Wall Street at the other. From the front windows
one looked across a little nineteenth century church, its spire absurdly
dwarfed by the gigantic newer blocks adjoining it, to where the masts
of ships and a ribbon of sea-water were eloquent of home. It saddens
me to think that I can never see it again; it was the scene of much
happiness not only for me, but for my wife and Lucy, for Peter and
his wife, and for many others to whom in later years Storer showed
kindness for my sake and their own.

From October onwards I was continually on the move, as indeed
that list of twelve Universities and Colleges mentioned above suggests.
But there were other journeys besides those. On the first weekend of
October Storer drove me to Princeton, where I enjoyed the spacious
grounds, the fine trees, the country-town atmosphere and the nicely-
faked Gothic and synthetic Tudor buildings, all of which suggested
Cambridge (indeed there was an actual copy of Trinity Great Gate at
one place) and made me wish I had gone there rather than to the urban

Columbia. From Princeton we drove on through rich and English-looking country to Wilmington, Delaware, to visit Storer's brother Dudley and his family.

The following week-end was the occasion of the most spectacular of all our trips: the pilgrimage to Vermont to see the autumn colours. As usual this was done in Storer's car, but this time his partner, Howard Wilson, came with us. I had, of course, often heard of the fall colours in New England, but the reality — for once — exceeded expectation. We had perfect, sunny weather, and blue skies against which the scarlets, salmons, crimsons and golds showed dazzlingly. The colours were at the height of their glory, and at Stowe, with its white-spired Church and high hills, rising here and there into blue mountains, we saw them to memorable advantage. The Inn and its food were of superlative quality, as were the sandwich-lunches it provided for picnics on two successive days. What with that, and the astounding pageantry of colour, and the pure mountain air, I returned to Babylon much strengthened and refreshed.

We hurried back to be in time for the great public event of the Columbia term, the installation of President Eisenhower as President of the University (on Columbus Day, 12 October). As I happened to be on the spot, I had been appointed to represent the University of Cambridge on that occasion, and to present the Address. This Address, composed in Latin by the then Public Orator, Professor W.K.C. Guthrie (now Master of Downing), awaited me on my return, packed in a registered envelope bearing three £1 stamps, one of 10s., two of 1s. and one of 3d. The packet contained a beautiful leather box embossed with the arms of the University, within which were three copies of Guthrie's Address printed on parchment, one of them bearing the University seal attached by a ribbon of Cambridge blue. It described me as 'virum doctum BASILIUM WILLEY', and went on in flowery rhetoric to say that since the closest links existed between our nations in a heritage of common language, what could be more opportune than that Cambridge should send Columbia its Professor of English Language [sic] and Literature, to testify to her goodwill, and as it were represent it in his own person. Having recently been awarded an Honorary Litt.D. by Manchester University, I decided to appear in a Manchester Doctor's gown, as likely to be more colourful than a mere M.A. one. In this wonderful city anything can be obtained at any time, and the campus store duly produced the Manchester apparel, though I was disappointed to find that only the hood was coloured.

Next day the hundreds of University Delegates all assembled at about 1.15 p.m. in the University Library, their multi-coloured gowns rivalling the autumn glories of Vermont. The Addresses were not presented by the delegates in person, but were handed to one of the

ushers before the procession began. It was ordained that the youngest
Universities should march in front, and so on by degrees back to the
oldest. Thus the Oxford and Cambridge delegates formed the last pair
but one in the file, only two older Universities, Salamanca and Bologna,
being represented that day. The Oxford man was the then British
Ambassador, Sir Oliver Franks, who was, I think, the tallest person in
the whole procession. Introducing myself to him beforehand, at a point
where Oxford's (alleged) seniority became relevant, I said 'Sir, I yield
precedence to the representative of Oxford with resignation, but I
follow the British Ambassador with humility and pride!' It was only
because of the chance absence of Paris and Florence that Oxford and
Cambridge marched as a pair that day; had they been represented,
Oxford (thanks to the accepted chronology) would have been with
Paris, while I should have had to content myself with Florence. It was
by another pleasant coincidence that the two Universities were
represented by members of sister Colleges, Queen's, Oxford, and
Pembroke, Cambridge. Sir Oliver, as Provost of Queen's, had been
present at the Pembroke Sexcentenary celebration the previous year
(1947).

We passed into the campus, and processed through a crowd of
20,000 spectators up to the stone staircase in the front centre. Here
President Eisenhower took his seat below the statue of Alma Mater,
which was decorated with branches of evergreen. Batteries of press
photographers, the Columbia Broadcasting System, and innumerable
private cameras and movies clicked, buzzed and flashed at us as we
passed. The sun came out, and the scene on which it shone was astonishing. All those 20,000 people were seated on chairs right across the
huge quadrangle, and across the road which runs through it; and
clusters of loud-speakers made the speeches clearly audible in the
remotest corners, a quarter of a mile away. We all rose for The Star-
spangled Banner. Then there was a prayer; then speeches by student
representatives (about liberty, basic human rights, and The American
Way of Life), then a speech by a Professor, then the presentation of the
Charter and Keys to Eisenhower, and lastly a long speech by
Eisenhower himself (about The American Way of Life, basic human
rights and liberty). He spoke in his usual manly, breezy style, and
although the matter was hackneyed enough, he succeeded in conveying
the impression of honesty and sincerity. Finally, after singing 'Stand,
Columbia', we processed in reverse, and the ceremony was over.

Soon after this Alistair Cooke, who had seen my name in the papers
in accounts of the Eisenhower affair, rang me up and asked me to
dinner. I accepted, and with his consent took with me Gordon
Sutherland who happened to be staying at my flat the same day.
Alistair had been my pupil in Cambridge years before, when he was

140 CAMBRIDGE AND OTHER MEMORIES

reading for English Part II at Jesus College, editing *The Granta* and founding the University Mummers. I had not seen him since those days, though like everyone else I had followed his meteoric rise to Anglo-American fame. I found him now living in a luxurious apartment just off Fifth Avenue, and the dinner he provided (complete with coloured maid-service) was as stylish as himself. It was interesting to find in him the same qualities, though now in full blow and exerted in far wider fields, as he had shown before: great cleverness, wit, imagination, and the up-to-the-minute alertness of the born journalist. I admired, too, his refined American accent (he was born in Lancashire), adopted with characteristic finesse so as to offend neither American nor British ears.

Another former Cambridge friend I met at this time was I.A. Richards, who had been a Professor at Harvard since 1938. At a cosy dinner in a Japanese restaurant, where we consumed very strange meats and liquors, he and Dorothea arranged a mountain walk for me and Storer in New Hampshire, after a visit to Boston which I shall describe later. Professor Henry Steele Commager, a former Pitt Professor at Cambridge, met me at the Faculty Club, and kindly put me up for temporary membership of the Century Club, the New York counterpart of the Athenaeum. About this time I received from the University of Virginia a paper called *The Cavalier* which bore on its front page the 'hot headline': 'BASIL WILLEY TO OPEN McGREGOR SEMINARS – Cambridge Professor Scheduled'. This was part of the 'build-up' for my impending visit to Virginia, arranged by that nicest of men the late Peters Rushton, whom I had known in Cambridge. He it was who, just before the war, had proposed the visit to Princeton which had had to be cancelled.

On the evening of the same day I was engaged to speak at a dinner arranged by Marjorie Nicolson in honour of Arthur O. Lovejoy. It was his seventy-fifth birthday, and my short speech was designed to be a tribute on behalf of the non-American world. It was on this occasion that Miss Nicolson described herself and her work as 'a footnote to Lovejoy', and added that when she had been his pupil, and even now, she was not a little afraid of him. This will surprise no one who knew that great scholar and formidable character. It was one of the proudest moments of my life when, on arriving at Baltimore to address the Tudor and Stuart Club of John Hopkins University, I was met at the station by this great man, and driven away in his car. He was all kindness and urbanity, but he looked like a Prussian general (his mother was German). From beneath his thick, smooth grey hair and military brow his blue eyes pierced into one's inmost being, and I felt that they could hardly fail to detect something shoddy or superficial in mine. However, although to my alarm he attended my lectures and took part in some of the ensuing discussions, I got through the assignment without being 'shown-up'. Lovejoy drove me out into the country one after-noon, and pointed out to me, amongst other things, Gilham School, where my son Peter was afterwards to be a visiting Master. When I left, he gave me as a souvenir a book which I prize, an inscribed copy of his *Essays in the History of Ideas*.

From this time until Christmas I was constantly travelling, on my spare days, to lecture at one or other of the Universities I have already mentioned. It would be tedious to describe all these visits in any detail; at every place I was received with infinite kindness, and flattered to the top of my bent. All this made me feel very grateful and humble, and I used to apologise for not bringing with me the kind of supernatural revelation which alone would have justified my having been summoned from so far and welcomed with such honour. At every one of these Universities, the lecture itself was only the centrepiece in a long series of social events: cocktail-parties, receptions, dinners, speeches and con-vivial evenings. I should be untruthful, as well as most ungrateful, if I were to make out that I did not enjoy all this; what human being could do otherwise? It excited and stimulated me, and challenged me to exertions of which I had not supposed myself capable. Never before, and only once since (on my second American visit, in 1953), have I lived at such a pace and pitch, continually on the stretch, with every faculty fully mobilised. This was something very extraordinary for a person of my reserved nature and recluse habits, and I admit that so much pushing and forcing against the grain wore me out. But I think it was good for me; it proved to me that my habitual inertia and diffidence *could* be overcome, and that the effort of overcoming them brought with it a pleasurable glow. Perhaps I ought *always* to have lived like this, with all my powers engaged and deployed, instead of relaps-ing, as I have always done when I could, into my natural, silent jog-trot? It may be so; perhaps then I should have lived a much more use-ful life, even if it had been a much shorter one.

Though these lecturing-trips were fatiguing, they were in the nature of things easier to accomplish than the daily routine of ordinary teach-ing, whether at Columbia or at Cambridge. They were 'hours of insight', without the usual intervening 'hours of gloom'. One simply flashed across the sky like a meteor, and was gone, whereas at home the light often burnt low and dim. The actual delivery of the lectures was quite enjoyable; it was like playing upon a musical instrument, of which one had the mastery, a piece which one knew by heart. What I found most difficult was the effort to assimilate, in a few hectic weeks or even months, a new and unfamiliar civilisation. I had known very little about America beforehand; and now, wherever I went, I had to be on the alert for the nuances, the allusions, and the ethos, which would open my eyes and enable me to divine the unspoken assumptions below the surfaces of American life. Each University, too, was a world in miniature; and at each one my powers of memory and sympathy were stretched to their utmost in the attempt to remember the names of the faculty members, their special interests and research-projects, what they had already published, etc. etc. All this, and my whole American experience, ought to have immunised me against all subsequent self-doubts, dreads and stage-frights; I knew now, I had proved to myself, that I could do what would once have seemed to me impossible. But was I so immunised? alas, no! Life is not like that, or at least not with me. After the 1914-18 War, whenever I found myself dreading a dental appointment, or a tea-party, or a lecture, or an interview, or a super-vision, I used to say to myself 'come on now, you fool; suppose you were going over the top tomorrow, what would you think of all these trifles then?' But it never worked; the peacetime 'trifles' still looked as grim as ever. The fact is that our feelings are continuously being adjust-ed to fit the context of the moment, and not to fit some larger pattern in which their true proportions would be obvious. And so now that I am a retired Professor, in spite of the Great War, and in spite of America 1948-9, and America 1953, and all the public duties that have fallen to me in Cambridge and elsewhere, I still undergo nervous apprehensions, and often physical upsets, whenever I have an outside engagement to keep.

I must say rather more of my visit to Charlottesville, at the begin-ning of November, than I mean to say of most of the other trips, because it left such a deep impression. Charlottesville was quite the most fascinating place I had yet seen in America. Almost the whole of the University building was designed and built by Thomas Jefferson to-wards the end of the eighteenth century, and it seemed to me a model of serenity and classic grace. The peace and quiet of it, in its rural surroundings, and with blue mountains close at hand, sank into me like a benediction. The main quadrangle, whither I managed to slip away alone in the dusk of a November evening, was quite silent, full of the smell of fallen leaves, and blue with haze. No, not silent, for there was one sound: the song of a mocking-bird, which seemed to mingle some of the tones of the thrush and the nightingale.

But the social whirl soon swept me away, and for three days I was almost killed with kindness. First, immediately following a seven-hour railway journey, a reception to which all the beauty and the chivalry of the University came thronging. Then dinner at a Professor's house; then my lecture to about 250 people; then a gathering at Peters Rushton's own place. After that, a blessed, blissful night's rest at a country-house inn, a lovely old red-brick colonial mansion like any eighteenth century English manor-house. It was so warm, on this night of 5 November, that I slept with a French window wide open to a balcony. Next

morning, an early rise and breakfast out with Rushton at his country
club, another and even finer old mansion, designed by Jefferson, with
dome and classical portico. The objectives that day were Williamsburg
and Jamestown, which meant a whole day's driving and sightseeing;
130 miles each way.

Williamsburg defies description. It is a thing which could only
happen in America, and only once there. It is a reconstruction, by
Rockefeller millions, of a whole eighteenth-century town, the original
having been mostly destroyed by fire (and the British). Although most
of the buildings are 'synthetic', the work has been done so well that
the illusion is perfect. There are even old-fashioned horse-coaches,
driven by negroes; there is even — oh, triumph of antiquarianism over
patriotism! — a Union Jack flying over the Governor's Palace, as in
good King George II's glorious days. At night all the buildings are lit by
candle-light.

Jamestown was the first permanent English settlement in America,
Raleigh's earlier landing on Roanoke Island having come to nothing.
Its site is on the broad estuary of the James River, half-way down the
Atlantic coast towards Florida. We had lunch and tea in Williamsburg,
and went dutifully round the show-places, conducted by lady-guides
(some of them 'Faculty wives' of William and Mary College, a real and
very fine antique of William and Mary's own time, said to be of Wren's
designing) dressed in brightly-coloured hooped skirts of Queen Anne
style. The contents of the buildings are mostly genuine antiques,
collected with scrupulous attention to period-accuracy, and checked
with the original inventories, which had been preserved. We had supper
at the State capitol, Richmond; and drove the 100 odd miles back to
Charlottesville in the dark, through torrential rain.

Next morning, Sunday, it was warm and crystal-clear, and remained
so all day. I was taken for a morning trip along the 'Skyline Drive',
which follows the ridge of the mountains for miles and miles, and
looks across the Shenandoah valley to the Alleghanies on the horizon.
Lunch, attended by many guests, was with the Dean of the English
Department, whose wife was the grand-daughter of a former President
of the U.S.A. The menage, with its eighteenth-century decor, displayed
the utmost dignity and elegance; the food, fit for royalty, had been
cooked by a negress called Beulah. In the afternoon: a trip to
Monticello, the mountain home of the famous Jefferson, and a national
shrine of the first order. Lastly: a tremendous social evening at a grand
country-house about fifteen miles away in the remote foot-hills:
turkey, ham, macaroni, pickled melon, apple-pie, and heaven knows
what else, served buffet-fashion: the host, a (to me unknown) novelist
and musician. Crowds, and music, and chatter, till 10 p.m., when it was
time for me to go and catch my night train back to New York. I sank

into my sleeping-bunk with inexpressible relief. But I did not sleep much; my brain was racing, and I had not only my routine Columbia Tuesday-morning lecture to give next morning, but the 'Bergen' Lecture to deliver at Yale the day after.

At Yale the routine was much less elaborate, for I was only away one night. But the kindness was just as lavish, and I felt very much at home in this place of Gothic Colleges, lawns and trees. The Hemingways (Sam Hemingway was then Master of Berkeley College) put me up in luxurious comfort at their Lodge, and even allowed me to have break-fast in my own room — which I regarded as a token of high civilisation and humanity. My room was known as The Prophet's Chamber, 'Prophet' having been their chauffeur's name for Provost J.T. Shepherd (of King's, Cambridge) who had recently occupied it. J.T. Shepherd, they told me, had been a resounding success at Yale and everywhere in America; his striking appearance, his wit, his learning, his oratorical brilliance and his eccentricities, had realised all the American notions of what a great English don should be like.

My lecture was 'covered' by the campus newspaper *Yale News* of which I treasure the relevant copy for its many inexactitudes. During the lecture a young man took a magnesium-flash of me, which appeared in next-day's paper, together with a write-up headed: "Willey Indicates Literature's Role in Setting Values: Oxford [*sic*] Professor Stresses Need for . . . " etc. The ensuing column was a masterpiece of mis-representation. Bits of my wording were used and garbled, and mixed up with the reporter's own (erroneous) summaries. I was even made to assert, as my own views, various opinions which I had quoted solely for purposes of refutation and derision.

At Princeton my kind host, Willard Thorp, vouchsafed me the unique concession of having no social function *before* the lecture. It was on this occasion that, finding myself in New Jersey, I drew the attention of my audience to my descent from the Jersey family of de Carteret, to which their first 'Lord Governor', Sir George Carteret, had belonged. I had come, I explained, mainly to see how, after having been left so long without the family's superintendence, they had been getting on; and I was glad to see signs that, on the whole, they had managed pretty well. I was surprised to see, in my audience at that lecture, not only my old pupil Eric Mackerness (now Dr. Mackerness, University Lecturer at Sheffield), but my Pembroke colleague the late Professor Alan Wace and Mrs Wace. Alan was spending a term at the Princeton Institute of Advanced Studies, where T.S. Eliot also was at that time.

During that same month I was invited to lunch by Reinhold Niebuhr and his charming English-born wife at the Union Theological Seminary (a department of Columbia). Two of their children were there, so the conversation remained human and light-hearted. The other guest was

W.H. Auden, who then, with his mat of tow-coloured hair and his pink complexion, still looked like an undergraduate.

The next big event was the trip to Boston. For once, this was not to give an ordinary lecture, but to be guest-speaker at a Dinner of the Colonial Society of Massachusetts – a far more alarming prospect. Like all such engagements, this one 'escalated' to include a Club Luncheon (with impromptu speech) and a tea with Ivor and Dorothea Richards – a unique gathering of 'Cambridge, Eng.' folks in 'Cambridge, Mass.', for besides the Richardses and myself there were Eustace Tillyard and Helen Cam.

At the big Dinner – and it was 'big' in every sense – I sat on high between Perry Miller and the Chairman, Augustus Peabody Loring, a Boston Brahmin of the highest caste, but 'Gus' to his friends. I had been told that the guest speakers at these Dinners of the Colonial Society were expected to talk, if possible, about some aspect of seventeenth-century colonial history. Now this, of course, was not in my power to do; the nearest I could get to it was Lord Herbert of Cherbury – *lucus a non lucendo*. I explained that while all the more virile and progressive spirits of the period were turning their thoughts towards colonising America, there were still a few reactionary and effete individuals left in England who were content to go on in the old rut, and it was of one of these that I proposed to speak. This, and the speech itself, received a warm response. But, in fact, so well had the guests been dined and wined that it mattered little what the speaker said. I heard next day that a member who was absent from the dinner asked another, who had been present, what the Professor had spoken about. The reply, as reported to me, was to the effect 'that Professor Willey had given a hell of a fine speech, but that on account of the number of cocktails consumed the member couldn't just recollect the subject.'

Early next morning (my digestive system was tougher in those days than it has now become) we (for Storer was with me) rose and caught a train to New Hampshire, picking up Ivor and Dorothea Richards at Cambridge Station, a few miles out from Boston. By lunch-time we were on the summit of Mount Monadnock, picnicking in brilliant sunshine, with Ivor frying bacon over a wood-fire. After a convivial evening, and a restful night at a remote farmhouse known to the Richardses, we set forth again next day, although it was now the 22nd of November, for a picnic on another mountain. Ivor had provided everything with the thoroughness of a seasoned mountaineer; indeed. if we had been about to repeat some of his famous Alpine exploits of former times, instead of merely walking up a mild upland in New Hampshire, we could hardly have been better equipped. Ivor carried a large Alpine rucksack, full of food, wine and changes of clothes. We all

K

wore the scarlet caps with heavy brims, which, in those hunting districts and at that season, were generally used as a precaution against being accidentally shot. The colour-slides I took of my distinguished friends, sitting round a camp-fire on a New Hampshire mountain-top, and attired as I have just mentioned, are among my more recherché possessions. I was back in New York that evening; gave my usual Tuesday lectures the next day, then packed and rushed off to catch the night train to Canada.

The Canadian invitation, which came from Toronto, was timed to coincide with Thanksgiving week, when the United States universities had a recess. I was in Toronto from the 24th to the 29th November. It was a week of incessant activity, for, owing to the energy and determination of my host, the late Professor A.S.P. Woodhouse, I was more fêted and exploited there than almost anywhere else. Take the first day: I arrived from my 'sleeper' train early in the morning, was met at the Station by Woodhouse and escorted by him to breakfast in the Hall of Hart House (a kind of residential College). A quiet morning was followed by a social lunch; then, *at 3 p.m.* came my lecture on Arnold, to a huge audience in a vast hall. After that was over, there was a social tea, then a sherry party, then dinner out with a Professor and two students. Next day: social lunch; afternoon visit to the Observatory; dinner at Trinity College. Here, at Trinity, I might have been at a Cambridge College, for we had Combination Room and Hall with high table; and gowns were worn by both students and dons. After dinner: an evening address to the English Graduate Union – an hour's talk followed by a longish discussion. Next morning: a two-hour seminar on Coleridge (attended by such high-powered dons as Northrop Frye, Woodhouse, Barker Fairlie, Priestley etc.); afternoon: attending a lecture by Van Doren; evening: dinner with the President of Victoria College, followed by a social at Woodhouse's home. The following day: a social lunch, after which I 'took the salute' at a sort of march past of Ph.D. candidates, trying to make some bright remark to each in succession; lastly a social dinner.

Sunday was my last day in Canada, and I had planned to visit Niagara that day alone, travelling by train. But news of my plan leaked out, and in the U.S.A. and Canada one has only to lift a finger or breathe a whisper, and someone instantly offers to do everything. So, sure enough, Professor and Mrs. Priestley, accompanied by their small son aged eleven, drove me the eighty miles in their car. It was not a good day to see the Falls; it was overcast and grey, and one missed the full brilliance, and the famour spray-rainbow (seen, however, on another visit five years later). What impressed me most was something I had not expected: the vast pyramid of spray rising from the base of the great Horseshoe Fall. It smokes up to more than twice the height of the

Fall itself (which is 160 feet), and hangs there in a great swirling cone like the steam from a cauldron. Near to the Fall, its thunderous noise makes speech impossible, except by shouting. Like most visitors to Niagara, I regretted the skyline of skyscrapers, chimneys and power-stations; and the tripperish atmosphere (produced, e.g., by placards inviting you to descend into the solid rock and see the Falls from behind, from a tunnel-shop in which English china and other souvenirs were to be obtained).

The Advent season was approaching, and I had to nerve myself up to endure what I knew it would bring: excruciating pangs of nostalgia. How massive the attack on the emotions would be I had not foreseen, for I did not know on how vast a scale the Americans celebrate Christmas. At a Hallowe'en party at White Plains a month before, to which Howard and Ethel Wilson had asked me, I had already had the annual forewarning that the night was far spent, and the supernatural about to break through. This intimation, with which every year the Eve of All Hallows suffuses the darkening weeks of late sutumn, came to me at White Plains that year in a new guise: the bonfires of fallen leaves, smoking at regular intervals all along Howard's quiet suburban street, and the parties of masked and dressed-up children who, every ten minutes, would knock at the door shouting 'Tips or Tricks' — to be admitted, of course, and offered something from the hospitable board which stood ready-loaded for them. But now, in early December, Christmas trees lit with coloured lights began to appear in all the main streets, sometimes along the centre, sometimes along the sidewalks, and often stretching for what seemed miles. The New York shop-windows put on carnival-dress, and in my favourite Lord and Taylor's, where I went to buy presents for the ladies, the upper air of the huge main-room was filled with floating angels, birds and coloured globes. At the Rockefeller Center, in the courtyard outside, there was a Christmas tree 95 feet high, covered with globes the size of footballs. Christmas carols pealed forth from loud speakers at the Grand Central and Pennsylvania Railroad Stations; and from my flat in Butler Hall I could hear the singing of University carol-parties in the streets fifteen floors below. That strangely powerful sense of imminent triumph, of ultimate homecoming, which stirs the heart at Advent, was now abroad, mingling with the stir of eager shoppers, the packing of parcels, and the departure of family-parties for country destinations. Foolishly perhaps, I went to a candle-light carol service at the University chapel. I doubt if the performance as such was very good, but it taught me once more, what I had discovered weeks before on hearing Serkin play the Brahms B flat Piano Concerto at the Carnegie Hall, that just below my placid and humdrum surface, and ready to break through unless sternly check-ed, lay an unsuspected reservoir of lachrymosity. But even now, a fortnight before Christmas, I still had all the Christmas parcels to send off, and several more engagements to fulfil, and this no doubt saved me from wallowing too much in Christmas nostalgia.

A few days before Christmas, New York had what was described as the third heaviest snowfall ever recorded there. Naturally, to my eyes its appearance was extraordinary; cars were buried up to the bonnets all along both sides of the streets, and the highly-efficient motor snow-shifters, which cleared both the roads and the sidewalks in no time, left mountains of snow piled head-high along the verges. I shall always associate this blizzard with a little adventure I had the next day. An acquaintance of my Pembroke friend and colleague Bryan King had invited me to attend a Christmas concert of the 'Schubert Society' (orchestral and choral) of which he was the conductor; his name was Edward Margetson. For Bryan's sake, I went; and I went all unsuspecting. Bryan, if he ever reads this, will, I know, forgive me in the charity of his heart if I say that, knowing the nature of some of his greatest interests, I might have guessed. Well! I took the subway to a place very far 'up town' in the northern suburbs, where the snows of yester-night were still largely untrodden and uncleared. Wading and crunching through them I reached the Hall, and found that I had arrived early — that I was, in fact, the only person, except for one or two negroes, in the building. I sat down and enjoyed the warmth and dryness. Presently, a few more people came in, who were also negroes. Presently again, the audience began to pour in, and they were, as I could not help noticing with some disquiet, *all* coloured persons. Eventually, when the auditorium was full, and the negro choir and negro orchestra and negro conductor (Mr. Margetson, Bryan's friend) had all taken their places, I found that I was one of two or at most three white people amongst all these hundreds of blacks. I felt very self-conscious and out of place. They must all be wondering what on earth I was doing there. But not one of them showed any surprise; in fact, they took no notice of me whatsoever.

Storer and I had talked over various plans for Christmas. One of his suggestions was Quebec, and I had quite seriously (though without real expectation) proposed to Zélie to come and join us. What happened in the end was that two of Storer's oldest and best friends, Charles and Mary Gregory, invited us both to spend Christmas with them in Chicago.

There is little more to relate. In the few weeks of the New Year that fell within my 'semester', I finished my Columbia courses, and lectured at Smith, Amherst, New Jersey and Connecticut Colleges. At Smith College I was entertained by the President, the late Herbert Davis, and his wife, in their delightful house commanding views of the Northampton Hills. It was here that I had one of the big shocks of my life, namely, when the President asked me casually whether I would mind 'taking morning Assembly' next day. I knew that this meant facing, alone, without defence, and at 8.0 a.m., about 2,200 girls, and I asked Davis what more it meant. Was the Assembly, by any chance, of a devotional nature? 'Only a hymn and a psalm, and then your address', he said. 'Yes, but the address – how serious ought it to be, to fit that context?' 'It needn't be serious at all!' I took him at his word, and made the girls laugh by telling them stories about 'Q', beginning by making them realise how shocked he would have been if he could have known what his successor was doing in that place, and at that unholy hour. It passed off all right, I think; but it was a daunting experience to stand up and face those troops of angel-faces, half of them looking up at me from the pit, and the other half looking down from heaven.

A farewell week-end in 'The Prophet's Chamber' at the Hemingways', and a lecture at Connecticut College, New London, were to have been my positively last public appearances. But at the eleventh hour I had an invitation from Cornell which – so as not to faint in the last lap – I accepted. And so, to quote from the Cornell University newspaper: 'After dark on a January evening in 1949, an unfamiliar figure made an appearance on the Cornell campus, and after a few short hours returned whence it came. "My American Odyssey", said the figure in a British accent to a Cornell assemblage, "ends at Ithaca".' By a strange co-incidence, it was at that selfsame place that my second American Odyssey began (1953).

I returned at the end of January in the Queen Mary, eager for home, and vowing to re-introduce myself as gently and unobtrusively as possible into a family now for six months accustomed to Life Without Father.

Chapter Eleven

The Second American Visit (1953)

1 The Voyage Out

Though I had returned from my American trip worn out, drained dry like a squeezed orange, I managed to persuade myself that I was ready to repeat the experience as soon as I could decently ask for another two terms' leave, and as soon as a suitable invitation came. It came four years later, from Cornell University, which invited me to go as visiting Professor for the spring semester (February to June) 1953. Apart from my as yet unslaked appetite for this kind of thing, there was the hope and intention that this time Zélie and Lucy would join me in the summer, when my work was done, for a month or two of holidaying in America. This was then a very unusual privilege for an English family; indeed, it was impossible unless one could count on hospitality, or unless one or more of the family was able to earn the necessary dollars.

I shall describe this second trip more briefly, since naturally it resembled the first in many ways. It differed from it, nevertheless, in its emotional colouring and in some of its outward circumstances, and it is on these differences that I want chiefly to dwell. Looking back upon it as a whole, I cannot think it other than a success, and the holiday at the end was stupendous. Yet I was not so happy at Cornell as I had been at Columbia, and suffered far more severely from homesickness. The reasons for this will appear, but at least one of them was constant fatigue. I had more lectures to give than at Columbia, yet I had not had time to prepare more than a fraction of them before sailing. This meant an unremitting struggle, lasting to the very end of the semester, to keep up with the 'schedule', with a few lectures in hand if possible. I knew, of course, that most of my American colleagues bore a much heavier 'teaching load' than I did, but I also knew that their lectures were largely informal and even conversational, admitting of discussions, questions, quizzes on the last class-topic, etc. Now I was not prepared to adopt this sort of approach; I lectured in my Cambridge style, from a carefully composed script. It was in great part the effort to keep to this standard throughout which nearly killed me, and which sent me home vowing that I would never accept another such invitation.

From the very outset, this trip was attended with adversities of all kinds. To begin with, the *Queen Mary* was delayed for a whole day at Southampton by one of the worst gales of the century, that fierce February northeaster which brought calamity to Holland and our own East coast, and sank the Stranraer-Larne boat (on which I had sailed a a couple of years earlier to lecture in Belfast and Dublin). I was surprised to find that all the way to Cherbourg the *Queen Mary* hardly quivered, but after that she began to roll heavily, and one heard repeated sounds of heavy objects sliding sideways, followed by crashes, and the tinkling of broken glass and crockery.

But there were other troubles ahead: the new immigration laws, and the tug-strike at New York. The so-called 'McCarran Act', regulating the import of foreign labour, had only just come into force, and I must have been one of the first Englishmen to enter the States under it. The Immigration Officer who boarded the ship outside the harbour had not yet mastered the new regulations; he held them in his hand and conned them with a puzzled look. Passing me a questionnaire, he exclaimed 'Say, I'd like to have you tell me which category you come in: is it "H(a), distinguished persons of exceptional attainments and merit", or "H(b), persons temporarily imported to fill a vacancy for which no unemployed labourer could be found in the locality"?' 'Well', says I, 'I'm a modest man; I suppose you'd better classify me under H(b).' So he admitted me, not without misgivings, as a 'skilled labourer'. But I was only allowed to land on a 60-day 'parole', or until such time as Cornell had succeeded in getting permission to import me. My passport and visa were kept in New York, and it was understood that I must report once a month to the Office in Columbus Circle to give my address and to see whether the forms in duplicate, and the supporting evidence in triplicate, had arrived from Cornell. When I told the Cornell authorities about all this they were horrified and mortified. The fact was that, owing to the extreme newness of the Act, they had not sent in the necessary application on my behalf beforehand; had they done so, all the fuss would have been avoided. As it was, I did not get my passport back until, long afterwards, I called at Columbus Circle and demanded it. But the whole episode was worth while for its subsequent value as anecdote.

During the voyage we passengers were wondering how we were to get ashore, for the *Queen Mary* was considered too unwieldy to dock without tugs in windy weather. The *Caronia* had attempted it a day or two earlier, and had damaged about thirty feet of the pier. As it turned out, the docking of the Q.M. on this occasion was headline news on both sides of the Atlantic. It was a masterpiece of navigation: performed without tugs, and with no longshoremen to manipulate the ropes. All the work on shore was done by Cunard officials: clerks, typists etc., many of them in city clothes and gloves. A large crowd watched the performance, which lasted for a whole morning. The ever-faithful Storer was there to meet me. This time he had reserved for me a small apartment, next to his own, in the Hotel Grosvenor; and there I stayed for a couple of days before proceeding by the Lehigh Valley line to

Ithaca.

2 Cornell

At Cornell, instead of living by myself in a flat — as I had done at Columbia — I was the invited guest of 'Telluride House' throughout my stay. Now this was an act of great kindness on the part of the young men who ran the House, and nothing that I may say must be taken to imply any lack of appreciation or gratitude on my side. Yet I found it a strain to live there, and this, added to the fatigues of lecture-writing and (as I shall explain) travelling, contributed to the depression from which I often suffered. Telluride House, I found, was a 'Fraternity', that is to say, a residential hostel run by a committee of its own members. It was like a College with no dons, in which the governing body was a group of undergraduates. It is, I know, one's duty — and it is essential to the art and science of living — to be adaptable to one's surroundings, to adjust oneself cheerfully to each situation that life presents; and I tried at Cornell, as always, not to fail too dismally in this respect. But perhaps I was a little too old, at fifty-six, and too accustomed to the traditional hierarchies of Cambridge, to feel immediately at home in the egalitarian world of Telluride. It was like starting life at a boarding-school, and reminded me of one of the recurrent dreams of earlier days, wherein I used to find myself, though middle-aged, sitting in a school classroom amongst the pupils, and subject to all the ignominies of boyhood.

I had a bed-sitting-room to myself, but it was not yet in order for the new term. It was dispiriting to find that it contained no bookshelf, no bedside lamp or table, no writing-materials, no vase for flowers; and that its furniture consisted of an old and battered desk and chest-of-drawers, and one worn-out easy chair. The bathroom-toilet was shared with two undergraduates who occupied the room opening into it from the other side. I hasten to add that the 'governing body' attended to all my needs most kindly, and soon had my room made much more inviting. Their evident anxiety that I should feel happy was indeed most touching; they were dear, good fellows, and did all they could. But they could not dispel the boarding-school atmosphere of the place.

At 'tea-time' on my first day I walked down the long and steep hill, through snow and slush, into the adjacent town of Ithaca, which turned out to be much further away than I had expected (I afterwards found that it was considered highly eccentric to *walk* as far as that, or indeed anywhere except within the Campus). Ithaca turned out to be a very second-rate little place; not a 'University town' in the Oxford or Cambridge sense. At Cornell the Campus was all in all: a huge, self-sufficient world, complete with 'campus-stores', theatre, concert-hall, chapel, hotel and restaurants. Life there, consequently, meant the

Campus or nothing. And as I came to discover more and more of the amenities of the Campus, the daily routine became much more pleasant.

Evening dinner proved to be a more orderly and civilised affair than breakfast or lunch, though there was no 'high-table' for the small group of seniors who, like myself, were guests at Telluride, and it was not considered good form for us to sit together. I found myself, however, within earshot of the English pianist John Hunt, who was teaching music at Cornell and staying at Telluride for a whole year. After dinner he took me under his wing, and showed me the resources of the Campus — such as cafés for morning coffee after lectures, and restaurants where one could escape for quiet meals when the hearty student-ethos became too oppressive. John, for whom I felt an immediate liking, was extraordinarily kind and sympathetic. Having himself passed through the stage of initiation, he could enter into all my feelings and misgivings completely. He said that he had hated the life at first, but that by now he had not only become reconciled to it but had come to like the Telluride men very much. It was to be the same with me. But whether it was because my Cambridge life had imbued me with a sense of what is and is not fitting, or whether I was just too old and set in my ways, I never could reconcile myself to the constant intermingling with students on terms of equality. A little of it is excellent and desirable; but the permanent blurring of the division between old and young seemed to me a defiance of taboos set up, not merely by social convention, but by nature itself.

I hope and believe that I let none of this feeling appear on the surface; but the inward conflict remained, unresolved and rather painful, to the end. The odd and paradoxical thing was that, in spite of this Telluride anomaly, the exact opposite seemed to be true of the University as a whole. Whereas in a Cambridge or Oxford College there is unbroken contact, hierarchically graded but real, between dons and undergraduates both socially and intellectually; at Cornell the student-body and 'the Faculty' (which in America means the whole teaching staff) constituted two distinct worlds, bridged only at lectures and seminars, and on set social occasions. For the most part the young lived on their own, under no Tutorial eye; and the dons scattered after the day's work to their own homes on Cayuga Heights, Ellis Hollow or elsewhere. The Telluride community was a peculiar *mélange*, with no parallel elsewhere. And this was because the governing body there, rightly considering their House to be the intellectual head-quarters of the campus, made a practice of offering hospitality to any senior visiting the University (including women), whether for short or long periods. Most of these invited guests came only for a day or two; the long-term guests, like Hunt and myself, were very few.

Through my friendship with John Hunt, I was quickly introduced to the inmost musical circles at Cornell. It was a delightful surprise, for instance, to find that Keith Falkner (a native of Cambridge, and now Principal of the Royal College of Music) was a Professor there. He and John used to give Lieder recitals to packed audiences in one of the large halls. Keith's singing, and John's accompanying, in Schubert and Schumann songs especially, were of so superlative a quality as not only to give all of us intense delight but also to fill me with pride in sharing my nationality with such artists.

A howling blizzard of wind and snow, the day after my arrival, ushered in what was to prove three months of almost unbroken winter. This was another contributory cause of my low spirits and nostalgia at Cornell. The University stands on a hill-top, nearly 1,000 feet above sea-level, and beautiful though its campus became in sunshine and warmth — with its rocky gorges, waterfalls, neighbouring lakes and surrounding hills — it was sombre and dreary under the grey and brown skies which brooded over it all that winter. From my window, for days on end, I could see little through the clogging mists except a slope of dun-coloured, faded grass or slushy snow, surrounded by the silhouettes of ugly buildings. Walking, one of my chief consolations, was impossible. As the days lengthened, I heard from home of the aconites and snowdrops in February, followed by the crocuses and daffodils and bird-choruses of March and April, and my heart nearly broke with exasperation as I looked out upon the unchanging wintry aspect of Cornell. Indeed, there was no spring at all there; only winter till the beginning of May, and then all at once, without warning or preparation, summer heats. In April I several times met the spring in the more genial climates of Virginia, N. Carolina and Washington, D.C.; but each return to Cornell was a return to winter.

Within a short time of my arrival at Cornell I had received ten invitations to lecture at other Universities, some of them many hundreds of miles away. Seven or eight more followed soon after. As before, I made a point of accepting every one which could possibly be fitted in, and Cornell was most generous in allowing me to miss lectures whenever (as often happened) my absences coincided with lecture-days. These journeys were of the greatest interest to me, and provided a very welcome relief from the monotony of the wintry campus. But the planning of them was a major operation, and I often felt like the clerk in a travel bureau. I sat at my table constantly, surrounded by letters giving alternative dates, and by railway timetables, trying to work out how various visits could best be combined with each other and with my Cornell duties. Ithaca was very different from New York as a starting-point; there were only two (slow) trains a day in either direction, and the travel-office was far away at the bottom of that long, snowy hill. The complications became much more formidable when 'summer time' came into force, because in America (as I found to my alarm, and sometimes to my cost) there are not only the natural time-differences caused by the immense east-west extent of the continent, but a lack of uniformity between adjacent States (even, sometimes, between different parts of the same State), one adhering to 'winter time' longer than another, and so forth.

The extent of my travels can be seen from the list of Universities and Colleges at which I lectured (a few of them, but not many, places I had visited in 1948-9): Bryn Mawr, Rochester, Columbia, Hamilton, Amherst; Wooster, Columbus and Oberlin in Ohio; Champaign – Urbana and North Western in Illinois; Wayne (Detroit), Ann Arbor and the State University (E. Lansing) in Michigan; Johns Hopkins, Duke University, and Charlottesville. The mid-Western Universities (Ohio, Illinois and Michigan) were included in a combined tour involving a week's absence from Cornell. From all these visits I will select a few memories that remain.

Bryn Mawr, the women's College near Philadelphia, was as different as possible from Cornell. It was quiet and exclusive, with only 500 students as against Cornell's 10,000; and its campus, with fine trees and rolling grassy slopes, was like an old-fashioned English park. Professor Sprague met me at Philadelphia station, and took me the last sixteen miles by suburban train, he being that almost unknown thing: an American without a car. Even his wife 'Posie', though twenty-seven years younger than himself, did not drive. But she turned out to be a Gilbert and Sullivan enthusiast and the following morning, before the civilities and academic exercises, we went off to the College music room and played through *Patience*, I at the piano and Mrs. Sprague singing and playing the flute.

At first I felt shy of asking Cornell for leave so often. But Francis Mineka, then acting for Henry Myers as head of the Department, gave me what amounted to *carte blanche*. With consummate tact, he even hinted that my being so much in request brought lustre to Cornell; and as for my poor hungry, unfed sheep – 'Guess you can give the children sumpn to keep 'em quiet!' On this latter point I soothed my conscience by reflecting (truly, as I do believe) that 'quiet' was what the 'children' most needed, and lacked. What with incessant lectures on the one hand and 'extra-curricular activities' on the other, they lived in a perpetual stampede; and half of them seemed to get very little sleep. Most of them were engaged in all sorts of semi-commercial affairs in addition to their studies. For instance, they ran a local wireless-station (profit-making), with the usual accompaniments of commercial advertising etc. In the various fraternity-houses they managed their own finances and culinary arrangements, and 'screened' their own candidates for admission. At Telluride, the table-waiters were undergraduates who needed extra money to support them at the University. This seething student-life, so autonomous and so demanding, made the dons seem very remote and ineffectual. Far from being in effectual command, as they are in Cambridge, they seemed rather to be called in from afar, at the behest of the sovereign people, to spoon-feed them with the minimum requirements for a 'grade'. All this tended, I thought, to make the students very mature, competent and self-reliant in practical affairs, and rather naive on the academic side.

In between my many journeyings, life at Cornell went on smoothly and very busily. On one occasion I was asked to give a public lecture before the University, which was attended not only by many Faculty members, but by the President of Cornell himself. I was still innocent enough of American ways to be surprised, and slightly shocked, at the total unconcern of the large audience when the President came in. They took no notice of him whatever. He just entered, one of the throng, in a lounge-suit, and took his seat unobtrusively on one of the back benches amongst the students. At Cambridge, of course, if the Vice-Chancellor, or still more the Chancellor, had attended a lecture, he would have worn academic dress and bands, and been ceremonially escorted to a front seat. The audience might very probably have risen at his entrance. I soon learnt, of course, that the President of most American Universities is a public-relations and propaganda official, with no academic prestige and neither commanding nor expecting any special deference. This particular President was, if I remember aright, a pineapple king.

I will describe here a few scattered events which happened during those quieter intervals, which, owing to my incessant travelling, became almost the exception rather than the rule. Cornell was a secular found-ation, and consequently had no religious basis or establishment. There was, however, a campus chapel, in which the Sunday services were con-ducted by a series of invited preachers, each week of a different relig-ous denomination. This sort of syncretism, however, was still more strikingly displayed in another building, called 'Religious Work', which had been 'donated' to Cornell by a rich benefactor. This contained a chapel with a revolving altar, designed so as to be capable of serving for Christian, or Jewish, or other requirements. It had three sides, and stood normally at Christianity. But by pressing a button, it could be turned round so as to present Hebrew symbols; or again, its third side was intended to be acceptable to devotees of other world-religions. One day we had an Oxford visitor at Telluride, K.M. Turpin, now Provost of Oriel. As he was new to Cornell I volunteered to show him round the campus, and this altar was one of the exhibits I particularly wanted him to see. It was late in the day and getting rather dark; nevertheless we went into the chapel and I pressed the magic button. No sooner had the altar begun its slow apostasy than the bell rang for the closing of 'Religious Work' for that day. The electricity was turned off, and we fled precipitately, leaving the altar at a halfway position between Judaism and Christianity.

In my lectures on the Victorians I used to take every possible opportunity to relate the literature to its natural setting by describing what England really looked like. For the benefit of the many who had never been there, and who imagined it to be a small patch of flat green fields, easily traversable by car in one day, I developed the theme of 'infinite riches in a little room', dwelling especially on the immense differences, reflected in the varying imaginative qualities of Tennyson, Hardy and Wordsworth, between Lincolnshire, Wessex and Lakeland. I tried to make them realise that in an ancient land, dense with history, a journey of a few miles was often a journey through a thousand years, and psychologically more than the equivalent of 300 miles of speedway driving in America. I enlarged upon the subtler gradations in tone, texture, building-materials and styles, which differentiate one county or region from another; and I explained that these are traceable not only to history but also to geology, which in Britain is more diversified than in any other country of comparable size. After one of these lectures, in which I had discoursed feelingly about Lakeland, a student was reported to have said that he thought Professor Willey must be homesick. Another, more cynical, had said that he *had* been to the Lake District, and it was all coca-cola stands, postcard-shops and gas-stations. Which showed that his explorations in Lakeland had not proceeded far beyond Bowness pier.

About the middle of March, Fritz Stern and his wife, noticing that I seemed overworked, asked me if I would enjoy twenty-four hours of complete silence and solitude. They lived in an isolated house, some miles out in the country, and offered to let me occupy it while they were away for a weekend. I jumped at this kind offer, and went to see them there beforehand to learn how to tend the boiler. It was about thirty times larger than our own, and very intimidating. When the day came I was driven out to my rural retreat by Mrs. Winter, one of my seminar-members, who also came the next day to fetch me back.

There had been a slight thaw, and after settling into the empty house I thought that, for the first time since I had been in America, I would try a country walk. But it was not a walker's country. There was only one road, running as straight as a die both ways, and it was sticky with mud from the thaw. There were no hedges and no field-paths, and the waterlogged fields were too squelchy to walk in. A few willow-buds just showing, some starlings, one blackbird, one pigeon-call, and some catkins in the distance looking yellow – these, on that bleak upland of New York State, were all the signs of spring I could see.

I settled in, and prepared to revel in the silence of the countryside, far from the tumult, the voices and the nagging bells of the campus. At first, the only sound I could hear was the endless ork-*woink*, ork-*woink* of three guinea-hens who were picking and prying in the yard, reminding me of our Cornish farm. But I had forgotten that all American houses contain several different kinds of thermostatic gadgets, and that these carry on an intermittent conversation, day and night. There were the deep-freeze, the refrigerator, and the heating apparatus; first one, then the other, would go '*Click*! oi-oi-oi-oi-oi-oi-oi-*click*!' or '*Ah*! woo-woo-woo-woo-woo-woo!' I had switched on the heat (as instructed), for half an hour, after feeding the monstrous dragon of a boiler. What happened first was that a little baby gadget sprang to life, said 'Tss-deedle-deedle pring - pr-i-i-i-i-i-ing!', and then pulled up the massive draught-gate. Within fifteen minutes the electric bellows began to blow hot air through the grills in the floor of each room, and the temperature became tropical. In vain did I switch off the draught; in vain did I open the front door of the house (the only means of ventilation, as the windows were unopenable). Hot air continued to pour up like a blast from hell, accompanied by the snuffling, worrying, animal-breathing noise of the bellows. I hoped that as the thermostat cooled down the bellows would stop. They did, but they started again in thirty seconds, then stopped, then started again; and this kept me awake listening for half the night.

On returning to the Campus, the first thing I did was to go with John Hunt to the student-performance of *Patience*. Many practices for this had been going on in the Telluride music-room since I arrived, and as this room was immediately below my own the sounds had both interrupted me and aggravated my homesickness (*Patience* was one of the operas we had done in our Cambridge drawing-room with our undergraduate group). There was to be a party for the cast at Telluride after the performance, and foreseeing another sleepless night I decamped to the Statler Club Inn, which was the University Department of Hotel Management and was run, of course, by undergraduates. Here I had a truly delicious meal. But when I went to bed I could not find the bed, although (or rather, because) the bedroom was ultra-modern and streamlined. Of course the 'sofa' was it; but where were the pillows? Prolonged fiddling with buttons and handles produced no result at first; but a chance turn — and behold! the 'sofa' slid softly out into the room on grooved tramlines, and the pillow was discovered inside a wooden box. Even in this palatial retreat the electric night-noises were incessant.

To illustrate the pace of Cornell life, I will add that the next day I was summoned by the bells of the Library tower to one of the Hunt-Falkner Schubert recitals. These bells used to infuriate me by playing 'Maryland' every morning as a kind of campus-reveille; but on special occasions they played something appropriate, e.g., *Patience* tunes last week, and Schubert tunes today. One of the songs Keith sang was 'Der Doppelganger', which always sends icy shivers down my spine. Keith said afterwards that it was the finest song ever written, and, for the moment at least, after hearing his rendering, I agreed.

So far I had seen very little of Storer. But now the Easter recess was at hand, and he had arranged to come and stay the night of 26 March at Telluride as my guest, and then drive me to Virginia for a week with the Gregorys at Charlottesville. We drove the 600-odd miles in two hops, staying a night en route at Harrisburg, the capital of Pennsylvania. Going so far south from Cornell at that time of the year was like traversing France from Calais to the Côte d'Azur; we left winter still prevailing at Ithaca and entered the spring by rapid strides as we sped south. Peach-blossom, forsythia, daffodils and bright green grass appeared one after the other — how gratefully to my jaded eye! — and by the time we reached Virginia we had entered a zone of summer, where it was almost too hot to sit out in the sun I had pined for. The Gregorys, whom I had last seen as my kind Christmas hosts at Chicago in 1948, now lived in a beautiful country house outside Charlottesville, surrounded by thirty-five acres of heath and wood and field. All around were lumpy hills like the Quantocks; and far away, stretching right across the panorama like a larger version of the Malvern Hills, lay the Blue Ridge Mountains. Mary Gregory's father Professor Palache, whom I had met at East Jaffrey over four years ago, lived close by in a recently-converted farmhouse, with silo adapted as a large circular living-room. In this house I was installed with him, occupying a separate suite with my own bed-sitting-room and bathroom. Mr. Palache was now an old man of 85, mournful, dignified, shy, and gracious; and he looked more than ever like a Hebrew prophet. All day long he used to work in his garden, not forgetting to feed the scarlet-feathered cardinal-birds which came to his window-sills. In the evenings, when I was not furiously scribbling lectures on Hardy to see me through the second half of my marathon, he would relax with me by playing gramophone-records, of which he had a magnificent collection. Though we did not speak much, we felt an intuitive sense of kinship, especially when we shared the delight of listening to Brahms's F Major cello sonata.

The Gregorys took us out twice into the neighbouring woods and glens in search of some of the American spring rarities; and Mary, deeply versed in nature-lore (as in music, and architecture, and all good things) pointed out to me the 'mayflower', a tiny pink-flowered arbutus hugging the ground; the 'Dutchman's Breeches' (why so-called I do not know — for it was a small, white 'bleeding-heart'); the *erithronium* ('dog-tooth violet'); and the wild Judas trees, whose pink smoke-clouds were afloat everywhere. Even on this southern holiday I was unable to avoid giving a lecture at the University, but it was an informal, light-hearted affair, and served mainly as overture to a cocktail party. Storer had to return by car some days ahead of me, so I went back to New York by train, breaking the journey for a few hours at Washington to see the famous mile of cherry-blossom along the Tidewater.

Back at Cornell, after all this sub-tropical luxuriance, I found that the spring there had gained no painful inch. But engagements now crowded in so thick and fast that I had no time to deplore the drab skies and the fog. I had, as immediate prospect, a dress dinner, followed by my public lecture to the University, followed again by a party in my honour. A day or two later there was to be a Phi Beta Kappa luncheon, and an evening banquet for the poet Louis Macneice. The day following, I was to be driven 100 miles to lecture (twice) at Hamilton College; thence, to go on by train to Amherst to lecture there (twice also). Back to New York by night train, to be in time for my Cornell class next morning. If I do not always mention these things it is not for want of gratitude, but I have a specially warm place in my heart both for Hamilton and for Amherst, at both of which places the hospitality and friendliness shown me were outstanding — even in a country where this is universally true.

At the end of April another lecture-tour took me as far south as N. Carolina, where Duke University had invited me to lecture. On the way I re-visited Johns Hopkins, lecturing and speaking at a banquet, and, on the following day, Washington. Both in Baltimore and in Washington the early summer had already unfurled its glories: everywhere I saw masses of azaleas in blossom, pink and white dogwood trees, lilacs and even roses flowering, and avenues shaded by full leaf-age. In Washington it was so hot (88°) that my host and hostess allowed me to spend an afternoon resting on my bed. Fortunately for me, John Clendenin (my host) knew the celebrated scholar and writer Edith Hamilton, then living in Washington, and next day he took me round to see her. I had met this fabulous old lady four years before in Maine. She was now 86; but her mental activity was as prodigious as ever, her talk fresh, brilliant and incisive, and her range of interest panoramic, stretching from Ancient Greece to the existentialists. In appearance she was grand and masculine, her great eyes and noble brow eloquent of wisdom and intellect. She reminded me a little of Ethel Smyth, though she was more imposing, and dwelt in a serener element.

Duke University appeared to me like an Aladdin's palace called into being by the wave of a millionaire's wand. It was founded and built at breakneck speed by Mr. Duke, a tobacco-king who was also a keen Methodist. The buildings, grandiose in scale, and standing in about 1,500 acres of forest, were built to a unified plan and in a uniform Tudor style. At night, when the great gothic chapel-tower was floodlit, it appeared unreal and dreamlike. Here I had a guest-apartment at the top of a 'Tudor' tower, looking down upon rich lawns, trees, and flower-beds, all in the full beauty of early summer, and upon the statue of Mr. Duke holding a cigar in his hand. I was told that when this statue was first commissioned, it was disputed whether the Founder should be represented with some symbol of his worldly avocation, or carrying a Bible to denote his spiritual calling and election. I felt rather glad that honest realism had won the day. Believe it or not, when I got back to Ithaca early next morning I found frost on the ground. I had seen *two* springs come *and go*.

The very day I returned (so the whirligig span on) I lectured at 11 a.m., took a seminar from 2-4 p.m., and spoke at a dinner in the evening on 'Religion and the University'.

In early May came the most ambitious of all my efforts: the tour of seven mid-Western Universities and Colleges, for which Cornell most magnanimously granted me a fortnight's leave of absence. The first three places were all in Ohio: Columbus, Wooster and Oberlin, and in travelling from each of these to the next I made use for the first time of 'Greyhound' buses. Of the Universities I remember Oberlin best, partly because there I had to put on an American Doctor's gown and deliver the 'Honors Day' Oration before a huge audience in the Finney Chapel. Also, it was here that the inter-state discrepancies over 'summer time' caused a breakdown in my arrangements. My next halt was to be at Ann Arbor, Michigan, where I was not only to lecture but to stay for several days with our friends Gordon and Gunborg Sutherland, using their home as a base for my further operations in Michigan and Illinois. One of the Oberlin dons kindly drove me to the railway station to catch a train which would take me to Ann Arbor (changing several times) in five hours. When we got there, we found that the train, adhering to another time-scheme, had left an hour ago. My friend did some quick thinking and after consulting the Greyhound time-table, set off with me at top-speed to intercept the last bus, which had already left Oberlin. We drove for miles across country, at such a pace that on one hump-bridge I verily believe that all four wheels left the ground. But I picked up the bus, with devout gratitude to my noble benefactor. Late that evening I knocked at the door of 2109 Copley Avenue, the Sutherlands' delightful house in Ann Arbor, and received a welcome that I shall never forget. True, I had been overwhelmed with kindness and hospitality wherever I went, and was to be so many times again. But this was like a real home-coming, and it warmed my heart. Gordon had been a colleague at Pembroke from 1935, and he and his charming Swedish wife, and their three beautiful daughters had been greatly missed by us all when he accepted a Professorship at Ann Arbor.

I find that my memories of the lecture-occasions at Ann Arbor, East

L

Lansing, Wayne (Detroit), Champaign-Urbana and North Western (Evanston) have become blurred and intermingled. At each place there were parties and dinners at which I met all the Faculty members in the English departments, and I sincerely tried to remember them and the various projects they outlined to me. But I was doing too much, and my brain had become like a piece of blotting-paper many times used and no longer absorbent. But the household at Copley Avenue is not among the memories that could ever grow dim.

Within about two months I was to return there, with Zélie and Lucy, in the course of our united holiday; but this visit I will describe later. Meanwhile I had been working out the itinerary for the holiday, and had by this time fixed nearly all the dates and reservations. My glimpse of home-life at Ann Arbor, comforting and restorative as it was, had in the long run intensified my longing for my own home-circle, and the impending trip to the Far West — for all its promised and expected thrills — seemed just a huge obstacle in the way to reunion. But I knew by now that my lectures at Cornell would be over sooner than I had expected, and that a whole month would have to be filled before my ladies arrived at New York (23 June). Storer's offer to drive me, with Howard and Ethel Wilson (in their car), right through the Rockies to San Francisco, was therefore most opportune, and was in any case far too good an opportunity to be missed. But I was sorry to be doing it without Zélie and Lucy, who would have to be content with lesser glories down east.

When I got back to Cornell from the Middle West I had only about a fortnight's routine teaching left to do. In Whitsun week (25-29 May), which was my very last week of duty there, I was given a series of good-bye parties every evening. One excursion I must mention, because it did much to efface the wintry image produced by the earlier months. That most kind and charming man Donald Grout, the Cornell Professor of Music, took John Hunt and me out on Whitsunday for a picnic at his cottage on Lake Skeneateles (pronounced Skenny-attalis), about forty miles away in the 'Finger Lake' country. It was a day of perfect May weather, and the whole countryside was transformed beyond belief. Skeneateles was sapphire-blue under a cloudless sky, and was like the southern reaches of Windermere — that is, Windermere without its northern skyline of fells. Mrs. Grout had prepared a lavish lunch and supper (but it was called a 'picnic') and electric stove, refrigerator and spring-water were all ready to hand. We spent long afternoon and evening hours strolling through deserted woods and sunbathing by the lakeside, and finally returned by moonlight. I had such a wonderful send-off when I left Cornell that I was made to feel as if my stay there had not been a complete failure.

3 The Far West

I preferred not to drive to California all the way from New York, so I had arranged with Storer to meet him and the Wilsons half-way, at Denver, Colorado. Accordingly, I went up to New York on 29 May and spent a day in Storer's flat, where in his absence (for of course he had already started on the long trans-continental journey) I was looked after by his aged cousin Anne Carroll Moore (well known as a biographer of Beatrix Potter). Thence I went on overnight to Chicago, where I had six hours to spend, in grilling heat, with a hot gale blowing dust and newspapers sky-high. Along the shore of Lake Michigan, where four and a half years ago I had felt a polar blast blowing in across lines of frozen spray, I now walked perspiring, and watched the speed-boats on the Lake and the crowds of people trying to keep cool by the water's edge. On again by another night-train, this time a very special one, all gleaming white metal, called the 'Denver Zephyr', which covered the 1,017 miles at an average speed of 83 m.p.h. I had breakfast on this train at daybreak, in the heart of the Nebraska-Colorado plains: endless stretches of treeless prairie, merging sometimes into sandy desert; or sometimes green, with herds of cattle and with occasional lonely ranches screened by stunted poplars.

As I sped westward across the plains I seemed to be leaving home an infinite distance behind; and yet at The Brown Palace Hotel at Denver, where the snowpeaks of the Rocky Mountains were visible from my window, I found letters from England awaiting me. In a sense, England itself was awaiting me, for it was the eve of the young Queen's Coronation, and all America seemed to be on tiptoe with the excitement of it. Here at Denver *The Rocky Mountain News* was splashed with Coronation headlines, and I found most of the hotel guests preparing to stay up all night to hear or see the ceremony on radio and television. It was most affecting to me, an exiled Briton, to find myself encompassed with so much good-will towards the Throne of England. No fierce light beating upon it from these republican heights! — nothing but warmth, and affectionate respect for the shy and graceful girl upon whom, at the centre and heart of so much pageantry and symbolism, the eyes and thoughts of all were fixed. As if to fill my cup of national pride to overflowing, the newspapers carried next morning not only Coronation pictures and headlines, but also the news of Hilary's ascent of Mount Everest. As Storer and the Wilsons sat at breakfast with me that day (2nd June), one of the waitresses (thinking my companions were as British as I) said to us 'Gee, you fellers must be feeling pretty good today!'

One more Coronation incident remains unforgotten. Our first day's drive took us through some remote Colorado villages, many thousands of feet above sea-level, and in all of them (until the ceremony in West-minster was over) there were wireless commentaries sounding from open windows. At one of the loneliest of these villages, a humble inhabitant shouted to us as we passed, in a voice vibrant with emotion, 'My! if you'd been around five minutes ago you'd have heard them putting the crown on that l'le girl's head!'

We drove over the snowy 'Continental Divide' at Berthoud Pass (11,000 odd feet), where my geographic imagination was stirred by the signboard pointing to 'Pacific' in one direction and 'Atlantic' in the other. Thereafter, we covered the remaining 1,500 miles to Portland, Oregon, in five days, following first the line of the Colorado River, then turning northwards to visit the Yellowstone Park, and continuing thence westward by the Snake River and Columbia River valleys. I sent Peter a birthday-greetings telegram from Twin Falls, Idaho. Among the many rather blurred impressions of this journey a few stand out clearly: pink cactus-blooms beside the Colorado River; 'Old Faithful', the geyser in Yellowstone Park (which 'erupts every 66.3 minutes and attains an average height of 150 feet'); the Yellowstone River Canyon; the steaming waters and valleys round the Yellowstone Lake; the heaving, spluttering mud-springs; and lastly — also in Yellowstone Park — the brown bears which came to the roadside to be fed by passing motorists. In the mountain-country the grandest scenes, I think, were the Berthoud Pass and the majestic Tetons. I was surprised to find how much of the Rockies consisted of vast flat or rolling plateaux covered with the blue-green 'sage-brush'. But even when crossing these great expanses one was seldom without a glimpse of snow-capped ranges, serrated and scooped, notching the horizon perhaps fifty miles away. In Pendleton (Oregon), one of the many small towns we passed through which might have figured in a 'Western' film, I was made to go into a shop and ask to be allowed to try on a cowboy hat. The salesman agreed most readily, although the transaction ended, as it was meant to end, not in a purchase but in a photograph.

At Portland, Storer and I left Howard and Ethel Wilson at the home of their married son Steve, and finished our journey to San Francisco by train through the Cascade Mountains and down the Sacramento Valley. Storer had booked our rooms at the luxurious Hotel Claremont at Berkeley, where my window overlooked the magnificent bay of San Francisco, with its jutting promontories, islands, bridges, gleaming-white buildings and encircling hills. Just below the window were great palm trees, and far across the water I could see the Golden Gate, then the world's longest suspension-bridge, spanning the outlet to the Pacific Ocean.

San Francisco was the first large American city I had seen (other than New York) which, quite apart from its setting, had real beauty and charm in itself. It seemed to me like a Mediterranean Riviera city: dignified, civilized and gay; and the sight of it was all the more cheering after the 'cowboy' western towns through which we had been passing, and in which we had stayed, for the past week. Here Storer, with his usual magic touch, borrowed a car (the original one having belonged to the Wilsons) from one of his numberless friends; and in this he took me to see some of the special glories of California: the Yosemite Valley, the Giant Forest (the 'big trees'), the country of R.L. Stevenson's *Silverado Squatters*, and the Grand Canyon (this last reached by train). The Grand Canyon, that mile-deep abyss, fifteen miles across, cutting down right through all the sedimentary rocks to earth's basic rind, and unrolling from sky to sky its immense panorama of cliffs, domes, temples and chasms tinted with every rainbow hue — this is among the world's greatest wonders. But I think with greater fondness of the Yosemite Valley with its enchanting blend of grace, freshness and majesty; its many waterfalls; El Capitan, that sheer wall of grey granite polished smooth in the Ice Age: 3,000 feet of vertical rock, yet graceful rather than terrible; the strange, Sphinx-like Half Dome; the meadows by the river, their rich green contrasting so strongly with the dried browns of the outer lands; and always in the background, both here and in the Sequoia Forest, the snow-topped range of the Sierra Nevada.

We boarded one of the 'crack' trans-continental trains at Williams, Arizona, and returned thence to New York. Of that long, restful return journey which had really begun at Berkeley, I have two special memories: the glimpse of the sinister, cactus-ridden Mohave Desert which we crossed on the way to Arizona; and the appalling heat of Chicago, which smote us when we stepped out of our air-conditioned train there to change for New York. It so happened that a fierce heat-wave was devastating the city just then; and to emerge from our artificial train-temperature of 70° into a natural 110° was an experience I shall not forget.

On 23rd June I met Zélie and Lucy at the New York Pier 90, where they disembarked from the 'Queen Mary' after a prosperous voyage. Though we had only been separated for four and a half months, it seemed to me more like years, and the re-union was one of life's great moments. Storer did the honours in his most princely style, putting on a celebration dinner and afterwards taking us to the top of the Empire State Building. Here the newcomers, only a few hours after arrival, received their first impression of the city in the most striking manner conceivable: looking down and around over the vast panorama with its myriad lights at late dusk on a midsummer night. I will pass over the happy weeks we spent in the mountains of New Hampshire, by the sea at Martha's Vineyard, and with the Sutherlands in Michigan. A few days before our return voyage in the *Queen Elizabeth*, I paid my duty-visit to the Income Tax office in Detroit, to get my 'quittance' for the embarkation. When the very courteous official saw my name on the form he looked up sharply and said 'Not the author of *The Seventeenth Century Background*? I read that when I was a student at College.' The interview ended on a note of cordiality unknown to me in any tax office at home.

Chapter Twelve

The Remaining Particle of Futurity:
A Layman's Thoughts about Immortality

During the years that have followed 1953, life has pursued an even tenor, and there is nothing that I wish to record here and now. I have been looking back long enough, and it is time that I took a glance towards futurity.

I have just reached the age of seventy: just passed that milestone beyond which, as the Psalmist says, all 'our strength is but labour and sorrow: so soon passeth it away, and we are gone'; and therefore I ought to be, in Sir Thomas Browne's words 'naturally constituted unto thoughts of the next world, and cannot excusably decline the consideration of that duration, which maketh pyramids pillars of snow, and all that's past a moment.'

And do I in fact think about the next world as I should? Can I say, with Donne,

> Since I am comming to that Holy roome
> Where, with Thy Quire of Saints for evermore
> I shall be made Thy Musique; As I come
> I tune the Instrument here at the dore,
> And what I must doe then, thinke here before?

Not as I should, God knows; not as the saints and mystics have done. But without any spiritual pride I can state, like anybody else of my age, that the rapid shrinkage of my residue of days has been for some time, and is now more than ever, forcing itself upon my attention. How could it be otherwise? It is not as it was in the days of thoughtless youth, when life lay ahead in an endless-seeming perspective, and time could be squandered without qualm. No; I am now 'necessitated to eye the remaining particle of futurity'; these are the autumn days, the evening hours; winter and darkness are coming soon. This realisation, I find, as I peer into the ever-shortening future, invests all existing things and people with a new pathos and preciousness. These aconites and snowdrops, which are flowering now as I write, are no longer just units in an endless recurrence; it will not be so many more times, probably, that I shall see them flower, or the daffodils begin to peer; and not so many years or days may remain of companionship with loved ones. Day succeeds day as of old, hearts beat and nostrils breathe; but these can no longer be presumed upon or taken for granted. Each day, each heart-throb and each breath of my beloved, is one of a numbered and ever-diminshing series; and there is no big balance left in Time's bank from which I can repay the debts of a lifetime. So far am I from feeling any world-weariness, or the ennui of a Hamlet —

> *How weary, flat, stale and unprofitable*
> *Seem to me all the uses of this world! —*

that age has brought me a heightened and deepened sense of the value, of each moment that remains. Perhaps this is not quite the mood in which a Christian should approach the end of his alloted span. Is there not in it too much of the pagan regret and wistfulness, the pagan clinging to what is perishable and fugitive? Should I not rather be nerving myself up to say, with Newman's Gerontius,

> *And with a strong will I sever*
> *All the ties that bind me here?*

I am not competent to say; but of one thing I feel assured: whatever deepens love, increases tenderness, enhances reverence for life, and shifts attention from self, cannot be wholly amiss.

Since in this Chapter I am only passing on some Thoughts of a Layman, not rehearsing the history of the belief in Immortality, nor expounding its philosophy and theology, I shall begin by simply trying to describe what I have been feeling and thinking about it all my life. I must plead the privilege of age if I indulge too freely in reminiscence; my excuse is that sometimes a few concrete examples from an individual life are more instructive than abstract reasoning.

It is not at all easy to say on what presuppositions, or with what purpose or aim, one's life has been lived. Often, perhaps always, the master-currents flow deep below the surface of consciousness. For example, I should not be surprised if a great part of my childhood and youth was unconsciously controlled by the thought of heaven and hell, or shall I say by the unquestioned assumption that I should have to give an account of myself hereafter. I did not, of course, reflect much or often on this, but I was brought up in a Christian home in which, although the traditional imagery of the future life was discarded, the eternal significance of every moral choice was never forgotten. I think that in that home the longing to deserve the Eternal Judge's 'Well done, good and faithful servant!', and to avoid his condemnation, was real and operative, though never mentioned. And what was true of that home must have been true of millions of others, even in those latter days (say sixty years ago); and if true then, how much more abundantly so in the centuries of faith, when all the doctrine and art of Christendom pointed to the Last Judgment as the destiny of man and the end of history, to Beatitude as man's appointed perfection, and to everlasting pain as its dread alternative. Whatever we may think now about the future life, we cannot doubt that the Christian versions of it, as presented in the New Testament, in the Creeds and liturgies, in sermons, in poetry, in sculpture and painting, for at least 1500 years, supplied the most powerful moral sanction ever known to man. This did not mean that all believers (i.e. virtually everybody) lived good lives; but it did mean that they acknowledged their accountability before God. They might forget or evade the thought of The Great Assize, but the tremor of it may be felt in such poems as *timor mortis conturbat me* and the terrible *Dies Irae*.

The evaporation of this belief in a future state of rewards and punishments has been going on, silently and imperceptibly, all through our lifetime; and by now there must be a very few Europeans left outside the Christian churches (and perhaps not so many within them) who still believe in it or indeed think about the matter at all. For the mass of our neo-pagans today I imagine that the belief in a future life is non-existent, or at most an antiquated fable, like religion itself. They do not believe in it, 'neither will they be persuaded, though one rose from the dead'. They would not even welcome it if they were so persuaded. Anyone who looks round aghast upon the contemporary disintegration of morality, is free to attribute it, in the last analysis, to the repudiation of all traditional rules, codes and standards, and above all of this ultimate belief, the former basis of it all.

In early manhood I thought that I had outgrown my childhood belief in a future life; I had put this away, along with Father Christmas and other childish things. I remember the feeling of mingled surprise, incredulity and contempt, with which I heard the reply of a fellow-undergraduate to my disclaimer of all belief in immortality: 'Oh, really? The future life is *very* real to me.' I thought this mere humbug, and could only excuse my friend by reminding myself that he had not been in the War (this was the year 1919), whereas I had. I also remember the approval with which, some years later when I was a young don, I heard a colleague say 'I sincerely *hope* death ends all.'

I have spoken already of the 'wave of panic' which overwhelmed me after my thirtieth birthday, and of how it led me to start writing, in the hope of checking the acceleration of the years. Let me now, leaving chronology and reminiscence behind, begin to ponder some of the considerations which have weighed with me (as with so many others), tipping the balance sometimes towards belief and sometimes towards incredulity. Perhaps there may emerge some of the senses in which immortality seems incredible and undesirable, and some in which it seems acceptable and desirable beyond all else.

For Christianity the Life Everlasting has never been in doubt; it has been an unquestioned article of belief from the beginning. 'I

M

believe in the resurrection of the body, and the life everlasting'; 'he that believeth on me hath everlasting life;' 'death is swallowed up in victory' — I need not repeat any more of the familiar utterances. Plato and others had laboured to demonstrate the soul's immortality by reasoning, and had failed, but Christ had brought life and immortality to light. And Christians to this day are committed to this faith, if they mean what they repeat in Church every Sunday; it is not an open question: it is a *datum*. Why then should they still discuss it amongst themselves? why are books still written, and lectures delivered, on this theme? I think it is because the Life Everlasting is an article of *Faith*, like the belief in God; and like every article of faith, it cannot be proved by demonstration, like a mathematical proposition. The truths of mathematics, as Coleridge said, are such that they cannot be denied; those of religion are such that they *can* be denied, but *will* not be denied by the good man. We do not have to renew our belief in the multiplication table by frequent examination; but religious faith must be daily reborn and re-lived: it must for ever become what it is, and be proved, not by reasoning, but in the refining fires of experience.

Articles of faith, however, are not all of the same class; some, as the belief in God, are primary; others, like perhaps the communion of saints, the resurrection of the body and the life everlasting, secondary. At least, it has seemed possible for many to believe in God but not in the life everlasting. I was once one of these. Was my position tenable? Perhaps my belief in God was too superficial to reveal all the depth and range of its implications; and perhaps my notions of everlasting life were crude and foolish? Here, at any rate, are some of the difficulties I have felt, most of them — I am sure — shared by others.

First I will refer to the difficulty of believing in the individual soul's survival after the death of the body — and let us be quite clear that survival in this sense is not the same thing as Eternal Life in the true and full religious sense. Soul, mind, life (call them what you will) seem to be so closely dependent upon the brain and body that the death of the one must mean the extinction of the other. We know what happens to the body after death; we neither know nor can ever know what happens to the soul. We do not even know that 'soul' is a real entity capable of survival; indeed, we have strong evidence suggesting that what we call 'soul' is a function of the body. An injury to the brain, or manipulation by surgery or drugs, can annihilate or permanently change a personality while the body still lives. Genetic science may some day (though God forbid!) make possible the laboratory production of moron-slaves and higher stereotypes (as in *Brave New World)*; what sort of heaven could be open to such as these? Putting aside these considerations, however, there are yet other difficulties. We have all known people who in old age have lost, not only sight and hearing, but their memory and virtually their whole mind. If they survive death, what is it which will survive? Not, one feels, the vestigial and almost extinguished personality of decrepitude; and if not, then what? some revived simulacrum of their earlier selves, arbitrarily selected from the best moments of their prime?

Another great difficulty arises, for me at least, when I consider the sheer numbers of the human race. If the latest evidence is valid, and beings classifiable as human have existed on this earth for twenty million years, the imagination reels at the thought of all those souls for whom appropriate accommodation has already had to be provided; and what if we extend our view forward, to the time — alas, nothing like so far distant — when there will hardly be standing-room on this planet for its teeming populations? No doubt there are many mansions in Heaven, but can all these souls, mass-produced and necessarily very much alike, and mostly of a low-grade type, be *worth* preserving? At what point in evolution, moreover, did primitive man rise far enough above the ape to qualify for a soul? Or have we been wrong in assuming a hard-and-fast line dividing 'human' from 'sub-human', and denying immortal souls to the animals — at any rate the more intelligent animals? An Anglican clergyman once seriously asked me whether I thought certain dogs could possibly be refused admittance to Heaven, if certain human beings were eligible. Clearly he would not have put in any such plea on behalf of cats, still less frogs, wasps or bacilli. And so it is with our imaginings about human survival; as long as we confine our thoughts to a few selected individuals, products of high civilization — bishops, sages, men of genius, University professors or just our Christian friends — the idea of a life hereafter for them seems not incongruous; but when we try to take in the larger panorama our imagination turns sick and swoons. How strange it would be if Heaven came as a *surprise* to any of those admitted there! Yet surely it must be so to all those palaeolithic savages of 20 million years ago, not to mention those of today, and of our own country, who have lived their lives with just as little thought of heaven as their ape-like progenitors. How strange, if Heaven be a Christian domain, for all those proto-men to meet Christ there, having never heard of him on earth; or indeed — to extend that thought a little — how strange, if Christianity be the only true religion, for all the deceased pious Hindus, Buddhists or Mohammedans to find themselves unexpectedly in a Christian entourage!

As long as we remain on this level of conjecture we may meet with another kind of objection — that of those who, while not utterly denying the possibility of survival, regard the prospect as uninviting and even abhorrent. Such people are usually thinking, not of the torments of

Hell, but of the ennui of Heaven. They will tell you that they cannot endure the idea of sitting for ever and ever on a damp cloud and playing the harp; or the more literary ones may add that Adam ate the forbidden fruit through sheer boredom with Eden, and that even Milton fails to convince us that the loss of Paradise was a bad thing. Some very high-minded sceptics, of the J.S. Mill type, may say that Heaven would be no Heaven for them if a Hell existed too; they would be thinking of the under-privileged all the time. A depressing aspect of the popular image of survival was revealed to me lately, quite by chance, in a remark by Winston Churchill in his booklet on painting. He would like, he said, to spend the first million or so years of the future life perfecting his control of the brush. The thought of a life hereafter which was merely a prolongation, through endless years and aeons, of the sort of life we live now, but in a disembodied state and without the comforts and joys of this too-much loved earth, seems to me appalling.

Of course we have no right to assume that the future life, if any, will be of the kind we now think we should *like*. We must not arrive at our belief in immortality by merely putting together all our notions, even our most exalted notions, of what we consider the most satisfactory state of being for a departed soul. God, whose thoughts are not as our thoughts, may have quite other designs. One of C.S. Lewis's insights on this theme was to suggest that many people disbelieve in immortality, not because they find it incredible, but because they find it alarming. They shrink, not so much from the prospect of eternal punishment (this sort of grave *has* lost its sting even for most of the orthodox now), as from the prospect of having to nerve themselves up to a level of spirituality they have hitherto managed to avoid. It is indeed a terrible thing to fall into the hands of the living God. We all know what Lewis meant, I think. The other day I found myself unwilling and unready to say my prayers. 'You'd better get used to God's company while you can', I said to myself reprovingly; 'soon you'll have no other'.

I remarked a short time ago that we neither do nor can know what happens to the soul after bodily death. As this statement may be challenged by some who are interested in Psychical Research, Spiritualism etc. I must just explain myself briefly on this point. Those who have read any of the Proceedings of the S.P.R., or such a work as F.W.H. Myers's *Human Personality and Survival* or any kindred books, will know the sort of evidence that exists for ghostly appearances, telepathic messages, communications with departed souls through mediums, table-rapping etc. I am not qualified to judge the validity of such evidence, though I can see how much disinterested endeavour has gone into sifting it and eliminating, as far as may be, whatever may

CHAPTER TWELVE 173

have been fraudulent or merely superstitions. I can also see that much
of this endeavour has sprung, not only from the yearning to keep in
touch with departed dear ones, but from the more philosophical desire
to undermine the arrogance of dogmatic positivism. Nevertheless I cannot find any comfort in evidence of this sort, nor any confirmation of
the only view of eternal life which I have come to find acceptable.
Granted that I knew, beyond possibility of doubt, that the soul of my
departed loved-one lived on, and could speak to me through a medium,
what would this profit me? I should merely know that my beloved
was a pathetic ghost hovering round its former habitations; I should
not know that he or she was living a new and glorified life in fellowship with God. But this is what I have come to understand by Immortality; I understand it as Eternal Life, life with God, not just as living on
and on in some melancholy Sheol or other underworld of Shades. I do
not want to go back to the animistic delusions catalogued in *The
Golden Bough* or the ancestor-worship of the ancient Romans; I
prefer to accept the words ascribed to Christ by the Johannine evange-
list: 'This is life eternal, that they might know thee, the only true God,
and Jesus Christ whom thou hast sent,' I want my belief in life eternal
to be rooted and grounded in my belief in God, not in any pseudo-
scientific results; I want it to remain an article of religious faith and not
become a matter of mere knowledge; I want to believe in it because I
ought, not because I must.

But before I stop I must try to say, a little more explicitly, what I
understand the belief to mean. The vain imaginings I have rehearsed all
lead to incredulity or despair; either there is no immortality as so pic-
tured, or it is an undesirable one. But there is another possibility; our
speculations may have ended, as they did, in absurdity, because we started with wrong assumptions. One of these assumptions, perhaps the
commonest one of all, and the hardest to eradicate, is that the human
soul has a natural or inherent immortality in its own right. It was the
belief that the soul is a separable spirit, immaterial and undying, which
at death floats away from the body and takes up its abode in the grave,
or in the underworld, or in other bodies – it was this which formed the
basis of most of the notions and practices studied by anthropologists
amongst primitive peoples and the civilizations of antiquity. The same
belief, immensely refined and sophisticated, underlies the attempts of
Plato, and other philosophers both ancient and modern, to 'prove' the
immortality of the soul. The One remains, the Many change and pass;
and Soul is to Body as the One to the Many. There are two realms: the
world of Being, where dwell the eternal and immutable Ideas or Forms;
and the world of Becoming, our own world, where flitting shadows are
mistaken for realities. Socrates in the *Phaedo*, himself face to face with
death, asks to which of these realms is the soul of man more akin?

And the answer comes, of course, that the soul, which can reason, and remember, and know, is akin to the heavenly world and will at last — though not till after many cycles of re-incarnation, and when purged of all its dross, enter upon the life of heaven. Of all the arguments used by Plato and his followers, most of them quite unconvincing, this is perhaps the best — if only because it is the least argumentative and the most intuitive. The pure and illuminated soul *feels* its kinship with the skies. Never has this kind of insight been more beautifully expressed than by John Smith, the Cambridge Platonist of the seventeenth century — Platonist and Christian — who in his Discourse *The Excellency and Nobleness of True Religion* says:

> 'It is not an aiery speculation of Heaven as a thing (though never so undoubtedly) to come, that can satisfy [man's] hungry desires, but the real possession of it even in this life. Such an happiness would be less in the esteem of Good men, that were onely good to be enjoyed at the end of this life, when all other enjoyments fail him. I wish there be not among some such a light and poor esteem of Heaven as makes them more to seek it as a thing to come, then after Heaven itself; which indeed we can never well be assured of, untill we find it rising up within ourselves, and glorifying our own Souls . . . This holy Assurance is indeed the budding and blossoming of felicity in our own Souls; it is the inward sense and feeling of the true life, spirit, sweetness and beauty of Grace powerfully expressing its own energy within us.'

It is then, I think, safer and wiser, and more orthodox, to take our stand here, rather than upon any alleged immortality of soul-substance as such. No argument based on the supposed incorporeal and incorruptible nature of the soul can in itself have much weight; it cannot be carried to the point of demonstration; it is always open to materialist attack; and even if it were convincing it would not prove the kind of immortality offered us by the New Testament. 'This is life eternal, that they might know thee, the only true God, and Jesus Christ whom thou has sent.' 'He that believeth on me hath everlasting life.' To hold that the soul survives the body because it is made of something undying leads only to the ghostly world of spiritualism, the modern Sheol. To know that my friend's soul survived thus would give me small comfort; I should still wish him a taste of real heaven.

Are we, then, to commit ourselves to the doctrine of 'Conditional Immortality' — that is, to the view that the life eternal is reserved for those alone who deserve it, or who can attain to it? There seems to be New Testament authority for that view. Jesus, answering the Sadducees on the question of marriage after the general resurrection, said 'they which shall be accounted worthy to obtain that world, and the resurrection from the dead, neither marry nor are given in marriage'

(Luke XX 35). And there is St. Paul's memorable disclaimer of all legal righteousness in favour of winning life in Christ: 'That I may know him, and the power of his resurrection. . if by any means I might attain unto the resurrection of the dead. . not as though I had already attained. . ' (Phil.III 10-12). If we do adopt this view, we are left with no answer to the question, what then becomes of all those who are *not* 'accounted worthy', and to those teeming millions previously mentioned, who cannot be supposed to have attained the saving experience or knowledge? I think we have here come to the extreme borderland of legitimate speculation, and must rest in Christian agnosticism. It does not appear that we have any scriptural guidance on this matter, nor has the Christian Church spoken with a united voice. Not only so, but it is not easy to be sure what particular views the Church holds and enjoins about the soul's destiny after the death of the body. It holds, and has held, differing views at different times, and the various sects have differed from each other: In New Testament times it seems to have been believed that the departed souls 'slept', perhaps in the grave, until the general resurrection, when they would arise at the sound of the last trumpet, be clothed with spiritual bodies, and receive condign reward or punishment. The Johannine Apocalypse looks forward to a millennial reign of Christ after a first resurrection of the saints and martyrs; then to a second resurrection for the remainder of the dead; and finally to the Last Judgment. The Catholic Church introduced the rational and charitable, though unscriptural, doctrine of Purgatory — that interval of further education and purification for the soul before it can approach its Maker. (It is a doctrine which Newman's poetry and Elgar's music have always tempted me, and almost persuaded me, to accept.) The Protestant churches have on the whole taught that all souls, on leaving the body, go straight to heaven or hell; but that they will be re-united in some mysterious way with their bodies — presumably now rendered incorruptible by divine agency — at the Last Day. Nowadays there is a great uncertainty amongst ordinary people as to what they can believe or ought to believe; and perhaps the majority have dismissed the subject from their thoughts altogether; Ask even any average Protestant Church-goer what is the received doctrine in his Church, and he will probably be uncertain what is taught about the meaning of immortality, its distinction from 'life eternal', what happens to the soul between death and judgement, and what is meant by 'resurrection of the body'.

Attractive though 'Conditional Immortality' may be and is, it offends the conscience of some because of its apparent exclusiveness; 'what', they say, 'is this a privilege to be enjoyed only by the Best People? Are the lesser breeds and the underprivileged to be excluded? Such critics prefer the Universalism of Origen, according to which all are eventually saved, including even the Devil himself. I have already suggested that Christian agnosticism is the only rational, as well as pious, state of mind to cultivate here. 'The souls of the righteous are in the hands of God', and God, not we ourselves, is the judge as to who these are.

> *All is best, though we oft doubt,*
> *What th' unsearchable dispose*
> *Of highest Wisdom brings about*
> *And ever best found in the close.*
>
> *(Samson Agonistes, l. 1745)*

Nevertheless, leaving aside these profitless speculations, we can be sure of our present duty. What we have to do, I think, is to discipline our own lives so as to experience, here and now, some foretaste of the Life Eternal. That this is possible, a whole cloud of witnesses can testify. We can and must *practise* the life eternal, just as we ought to practise the presence of God; indeed the two practices are one, for there is no meaning of 'life eternal' which does not involve God's presence. We are not to expect beatitude beyond the grave if we have not already glimpsed it − however distantly and momentarily − in this life. As Fichte said, 'blessedness exists also beyond the grave for the man for whom it has already begun here; and it exists there in no other way and kind . . .; by the mere getting oneself buried, one cannot arrive at blessedness' [quoted in von Hügel, *Eternal Life*, 1912; p.176]. And, said Sir Thomas Browne, 'if any have been so happy as truly to understand Christian annihilation, ecstasies, exolution, liquefaction, transformation, the kiss of the spouse, gustation of God, and ingression into the divine shadow, they have already had a handsome anticipation of heaven. . ' [*Urn Burial, ch. V*]. But we are not bound to be advanced mystics of this kind in order to have that communion with God which is life eternal; the humblest and most unpretending can enjoy it. Adumbrations of it can be found in aesthetic experience, where a sense of deep indwelling order may sometimes supervene upon the multitudinousness of things. A sudden cessation of what has been called 'clock time', and its replacement by an apparent pause in, or oblivion of, the successiveness of daily living, may come in communion with art or nature. There is a passage in the slow movement of Brahms's Second Piano Concerto (B flat), where motion is stilled and time seems to have a stop, the music taking on the entranced calm of adoration or deep rapture. I am never sure whether this passage means worship or love − but it could well mean both, for what is worship without love? Or Wordsworth can say of his early-morning communing with nature at Esthwaite:

Oft in these moments such a holy calm
Would overspread my soul, that bodily eyes
Were utterly forgotten, and what I saw
Appeared like something in myself, a dream,
A prospect in the mind.

[Prelude II, 348 (1850]

Since I have already used the phrase 'Intimations of Immortality', I think I ought here to say a few words about what is, I suppose, the most celebrated poem on the subject in the English language, Wordsworth's great *Ode*. In that poem, as you will remember, Wordsworth laments the passing of that childhood vision which had once invested earth and every common sight with visionary glory. Looking back, at the middle of life's journey, upon his memories of childhood, he knows that 'the things which I have seen I now can see no more'; 'there hath past away a glory from the earth'. And although for this loss he finds abundant recompense in 'the faith that looks through death' and in 'years that bring the philosophic mind', still the fact remains that 'nothing can bring back the hour Of splendour in the grass, of glory in the flower'; and the poem, though it ends bravely, remains a lament. The point that concerns us is this: Wordsworth values so highly the great imaginative moments of his childhood, and still derives such strength from recollecting them, that he is constrained to express himself in the form of a myth — a myth which shall bring home, in the most vivid possible way, his sense of the contrast between childhood and maturity, and the distance he has travelled from the dayspring. He has adopted one of the myths of pre-existence according to which 'our birth is but a sleep and a forgetting'; we come 'trailing clouds of glory' from our heavenly home, and in the days of our angel infancy we still see earthly things in a celestial light. The visionary gleam lasts for a while, but in due time the years bring 'the inevitable yoke', and finally

'the Man perceives it die away
And fade into the light of common day.'

There is profound psychological truth in all this; no one has known more than Wordsworth about the imaginative consequences of growing up. But do we learn anything from him on the topic of this chapter? No more, I think, than we know already, namely, that there are moments in our lives ('spots of time') when our soul seems more alive, more awake and more creative than usual; moments when 'our noisy years seem moments in the being Of the eternal Silence'; when the flux of time seems arrested, and we have inklings of another, a higher and more enduring, level of existence. As for the pre-existence story, Wordsworth himself did not take it seriously, except as a piece of poetic machinery. In a note dictated late in life to Isabella Fenwick he said:

'To that dream-like vividness and splendour which invest objects of sight in childhood, every one, I believe, if he would look back, could bear testimony . . . : but having in the Poem regarded it as presumptive evidence of a prior state of existence, I think it right to protest against a conclusion, which has given pain to some good and pious persons, that I meant to inculcate such a belief. It is far too shadowy a notion to be recommended to faith, as more than an element in our instincts of immortality . . . when I was impelled to write this Poem on the"Immortality of the Soul", I took hold of the notion of pre-existence as having sufficient foundation in humanity for authorizing me to make for my purpose the best use of it I could as a Poet.'

But these are only hints and glimpses. The truer intimations of immortality are granted to the soul which, in humility, love, repentance and faith finds, not all things absorbed within itself (as in Wordsworth's *Prelude* passage), but the Self extinguished in contemplation of transcendent Being or as some would prefer to say, in loving identification with our fellow-men. This is that death-in-life which leads us to hope for a life-in-death. For St. Paul, as we know, to be made 'conformable' to Christ's death was the necessary prelude to sharing his resurrection. If we wish to be candidates for eternal life we must go into training for it now; and that means not only prayer and spiritual exercises directed towards God, but charity and neighbourliness in all our individual and social relationships. If we love not our brother whom we have seen, how shall we love God whom we have not seen?

I have time for only one more observation. I can well imagine some readers of these remarks saying to me 'Ah, yes! you are just like the rest of them. You pretend to know something about immortality, or at least you presume to air your views about it. And yet what do you give us? The usual evasions and fine words! You don't seem to believe in the after-life — that is, you don't hold out any hope that I shall meet in heaven those whom I have loved long since and lost awhile — and meet them as the very same personalities, remembering me and their past lives, that I knew on earth. You flinch from this, and make your escape behind a smoke-screen of words about eternal life as something already experienced in this life. We all know that we can lose ourselves in art, or love, or worship; we don't need you to tell us this. What we want to know is whether there is any life beyond the grave, or whether George Borrow's gypsy friend was right when he said "When a man dies, he is cast into the earth, and there's an end of him, brother, more's the pity." And this you haven't told us.'

No, my friend, I have not, because I don't know; nobody knows; only God knows. All I know, all anybody knows, is that we can begin to know God in this life, and that no eternal life is conceivable or desirable apart from him. Again my objector may say: 'why speak as if communion with God in this life furnished grounds for believing in its continuance after death? Would not such communion still be worth sharing even if it ceased with this life?' To this last question I can only answer 'Yes, it would; but experience of this communion, and of the quality of life which belongs with it, render it very hard to believe in the extinction of all the values summed up in the word "personality" '. If we believe in God, we must believe that the world is administered in the interest of all that we value most; that a universe which has produced free and responsible moral agents must itself be morally governed, and that the God who made it will not suffer its choicest products to be extinguished, even if the great globe itself shall perish in the frosts of entropy. Hear again the voice of John Smith, whose words are as much sweeter and more compelling than mine as his faith is more serenely assured:

> '[The soul] knows that God will never forsake his own life which he hath quickened in it; he will never deny those ardent desires of a blissful fruition of himself, which the lively sense of his own Goodness hath excited within it: those breathings and gaspings after an eternal participation of him are but the Energy of his own breath within us; if he had any mind to destroy it, he would never have shown it such things as he hath done; he would not raise it up to such *Mounts of Vision,* to shew it all the glory of that heavenly *Canaan* flowing with eternal and unbounded pleasures; and then tumble it down again into that deep and darkest Abyss of Death and Non-entity. Divine goodness cannot, it will not, be so cruel to holy souls that are such ambitious suitors for his love.'

> [Discourse *Of the Immortality of the Soul,*
> *ch. VII.*]